SECRETS AND LAWS

7 Day

SECRETS AND LAWS

COLLECTED ESSAYS IN LAW, LIVES AND LITERATURE

Melanie Williams

UCL PRESS

First published in Great Britain 2005 by UCL Press
an imprint of Cavendish Publishing Limited, The Glass House,
Wharton Street, London WC1X 9PX, United Kingdom
Telephone: + 44 (0)20 7278 8000   Facsimile: + 44 (0)20 7278 8080
Email: info@uclpress.com
Website: www.uclpress.com

Published in the United States by Cavendish Publishing
c/o International Specialized Book Services,
5824 NE Hassalo Street, Portland,
Oregon 97213-3644, USA

Published in Australia by Cavendish Publishing (Australia) Pty Ltd
45 Beach Street, Coogee, NSW 2034, Australia
Telephone: + 61 (2)9664 0909   Facsimile: +61 (2)9664 5420

© Williams, Melanie 2005

British Library Cataloguing in Publication Data

Williams, Melanie
Secrets and laws
1 Law and ethics 2 Sociological jurisprudence
I Title
340.1'12

Library of Congress Cataloguing in Publication Data
Data available

Paperback ISBN 1-84472-018-7
Paperback ISBN 978-1-844-72018-7
Hardback ISBN 1-84472-019-5
Hardback ISBN 978-1-844-72019-4

1 3 5 7 9 10 8 6 4 2

Printed and bound in Great Britain

Front cover artwork *Shadows* © Sorcha Williams

Acknowledgments

Grateful thanks to editors and publishers who have kindly given permission to reproduce materials in whole or in part as follows:

A version of Chapter 3 first appeared in the *Australian Feminist Law Journal* (1998); the most recent version appeared in Desmond Manderson (ed), *Courting Death* (1999, London: Pluto Press), as 'The sanctity of death', and is reproduced with kind permission of Professor Manderson.

A version of Chapter 4 appeared first in the *Cambrian Law Review* (2004, Centenary Collection) as 'A lawyer drawn to fame: John van Druten', with kind permission of the editor, Richard W Ireland. Chapter 1 is an amended version of a much longer essay entitled 'Then and now: the natural/positivist nexus at war: Auden's "September 1, 1939"' appearing in the *Journal of Law and Society* (2004) 31.

Chapter 6 was first published as 'Cultivated citizen or popular savage? – the *Crash* of the moral mirror' in *Current Legal Issues* (2003): Law and Popular Culture (Oxford: OUP) and the version appearing here is with the kind permission of the editor, Professor Michael Freeman.

The essay contained in Chapter 7 first appeared as 'The law of marriage in *Jude the Obscure*' in 1996 – thanks to the *Nottingham Law Journal* for permission to reproduce the essay.

Chapters 8 and 9 both appear with the kind permission of Kluwer; the first was published in *Feminist Legal Studies* (1998) VI, as 'Medico-legal stories of female insanity – three nullity suits', the second in *Feminist Legal Studies* (1999) VII, as 'Is Alec a rapist? – connotations of "rape" and "seduction": a reply to Professor John Sutherland'.

Grateful thanks to Gordon M Williams for permission to quote from *The Siege of Trencher's Farm* (originally published 1969; now published as *Straw Dogs*, London: Bloomsbury (2003)).

Contents

Table of Cases

Introduction

This collection brings together essays and materials written over a period of approximately seven years, from 1997 to 2004. Though they are capable of being linked in terms of a methodology – the development of legal and ethical questions through the medium of literary texts and narrative histories – the issues addressed are varied, covering a range of topics: assisted suicide; sex, violence and media representation; rape and seduction; legal theory, war and politics; expert evidence and insanity; race and identity; censorship, fame and infamy. Most are also linked in the use of literary sources, sources rich in normative commentary and therefore fruitful as a means of extending the moral-philosophical as well as practical issues of law and ethics discussed therein. Many of the essays have a historical perspective, sometimes taking a broad 'history of ideas' approach, alongside individual stories. Tracing such developments through individual events, literatures and laws will – it is hoped – broaden the accessibility of debate for a range of readers with an interest in the topics as social and anthropological phenomena.

Works of poetry and literature can contribute to debate on many levels and, as will be seen, such materials provide solid sources of legal and social history, political and cultural commentary. The approach to literary sources and commentary adopted here – as a springboard in discussing the world of the *possible* – corresponds in particular to 'practical ethics' methodology, whereby ethical and moral questions are tested and developed against a model, metaphor or parable adapted or already prescient to, the issue in question. This model originates not merely in parallels between 'real' and 'imaginary' *stories* of human struggle, but in a singular relation to the texts in question, a recognition of their ability to contribute an additional quality or perspective to existing legal and ethical debate.

The collection is composed predominantly of work building upon essays already published in a range of book or journal productions. A quite separate, more thematically streamlined book, focusing upon different texts and concerns – *Empty Justice: One Hundred Years of Law, Literature and Philosophy* (2002) – was produced around the middle of the periods of production.

The chapters herein each provide a ready source of recent critical material, 'tying-in' and updating the original essays to current debate. The book is loosely arranged into three sections – Law and Poetry, Law and Popular Culture, Law and Prose Narrative – reflecting the nature of the literary sources drawn upon for each study. Though the subjects are diverse, a linked methodology can be found in each essay – using the literary source or approach to provide a springboard for tangential insights otherwise not easily realised in legal scholarship. This is undertaken in the belief that the worlds of legal and political doctrine and policy are much less removed from the 'inner' worlds of private thought, imagination and literary projection than traditional epistemology has suggested. Since this is essentially a diverse essay collection as opposed to a closely worked, choreographed thesis however, it would not seem appropriate to 'graft' an introductory or concluding theoretical *denouement* onto the book. The links to existing scholarship in 'Law and Literature' and 'Law and Popular Culture' are clear but do not claim a strategy of incorporation: no direct bibliography of such associated material is offered. That said, certain themes and characteristics will be noticeable to the reader, reflecting the current writer's response to text. For example, the methodology pays close attention to the original texts under discussion and tries where possible to link the resultant debate to concrete doctrinal questions in law. The materials have a strongly 'British' sourcing – in terms of texts and cases – though the perspectives derived are capable of much broader application. The approach attempts to broaden accessibility to debates, aiming to convey the 'stories' behind the studies. One or two chapters evince a loosely feminist perspective. Overall however the focus underlying 'concrete' doctrinal and policy questions tends to link to normative evaluations – a quest to better understand how cultural and ideological attitudes in relation to a wide range of normative issues may impact in the texts of literatures and laws. Questions of gender identity are sometimes integral to this process.

The article at the heart of Chapter 1 considers a poem by WH Auden, a poem with resonances in key debates to legal theory and which has undergone countless colonisations for various political and cultural purposes and events – most recently following the haunting events of '9/11' and the subsequent debates in politics and law on the nature of law itself.

Chapter 2 recounts a personal story of domestic politics in correspondence with the poet RS Thomas, provoking re-consideration of identity and of cultural history, of the development of notions of 'otherness' in the private and political realms.

Legalisation of physician-assisted suicide is a source of much modern debate. Uncompromising to the claims of the terminally ill who seek such legalisation, most jurisdictions are caught in an ethical and moral stasis, between a fixed notion of 'sanctity' and a limited view of 'autonomy'. Chapter 3 juxtaposes two sources – a powerful poem by Jon Stallworthy with an article by Seamus Heaney – both concerned with the process of spiritual growth, bringing a kinetic power to the debate and widening the ethical vocabulary. The chapter also reveals an additional, somewhat antagonistic 'grain' to the argument, evoked by the correspondence with, and further poetry of, the poet himself.

Chapter 4 provides a brief biographical account of the life of John van Druten, playwright and lawyer, demonstrating the very recent encroachment of the laws of censorship in domestic drama, and the possible links between the personal and professional life of the playwright himself – the man whose work famously gave rise to *Cabaret*. Chapter 5 explores the legal issues in relation to the crime of rape thrown up advertently – and inadvertently – by the film *Straw Dogs*, of the hijack, or colonisation and re-colonisation of the idea of rape. Whilst feminists rightly object to perpetuation of myths asserting that woman's 'no' really means 'yes', an intriguing 'truth' may also arise from an involuntary physiological response – as yet only partially acknowledged in caselaw – suggesting that 'yes' can also mean 'no'. For completeness, the chapter also tells the story of the book which gave rise to the film, a book dealing with the quite different dilemma thrown up by householder self-defence. Chapter 6 reflects upon our current culture of mass media, sex and violence in an age of unquestioning consumerism and unquestioned individuals and reviews the potential message for such debates present in the novel *Crash* by JG Ballard – and the subsequent film of that name, proposing a 'practical ethics' fantasy to sound our understanding of the links between nature and nurture.

Chapter 7 is predominantly a straightforward study in legal history, prefaced by a short reflection upon current policy debates in relation to cohabitation and marriage. Prompted by Thomas Hardy's highly technical account in *Jude the Obscure*, it considers the 'collisions' between the law and individual legal subjects in the realm of Victorian marriage law and identifies the strategies adopted by individuals to circumvent or otherwise take control of legal constraints. The characters of fiction raise hypotheses concerning such strategies; hypotheses which are not readily invoked by examination of the legal-historical record, since by their very nature such activities are designed to evade the record. Chapter 8 is an account of three cases; it does not use literary material as a proving ground, but examines narrative processes in the cases *simpliciter*. Specifically it considers recent controversies relating to the law's reliance upon expert evidence and traces back to three Victorian legal cases: suits of nullity. A suit of nullity of marriage enabled a spouse to claim that the said marriage had not originated in a valid contract. If medical evidence demonstrated that a wife had been insane at the time of contracting marriage, then she lacked capacity to so contract, *ergo*, no marriage existed. In considering the three cases, the essay reviews the quality of the medical evidence brought at trial, the ethical dubiety of the expert evidence and the 'metanarratives' inferred in each case, providing possible alternative explanations for the behaviour of the women concerned.

Rape and sexual offences continue to maintain an odd position as a mirror to wider cultural norms – Chapter 9 (with clear linkage to Chapter 5) takes the form of a 'reply' graphically illustrative of this point. In his article 'Is Alec a rapist?' Professor John Sutherland suggests that readings of the 'rape/seduction' scene in *Tess of the d'Urbervilles* have been shaped by literary-political fashions, culminating, for Sutherland, in a modern interpretation which 'favours' rape and unfairly demonises the character of Alec d'Urberville: 'She who was seduced in the 1890s is she who is raped in the permissive 1960s.' The simple 'polarisation' of the notions of 'rape' and 'seduction' that this statement entails is dramatically undermined by Victorian caselaw, in which both 'rape' and 'seduction' could attract legal notice. This article takes issue with Sutherland's account, demonstrating a selective use of the evidence, and predisposition that is sadly still mirrored in modern court cases involving charges of rape.

No conclusion is offered in this book; the essays do however share a general recognition of the need to nurture a more active civic discourse which avoids sanctimony, but reclaims the right and responsibility of citizens to claim politics, and laws, as their own.

Melanie L Williams

Swansea, 2005

PART I

LAW, POLITICS AND POETRY

CHAPTER 1

JURISPRUDENCE, POLITICS, WAR AND THE MESSAGE – MESSAGES AT WAR: AUDEN'S 'SEPTEMBER 1, 1939'[1]

INTRODUCTION

A poem written by WH Auden at the outbreak of war in 1939 resonates so clearly with moments of crisis down the ages that politicians and the public alike use it as a touchstone for crisis – and it re-appears notably in the days following 9/11. Though at first sight peripheral to the larger-scale political debate, the semiotic message transmitted by the poetic use raises many questions – what is the meaning of this 'populist' attraction of the poem (and particularly, as will be seen, of the line 'we must love one another or die'); what other freight might it carry? To what extent might such a poem, given its ambition, present a meaningful 'snapshot' of the moment in the history of ideas? What – if anything – can the present moment learn from this – how far are the concerns and contradictions expressed in the poem redolent of concerns and contradictions in the wider discourse of politics and law and the narrow debates of theory?

Uncertainty in the West following 9/11 is exacerbated by uncertainty about both the provenance and reliability of international law and the integrity of the polity in such difficult times. Experts in the field of international law do not allay these fears – demonstrating the wide margin for interpretation afforded by the links between legal science and legal theory. The step into the unknown – that is the current threat of, and 'war upon' terrorism, presents questions that reverberate through notions of individual and collective identity, personal and community responsibility, political and legal integrity. The dominance of a kind of thraldom to the notion of terror itself compounds the *locus* of subjection to political accounts that capitalise upon the taint of uncertainty. Polarisations

---

1 The poem 'September 1, 1939' was published in *The New Republic* on 18 October 1939. It can currently be found in, amongst other collections, an anthology of poetry, *Astley*, 2002, p 357. A different version of the essay forming Chapter One of this book appears in the (2004) 31(1) Journal of Law and Society. The essay was first provoked by the odd conjunction of resonance and dissonance in the poem – a perpetual and ongoing resonance with developments in legal theory and politics, a dissonance in some awkward, rejected aspects of the poem, adapted to doubtful political use. The initial intention was to write a fairly straightforward account of how theoretical tensions and fractures in the poem might reflect in similar tensions in law and politics; however, the study developed disparate, intriguing and unwieldy strands and easily could have run to a book that looked at law and Protestantism, international law and war, the origins and offshoots of legal and political theories, and links between physics and metaphysics in personal and in public realms. The present essay is a much altered account.

deepen as credible views surface, which seem accurately to reflect fears as they materialise in the world of domestic politics. For example, Scruton,[2] writing about the conflict as it surfaces in the domestic tensions over the meaning of citizenship, states:

> ... while the newcomers seek the benefits of citizenship, they do not always accept the costs. The primary cost is the privatisation of religion and the public endorsement of the secular rule of law. The secondary cost is tolerance, which means living with free speech, alien manners, other religions and other tribes, Jews included.

Laudable as an attempt to reconcile the difficulties residing in a rapidly changing national and civic dynamic, the article – as the quotation betrays – suffers from a lamentably subjective belief in the originating and continuing integrity and stability of the rule of law, a controlled and sacrificial excision of religious power from public life and a partiality, indicated only by a parenthetic final aside, in relation to the Arab-Jewish conflict. Authentic debate, with the possibility of another point of view, is clearly disengaged, yet fully reflexive engagement might hold the key to a meaningful political and legal debate in this time of domestic and global conflict. Though the excesses of tabloid accounts and political pundits are frequently transparent in their partiality, it is sobering to realise the extent to which the problem is pan-discursive, affecting not only the journalistic musings of philosophers, but the interactions of conceptual worlds in general. As Chadwick (2003) points out, current discussions of the coherence and legitimacy of responses to terrorist threats are driven by 'contractual' models of the global stage insensitive to alterations in the political landscape, whilst noting that:

> The codifications negotiated before World War 1 were drafted by those 'civilised' capitalist states which possessed a degree of parity in (industrialised) armaments, and focused largely on specific weapons, or modes of military behaviour [p 238] ... An army would be foolish to observe non-reciprocated legal niceties, but also exposed is an attitude that subjugated; colonial peoples, for instance, were potentially of less 'worth' than their Christian cousins – a distinction which carries with it both economic and political undertones. The economic worth of the 'uncivilised' was generally to be found in vast stores of raw materials; their political worth, for the most part, was in the material acquisition ... lead[ing] in turn, to a consideration of ... the class interests and wishes reflected in the law ... Significantly, the appearance of a so-called 'new enemy', who operates violently from the 'grey zones' of international political and economic life, threatens many of the heretofore ascertainable frameworks of analysis. With access to important industrial-technological-economic resources, the 'new enemy' is a 'wild card', with utilitarian objectives all its own. [pp 243–52]

A warning of the unfamiliarity of this landscape, the discussion is also a reminder of the historical forces imposing subliminal status to now super-liminal actors – terrorists. Just as the theory of domestic contracts has understood such innate partiality only latterly – slowly recognising the largely mythologised rationale

---

2   Scruton, 'Friends, Muslims, countrymen, lend us your ears', *The Sunday Times* (2004) 15 February.

underlying parity of parties – so too the contractual basis of international law bears an historically tainted and obscure relation to political interests beyond its own intimates. Whilst presenting the coherence of instituted formality, the format of international law and politics is thus vulnerable because otiose, given its foundations in a bygone world. Similarly, the theorising of the agents identified as liminal and subliminal by the law is directed by an elderly myopia. Hess (2003) explains that scholarship on terrorism in the 1970s and 80s developed two models of terrorism (the psychiatric model, where 'there are always personalities prone to commit violent acts', and the sociological model, where personality factors are minimised and structural conditions – economic, social, political – are generative) and, whilst noting the desirability of a model which reflected both concerns, reflects that anyway (Hess, 2003, pp 346–51):

> The last decade changed the picture considerably. Terrorism became much more diversified, much more virulent, and much more dangerous. Political and ideological motivations which were, however far-fetched, still part of the venerable tradition of the Enlightenment, receded and are now overshadowed by regressive, fundamentalist religious ideologies with strong pathological complexions. And these ideologies fuel a much more virulent and lethal terrorism. Christian fundamentalists with right-wing inclinations, racist and white-supremacist, but – a particular American variety of right-wing ideology – anti-state. Jewish fundamentalists like Kahane's Kach Party and Messianic Zionism in general. And above all Islamist fundamentalists … I think that those new wars are a consequence of the breakdown of traditional authorities in the wake of decolonisation, from Britain, France and Portugal to Russia and Serbia, and a consequence of the onslaught of globalization and the establishment of a new worldwide authority … There is a tendency toward ever-larger political units with an internal monopolization of the legitimate use of coercive force, putting an end to wars inside the territory and trying to bring peace, law and order … The driving force is mainly economic …

Now, although Hess exhibits insight into the limitations of the 'old' models propounded by theory, his accommodation of the 'new' alongside a neutral and 'upbeat' account of the significant global actors demonstrates a less than complete digestion of the implications of his own theory; for his analysis presupposes that the 'ever-larger political units' have an ideologically pure foundation, carried forth in their law and politics; and that the 'fundamentalist ideologies' with their 'pathological tendencies' – albeit that some present as Christian ideologies, and American ones at that – are predominantly other: 'above all Islamic fundamentalists'. Surely, from the point of view of those 'others', the terrain appears very different, with an American president and British prime minister motivated, in part, by prayer, by territorial politics, by the hint of political pathologies and notions of legality which appear rather fluid. Hess recalls (2003, p 342):

> … Frantz Fanon's thesis that there is or should be an existentialist element driving actors in their violent acts, a kind of psychological liberation from a politically and culturally over-powering, arrogant, hated and at the same time admired opponent.

Yet, Hess fails to take account of how this translates to the application of violence by the apparently overpowering opponent. Nevertheless, his use of the word 'existentialist' is telling, for the word captures the crystallisation of ideological fracture, fearful autonomy and pursuit of reification, or 're-authentication' invoked by violence when experienced on either side of the 'divide' – whether dominant or subjugated polity. Interacting with this 'collective' perception of the threat from beyond are individuals subject to the pronouncements of their belief system with a concomitantly disabled *locus* of autonomy and authenticity within the system, as the violent and the rhetoric of violence dominates and drowns more measured discourse. Though Hess remarks upon the pathological nature of terrorism and notes (2003, p 348):

> A major factor in both brutality and suicidal nature are the vocabularies of motive and the techniques of neutralization supplied by fundamentalist religion. Religion is, as Freud said in *Civilization and its Discontents*, the collective delusion that saves the believer from having to develop an individual one ... the fundamentalist religion that takes the scriptures and commandments and prophecies literally, liberates the true believer from secular morals, from obligations to tolerance and other norms of the Enlightenment and allows him – even demands of him – to dehumanise the 'others' ...

Hess is blind to his own partiality in reading the provenance of these observations. Such interpretation is fuelled by what might be termed the 'internal narrative neutrality' promulgated by liberalism, with its self-declared dedication to the practice and perfection of impartiality, of adherence, regardless of interest drives, to the principles of justice and truth. As the following discussion of the Auden poem indicates, the search for an ideological base capable of delivering such integrity, whether individual, civic or state, has proved more elusive than our own epistemologies would have us believe ...[3]

THE POLITICS OF THE POEM: 'SEPTEMBER 1, 1939'

This chapter returns to a little examined moment in the history of jurisprudence. A moment fleetingly considered, it has been ascribed, nevertheless, an iconic status in that history,[4] and it is meet to return to it now, at the war-shadowed dawn of the 21st century, to consider how the juxtaposition of war with the positivist-natural law debate compares with the outbreak of an earlier war. The consideration of poetry, alongside philosophy and jurisprudence, permits reflection upon the history of ideas permeating many strands of thought and allows tentative conclusions to be drawn concerning implications for 'local'

---

3   The essay which follows is a much shortened version of the original.
4   Most famously in the Hart-Fuller debate, with especial reference to law under Nazism. This chapter will not be examining that theoretical enquiry directly. Whilst clearly galvanised by the work of Hart and Fuller, the broad question of the natural law and positivist nexus was in another sense somewhat distilled by the *perversion* of law their debate examined – see, for example, the discussion in Cotterell, *The Politics of Jurisprudence* (1989), London: Butterworths, especially at p 131, which emphasises the focus placed by Fuller upon *irregularities* of form (nevertheless begging the question, whether positive law would be law provided formally regular, though substantively doubtful).

theory – especially 'Anglo-American' debate and the influence of discrete aspects of theory as they impinge one upon the other. History also holds lessons for the very notion of theory itself – in the need to consider the 'tensile' properties of legal and political theory, any putative interactions between the formerly separate worlds of the analytic and normative, the 'natural' and 'positive' – particularly tested in the contingent event.

The *locus* for this study is Auden's 'September 1, 1939' – written in New York on the day war broke out. The poem clearly resonates with recent events and this resonance has not escaped the notice of the popular and official polity (of which more anon). For the moment, however, let us concentrate on those elements of particular relevance to the jurisprudence.

It is a commonplace of jurisprudential historiography that the events and horrors of the Second World War induced a revival of natural law theory.[5] Though there is some recognition that the failures of law in the first half of the 20th century were multi-factorial,[6] two concerns remain dominant and to some extent interconnected – a 'failing' Protestant rationalism and a return to natural law theory: both are reflected in the poem. First, the poem refers to the concern that the horrors of Nazi Germany could be attributable in some way to Protestantism, specifically Lutheran Protestantism: 'Accurate scholarship can/Unearth the whole offence/From Luther until now/That has driven a culture mad/Find what occurred at Linz/What huge imago made/A psychopathic god'. Though the reference to a 'huge imago' making 'a psychopathic god' bears some faith in the Jungian imagery of a damaging culture creating a damaged individual, there is a note of scepticism extending to sarcastic disbelief in the invitation to scholars to successfully locate 'what' made the *locus*: the several pressures elude the precision of scholarship (as if to say 'go on then – I defy you to show us this time *what* made it all happen').[7] This scepticism is further underscored by these rather offhand reference points – the improbable gumshoe image of 'unearthing' the 'whole offence', the lazy provocation to '*find* what occurred at Linz'.

Scholarship, rationality, analysis – the flowering of enlightenment skills in politics, creativity, intellectual life altogether – have failed: 'I and the public know/What all schoolchildren learn/Those to whom evil is done/Do evil in return'. The analysis provided by the political theory of Western liberalism, its claim to be able to trace a link between a crazed Germanic culture and Hitler's Nazism and thus safely 'locate' the enemy vis à vis ourselves, can be undone by

5   Morrison, *Jurisprudence: From the Greeks to Postmodernism* (1997) London: Cavendish Publishing, pp 312–21; Freeman, *Lloyd's Introduction to Jurisprudence* (2001) London: Sweet & Maxwell, p 367.

6   Freeman, 2001, p 123.

7   Hecht, *The Hidden Law* (1993) Cambridge, Mass: Harvard University Press, pp 156–57, seems to hold that this line reveals a sincere faith in scholarship, though it picks up a similarly 'gumshoe' flavour to the enterprise:

   The diagnostic skill implied in 'accurate scholarship' is a twofold aptitude: both historical and psychological. The investigation will perhaps begin in the realm of history ... 'Unearth' is a colloquialism for something as innocent as 'reveal', but it carries the murder-mystery overtones and criminal flavour ...

the public, even by schoolchildren. The lesson of the playground is played out in international politics – the stringent and punitive terms of the Versailles Treaty were bound to return evil to its makers. Positivism as rationalism fails. It fails to deliver a convincing account or remedy, and the positivism of an allegedly liberal international politics and law fails – in perpetrating a failed ethics under the guise of a 'reparatory' and corrective agenda. For Auden, and for many of his generation, and thus for the collective intellectual mind, this presaged a retreat into the classical notions of 'fundamentalist' values, either as religious or as metaphysical elementals. The 'challenge' of positivism – to adhere to the rationalist project 'through thick and thin', to adhere to it even when the physical world threatens imminent death and chaos – proves too great a challenge to the human psyche when positivism can only offer the tentative steps of the logician, without any accompanying promise of spiritual security or redemption.[8]

The fifth stanza concentrates upon the hopeless vulnerability of mankind and its tendency to seek security and stasis in an illusory world of material comforts – 'Lest we should see where we are/Lost in a haunted wood/Children afraid of the night/Who have never been happy or good.' Auden's view of human nature is essentially compassionate, but not particularly hopeful; persons, citizens, are 'children', never 'happy' or 'good'. This is followed, in the sixth stanza, with a reminder that these citizens suffer from a particular flaw – susceptibility to 'The windiest militant trash', which is 'not so crude as our wish/ … the error bred in the bone/Of each woman and each man/Craves what it cannot have/Not universal love/But to be loved alone'. This confirms the trajectory begun with an 'enlightenment driven away'; any collective project, any 'strength of Collective Man', is liable to be desiccated by the needy insatiable vulnerability of each of its constituent parts. As stanza seven reflects, individuals *do* apprehend the 'pull' of community ethics, of an ethical polity, and they make attempts to respond to it;

---

8   The third stanza – 'Exiled Thucydides knew/All that a speech can say/About Democracy/And what dictators do … [ending with]/The enlightenment driven away/The habit forming pain/Mismanagement and grief:/We must suffer them all again/' – reflects not only the historical lessons of the battle fought between claims to democracy and those of dictatorship, but heightens the sense that the cycle is possibly unavoidable, *not* susceptible to reason – that the 'habit forming pain' of contingent disaster is always liable to predominate, to conquer attempts to nurture rational progress. In times of crisis we cannot rely upon the salvation of reason, but return to our primitive selves. To a logician, this might simply provide a stimulus to rationalising how to overcome the failure – perhaps a central challenge to analytical positivists; to Auden, it seems to have presaged a retreat to religion as the only 'logical' outcome – an acceptance of our inability to control events.
     The fourth stanza – 'Into this neutral air/Where blind skyscrapers use/The full height to proclaim/The strength of Collective Man/Each language pours its vain/Competitive excuse/But who can live for long/In an euphoric dream/Out of the mirror they stare/Imperialism's face/And the international wrong' – again emphasises the failure of rationalism and liberal politics; differing explanations are, in the end, simply vain (useless) and also vain in the sense of ego-driven, as is emphasised with the immediate juxtaposition of 'competitive'. Intellectual debate cannot explain away the images which stare back at it – imperialism, with its full history of justification, and 'the international wrong' – the complicity which has led to a crisis which should be understood as a result of complex historical forces, rather than the easy depiction of 'us' and 'them'.

but such attempts are inevitably driven by small local and personal imperatives and by the pressures of daily existence, none of which are sufficiently responsive to a reflective ethical transformation: 'From the conservative dark/Into the ethical life/The dense commuters come/Repeating their morning vow/ "I *will* be true to the wife/I'll concentrate more on my work."' Now that large scale ideologies have failed, who can provide a workable template for salvation from such treadmill mediocrity – 'Who can release them now/Who can reach the deaf/Who can speak for the dumb?'

In stanza eight, Auden's response to his own question recognises its essential hopelessness. As a poet, any 'release' he can offer is merely an incantation, a 'voice', ending with an imperative. The material conditions of existence, social and physical – 'There is no such thing as the State/And no-one exists alone/Hunger allows no choice/To the citizen or the police/' – predicate one conclusion: 'We must love one another or die.' In this conclusion we see the seeds of both utilitarian pragmatic positivism – that we must have ascertainable rules and a willingness to abide by them – and of an appeal to naturalist metaphysics, and in a sense the trajectory of arguments leading to this anticlimactic climax encapsulates the history, the currency of the debate, the intransigent dilemma *and* its relevance to modern philosophical discourse in the face of similar crises. Yet, though for Auden the poem was a prelude to his rationalised journey to religion,[9] the conclusion does not herald a sentimental journey. Of all the poems, this was one Auden was to repudiate most strongly, and his repudiation lay in his identification of the hopeless collapse of rationality, the dangerous emotivism of 'We must love one another or die'.

Accounts of the poem, and of Auden's rejection of the poem, produce a fascinating insight into political and philosophical cultures. The poem in its entirety has been colonised and metabolised for a huge range of purposes, and indeed so lends itself to propagandist claims as to form a further insult emanating from the poem in the mind of Auden. A reflection upon the poem's resonance with the events surrounding 9/11 would be an 'easy' essay indeed. The poem chimes strangely with our time in many ways – most dramatically for some perhaps in its location in a New York of 'blind skyscrapers' which 'use/The full height to proclaim/The strength of Collective Man' where 'The unmentionable odour of death/Offends the September night' and marking the beginning of war; but a more interesting story can be retrieved from consideration, simply, of the conflict and collapse of ideas that almost certainly formed the core of Auden's own repudiation of the poem and the possible links to fields of conflict across theory in general. My title, 'The natural/positivist nexus at war',[10] is a reference to the link between the time of the poem and the time of ideological change in the

---

9 In fact, a fascinating journey can be tracked through his poetry – many scholars, such as A Hecht, E Mendelson, J Replogle, A Rodway and S Smith, have produced careful accounts of the developments, with varying emphases. Hecht, for example, concentrates upon the religious journey. Perhaps the most consciously political analysis is, however, provided by S Smith, WH *Auden: Re-reading Literature* (1985) (series edited by T Eagleton) Oxford: Blackwell.

10 As originally published.

teeth of war – jurisprudential historiography marks the event as a point of reference, as a time when, so it is argued, the alleged 'vacuum' created by positivism permitted the amorality, in Hannah Arendt's terms, the 'banality' of evil.

PROTESTANTISM, IDEOLOGY AND THE 'WRONG KIND' OF AUTONOMY

Broadly, the poem appears to corroborate – or at very least, not to contradict – that key folk tale of jurisprudence – of the link between Nazism and the natural law revival. Though Auden expresses scepticism as to the ability of scholarship to provide a convincing account of 'the whole offence', though *one* ultimate answer is the simple, playground answer that evil returns evil, the poem, by its very location of argument, gives some credence to the hypothesis concerning 'a' journey from Luther to Linz. In one sense, this feeds into contemporary theorising about the seductive capability of National Socialism and Nazism to metabolise those aspects of indigent culture and belief that will create the best composite ideology for popular German consumption – let the people hang on to some of their old icons, parade this popularised politics as an *ethical* and yet *spiritual* ideology, and attach it to their own Lutheran Protestantism.[11] But in another sense, Auden is perhaps playing out his own concerns about the trajectory created by Protestantism – the link between Protestantism and intellectual independence, its proto-political contribution not only to rationalism, individualism, liberalism, positivism (all creatures of an antic enlightenment period reaching full maturity in the modern period of his day) but thereby to a ludic, anarchic intellectual stage guilty of *complicity* in the assemblage of dubious ideologies from scavenged remnants.[12] Though perhaps no more than retrospective and impotent posturing, the 'low dishonest decade' of the 1930s, with its personal and collective ideological wars – via socialism, communism, fascism – and its claim to be able to *reason* solutions could be characterised as part of the offence compounded by Luther and exploited by Hitler. Ultimately, *this* reading of the link between

---

11   The impact of Protestantism, and of Lutherism, was widely discussed in the early 20th century. Reinhold Niebuhr, who became a friend of Auden and stimulated (though did not necessarily profoundly influence) his thinking (see Mendelson, *Later Auden* (1999) London: Faber), wrote prolifically in the 1930s and 40s. Niebuhr, *The Nature and Destiny of Man* (1943), p 198 bears a searching discussion of the difficulty for Lutheran Protestantism in the conception of law. A more recent, comprehensive critique is that of Witte, *Law and Protestantism* (2002) Cambridge: CUP.

12   The possible links to Lutheranism, Protestantism and Nazism are numerous. They include the Lutheran contribution of the separation of Church and state; the specific creed that individuals be responsible for their own moral decisions; Protestantism as anarchy leading to a vacuum; the anti-semitism of the later Luther; Protestantism as human intellectual vanity leading to the misleading 'pretensions' of positivism; for Auden, the Luther-Linz journey has personal implications, given his dalliance with aesthetic Germany; also on a personal level, this stage of Auden's life marked an incipient return to High Anglicanism (and the preceding failure of political ideologies – yet note Auden and Isherwood's later agreement that they might just as easily have 'fallen for' Fascism as a favoured ideology under slightly different circumstances); that rejection of Catholicism by Protestantism provides the 'latitude' or 'vacuum' for pseudo-ideologies, such as Nazism specifically or the general collapse of values less specifically.

Protestantism and positivism – the link between Protestantism as independent thought and rationalism as an empirical ethic – provided an essentialist retreat for Western intellectuals recoiling from Nazi atrocities, the 'return' to natural law. The stanza identifying a journey 'from Luther to Linz', invokes the preamble, so to speak, to the mechanics of the Hart-Fuller debate, where Hart and Fuller discuss the boundaries and meaning of the separation thesis in relation to dystopic legal systems, such as the system subsisting under Nazism. In the 1930s and 40s two debates raged that impinged more broadly upon any such separation. One debate was the impact upon epistemology created by the sciences of society, by 'accurate scholarship' and by science itself.[13] The other related question was how the separation of Church and state has assisted in the inception of such dystopic law. As Auden appreciated well, the challenge reaches beyond the realm of 'accurate scholarship' alone. The separation of 'fact' systems from 'value' systems – of 'physical' worlds from 'metaphysical' worlds – is characteristic in both fields; the consequent impact upon notions of individual and collective responsibility more than merely incidental, for each, and both together, create variants upon the notion of autonomy. A key factor in current debates upon how we model 'rights', and also in the way normative and analytical forms of jurisprudence are positioned in relation one to the other, 'autonomy' may be understood as the particle at the heart of competing theories of law. For Auden, the period presaged something very similar, turning to God via a rationale provided by Kierkegaard and closely mirroring Auden's personal experience – a journey from aesthetics (art and the Bacchanalian) to ethics (an engagement with politics) to God.

Auden's identification of the contribution of Luther, of a particular form of Protestantism to the inception of an aberrant order, keys into a still-debated fragment in the history of ideas concerning Protestantism more generally. Simmonds[14] traces the roots of the separation thesis via a recovery of the strands linking Aristotle to Grotius, Hobbes and Kant, demonstrating how early scholarship understood its own contribution to notions of the natural and the physical, the individual and the collective, and how this contribution has been misunderstood by subsequent transcription. Simmonds models the form of Protestantism which shaped a particular embodiment of autonomy as follows:[15]

> Retaining the Aristotelian view of humanity as essentially social, such late scholastics and early Protestants as Grotius found it natural to regard our moral nature as articulated in the form of our institutions. Such assumptions were fundamental to the Grotian origins of systematic doctrinal scholarship. The inwardness of Protestantism, however, was to undercut this position and encourage a perspective that regarded actual institutions as potential threats to autonomy, rather than as anchors of moral reflection ...

Simmonds demonstrates how this process is exacerbated by the distorting influence of the notion of the categorical imperative which fostered the *locus* of

---

13 Especially relativity – considering the range of works from Haldane to Whitehead.
14 Simmonds, 2001, pp 271–300.
15 *Ibid*, p 286.

that particular notion of autonomy within the separation thesis,[16] and shows how this trajectory of 'misunderstood' or unworkable Protestant autonomy leads directly to Dworkin.[17]

LOVE ONE ANOTHER *AND* DIE ...

After writing the poem, Auden was shocked into the arms of religious explanations by, in particular, his realisation of human weakness and his loss of faith in rationality as an *adequate* source of solutions. Yet his subsequent insistence that we must 'love one another *and* die',[18] that we keep justice alive through *ironic* points of light, relies upon a plea to rationality independent of essences. The admission that even a successful polity – 'love' – will *still die* – marks a refusal to pour the balm of a falsely Utopian *worldly* resolution or divine immortality upon the political wound. Given that law could be described as a system designed to contain the impact of the immanent and contingent, war – as we have recently observed – becomes its most rigorous test. Just as Auden's poem reveals this moment of ideological fracture – what might be described as the collapse of the natural-positivist *engagement* in human perception – with the loss of a credible secular rationality becoming overwhelmed by a tide of metaphysical neediness, so discussions of uniformity and contingency seems more relevant. In the endless recalibration of factors that forms the discourse between analytical and normative jurisprudence, the unpredictable nature of the contingent world is poorly debated.

---

16   *Ibid*, pp 285–87:

Kant's emphasis upon the detached and categorical nature of morality, ungrounded in either practice or desire, and the related detachment of the 'noumenal' self, rendered older forms of jurisprudential reflection unintelligible. The consequence of this Kantian perspective was a sense that only two forms of inquiry were possible, or even conceivable, for the philosophy of law ... one was a normative inquiry ... the other enterprise that survived Kant's grounding of morality in individual autonomy and radical detachment was an exercise in conceptual clarification.

17   *Ibid*, pp 293–94:

The problem of subjectivity makes law necessary; and doctrinal scholarship appears to extend and perfect the determinacy of law's governance. Yet how can it do this without falling prey to the very subjectivity that gives rise to law's centrality in the first place? Such a question should have been squarely raised in the debates surrounding Dworkin's theory of law ... The question was not ... adequately addressed because people were too busy asking whether Dworkin had refuted Hart's thesis that there are no necessary conceptual connections between law and morals ... A far more important question ... concerns the viability of Dworkin's account of legal doctrine ... Since Dworkin contemplates a liberal society where people may be expected to hold diverse moral views, we might have expected him to urge the importance of laws that are possessed of a content ascertainable independently of individual moral judgment. This is, however, not so: Dworkin adopts a 'Protestant' view of law in which each individual must rely upon his or her own moral judgment in deciding what the law requires ... Take [Dworkin's argument] that a shared sense of danger might protect us from the centrifugal forces of 'Protestant' interpretation. Dworkin simply ignores the fact that the situation he is discussing resembles in its structure the classic 'tragedy of the commons' beloved of economists and Hobbesian philosophers. Individual agents would have a strong incentive to proffer interpretations of law that favoured their own position and preferences ...

18   Altering the line in the poem from the original injunction to 'love one another *or* die'.

Attempts to formulate points of contact between analytic and normative models of philosophy and law may, with good reason, appear more sophisticated than those of the early 20th century. Identification of Dworkin's theoretical weakness as traceable to autonomy culture and decontextualisation (both of individual and semantic operations) is *part* of the story of current legal theory. The weakness is also a predictable outcome of the truncations in theory generally. Part of this may be traced to a mistaken Protestant inheritance, partly to the symbolic magnitude of war in relation to an overweening, ego-driven, mechanistic positivism; but less visible contingencies may also have been co-incidents.

REJECTION OF THE POEM, METABOLISATION, AND THE LESSON OF 'THE WINDIEST MILITANT TRASH'

Perhaps one of the most profound lessons for any analysis of unfolding processes of theory is not just the poem itself, but the subsequent rejection of the poem by Auden alongside its unending metabolisation, for varying purposes, by others. A poem most frequently referred to, adopted by popular causes and endlessly prescient of contingent events, Auden was quick to distance himself and attempted to excise it from the *corpus* of his work. Appearing at a crucial point in his own ideological crisis, the poem inhabits a space of transition, where adoption of a compelling but inauthentic synthesis is immanent. Two expressions in the poem were altered by Auden. The first related to the call to collective unity, to 'love one another or die'. The second alteration related to the notion of justice preserved through the dark days: the initial impotence of the agents of justice signalling their 'little' points of light were later modified as 'ironic' points – arguably a more potent vehicle for the preservation of justice, despite temporary suspension. He knew that the momentary zeal producing 'we must love one another or die' was logically, and ideologically, thin – altering it to 'we must love one another *and* die' before abandoning it altogether – and his apprehension was borne out by the successive generations of popular zealots, political spinners and desperate myth makers to whom such sentiments so readily lent themselves. Accounts of the significance of the poem, and of Auden's recoil, vary, and this variation, too, is a point of caution to analysis. Carpenter notes that:[19]

> The poem's closing words were echoed in a book review Auden wrote about two weeks later ... 'There is one way to the true knowledge and only one,' he wrote, 'a praxis which, if defined in terms of human relations, we should call love'. But there was still no question in his mind of this view becoming anything that could be called religious belief ... he suggested that belief in God as a conscious agent outside Man was 'dualist' and therefore wrong ...

Nevertheless, within weeks, the inexorable attraction back to a metaphysics, which would provide divine support, was completed when:[20]

---

19   Carpenter, *WH Auden: A Biography* (1982) London: HarperCollins, at p 274.
20   *Ibid*, p 282.

[t]wo months after the outbreak of war, in November 1939, he went to a cinema in Yorkville, the district of Manhattan where he and Isherwood had lived for a few weeks in the spring. It was largely a German-speaking area, and the film he saw was *Sieg im Poland*, an account by the Nazis of their conquest of Poland. When Poles appeared on the screen he was startled to hear a number of people in the audience scream 'Kill them!' He later said of this: 'I wondered then, why I reacted as I did against this denial of every humanistic value. The answer brought me back to the church.' He had been through many changes of heart since reaching adulthood, but all the dogmas he had adopted or played with – post-Freudian psychology, Marxism, and the liberal-socialist-democratic outlook ... had one thing in common: they were all based on a belief in the natural goodness of man. They all claimed that if one specific evil were removed ... sexual repression ... the domination ... by the bourgeoisie, or Fascism, then humanity would be happy ... [even his viewpoint in] the summer of 1939 ... which might be called liberal humanism with religious and pacifist overtones, was still based on a belief in man's natural goodness. Its message was, in the words of the poem which summed it up, 'We must love one another or die': that is, only the exercise of love between human beings would save humanity from self-destruction ... Auden's experience in the Yorkville cinema in November 1939 radically shook this belief. He now became convinced that human nature was not and never could be good ... 'The whole trend of liberal thought', he wrote during 1940, 'has been to undermine faith in the absolute ... It has tried to make reason the judge ... But since life is a changing process ... the attempt to find a humanistic basis for keeping a promise, works logically with the conclusion, "I can break it whenever I feel it convenient."'

This view was confirmed by Auden's reading of Kierkegaard, for whom the 'ethical' stage of experience (which followed upon the 'aesthetic' – note the similarities to Comte)[21] with its clear identity with politics and ideology:

> ... would soon in its turn prove inadequate, because it made no claims on any transcendent notion of eternity, and because its foundation, a belief in the individual's (or humanity's) basic righteousness would soon prove false – which was precisely what Auden had just realised.[22]

In a letter written to Stephen Spender in April 1940,[23] Auden writes:

> Just been reading Neville Henderson's book. What emerges most strongly I feel is that the basic weakness of the democracies is the failure to realise that if you give up Catholicism – and I think we must – one has to discover one's base again and that is a very long and very exhausting job. Henderson is the typical lazy Protestant living off the fat of his Catholic past and imagining that metaphysics and mysticism are unnecessary – the virtues will be kept alive by good form ...

---

21 Comte, a leading positivist, devised a linear philosophy which posited the development of human intellectual understanding in terms of a movement from a theological to a metaphysical towards a final positive, *scientific* phase. Kierkegaard similarly posited a linear development but beginning with the aesthetic, or sensory, moving on to the ethical, and concluding with the religious.

22 *Op cit*, Carpenter, fn 19, p 285.

23 Quoted in Bucknell and Jenkins (eds), *The Map of All My Youth* (1990) Oxford: OUP, p 73.

Yet retracing a workable lineage for a new belief system – trying to 'discover one's base again' – clearly proved too great a challenge for Auden himself. In a sense, the poem quite clearly flags this *moment* of ideological crisis, a moment visible in the chronology of reading and thoughts in Auden's personal accounts; and the symptom, the visible stigmata of this crisis, lies in the failure of thought at the heart of the poem. If Neville Henderson was a 'lazy Protestant', Auden was a hazy metaphysician. As Smith comments on the poem:[24]

> The only way to elude this power of positive lying, in which every text is subverted by its negation, is to speak with the irony and indirection that is linked to justice in the last stanza. But even here the lie suborns affirmative speech ... What the poem affirms, in effect, is its own desperate sense of failure, its yearning for a community and a succession, at the moment that it realizes this is no more than one grand rhetorical gesture before falling on the floor ... One can understand Auden's embarrassment in the grey light of dawn. But it is precisely its honesty in catching the duplicity and bad faith that makes it a fine and powerful poem ... The poem undoes the folded lie of the ideologically composed subject ...

Hungry for a *comprehensive* – transcendent – ideological pathway, a religious, or at any rate, metaphysically rich, 'solution' was perhaps incipient for Auden, as it was for many thinkers of the time. Yet he continued to grapple with the political implications of semantics, howsoever resolved his divine contract. In the 1950s Auden further crystallised and objectified the problem of the thin ideological seam. By this time, as Smith makes clear, Auden recognised the corruption of the word:[25]

> ... the song from the resonant heart in the grand old manner no longer work[s]. These forms have been hopelessly compromised by a mass society, where 'All words like peace and love,/All sane affirmative speech,/Had been soiled, profaned, debased/To a horrid mechanical screech.' In 1950–51, for veteran socialists like Auden ... such a profane language was not confined to the Eastern bloc, but was embodied in the United States by the horrid mechanical screech of McCarthyism, in a language 'Concocted by editors/Into spells to befuddle the crowd', 'pawed-at and gossiped over', leaving the only surviving civil style that of a marginalized 'suburb of dissent', wry, ironic, *sotto voce*. It is the quietness of Auden's dissenting style, in the fifties, which misleads the critic into believing he has renounced politics ...

Scholarly 'threads' on the internet indicate the extent to which Auden's poem has been adapted to political rhetoric, notably by a speech-writer for George Bush, Senior, and for Ronald Reagan.[26] Most dramatically however, Mendelson records that:[27]

> ... in 1964 ... the advertising consultant who prepared television spots for Lyndon Johnson's presidential campaign – a campaign that accurately portrayed Johnson's

---

24 *Op cit*, Smith, fn 9, pp 30–31.

25 Smith, p 169.

26 See D Lupher, internet thread 'Auden, *Sept 1, 1939*' (was: 'Re 9/11'). Was at http://omega.cohums.ohio-state.edu.

27 *Op cit*, Mendelson, fn 10, p 478.

opponent as eager to use nuclear weapons while inaccurately portraying Johnson as a committed peacemaker – produced a thirty-second film in which a young girl counted the petals she was picking from a daisy while a male voice-over counted from ten to zero. When the countdown ended, the image of the girl disappeared and a nuclear explosion filled the screen. Over the expanding mushroom cloud was heard Johnson's voice: 'These are the stakes: to make a world in which all of God's children can live, or go into the dark. We must love each other or we must die.' The dark, the children, and the night, together with the resonant misquoted line, were all lifted from Auden's poem.

An internet search for *September 1, 1939* reveals a mass identification of 1/9/1939 with 9/11/2001:[28] 'Auden's words are everywhere ... the Times Literary Supplement ... It was read on National Public Radio ... the Chicago area ... four blocks from ground zero in Manhattan ... newspaper cited one of the poem's most familiar lines, "We must love one another or die".' The thin ideological seam, its tensile weakness, continues to fracture with this benighted line, providing a muster station of collective emotivism.

CONCLUSION: THEORY THEN AND NOW – ANGLO-AMERICAN ALLOYS

The points of fracture in Auden's poem – and responses to them – reveal the network of ideological and historical factors besetting the development of functional notions of autonomy in a destabilised world. As in the world of pragmatic decision, so also in the world of theory, the claim to rational neutrality bound to the myth of the individual unfettered by prejudicial interests, holds great sway. Yet, whether in his juristic, political or philosophical mode, this 'creature' of autonomy is subject to poorly reconciled tensions between the inhibitions of mortal life and of personal, local and global polity. The pragmatic message, that we must love one another *and* die, remains submerged by competing claims to deliver an integrity of immortal magnitude.

It was Auden's fate – and that of developing theory itself – to encounter the fulcrum of ideas at a time when, to quote WB Yeats, 'the centre cannot hold'[29] – at a time of war. Like Wordsworth before him,[30] the excesses of visible collective human weakness drove Auden away from the pursuit of politics and rationality back into the private and, for him, the religious; and it is likely that not only the intellectual uncertainty of this encounter with *logic itself* proved too great. For a crucial period of this time, Auden had grappled with the philosophical picture advanced by AN Whitehead – Whitehead's *presentation* of the arguments may also

---

28 Sites continue to proliferate, but see, for example, items on *The Boston Globe* at www.boston.com.

29 WB Yeats, 'The Second Coming' was written in the wake of the First, 'Great', World War.

30 The poet William Wordsworth famously returned from witnessing the appalling excesses of the French Revolution and, despairing of his erstwhile hope of witnessing the birth of a new humanist polity, his poetry became markedly committed to the private, individual and domestic life.

have fuelled the failure to sustain a philosophical perspective.[31] Nevertheless, Whitehead's discussion of our engagement with the contingent world around us provides a conception of the appalling range of factors to be apprehended in the understanding of any moment, or cluster of moments. War is the result of a tension between a collective prehension and apprehension, in a world of distant 'perceptual objects' and unpredictable 'ingressions'.[32] Add to this the elements of human nature contributing to the inception of war – aggression, territoriality, passionate ideological identities, greed, anxiety (all identified as competing claims in Auden's poem) and the challenge facing the philosopher and jurist is significant indeed.[33] The 'vertigo' of this incredible metaphysics of physics steered Auden away from faith in rationalism towards a more tenable rationalism of faith, which he soon found in the more comfortably *linear* approach of Kierkegaard. The poetic, moral and rational failure embodied in the line 'We must love one another or die' is symptomatic of the crisis. Arguably, it exemplifies a collapse of reason into a sea of sentiment. More profoundly, it heralds the further separation of belief in systems and systems of belief that characterised intellectual thought in many fields from that time on. The process-driven argument was overshadowed by that forerunner of postmodernity, the threat of relativity – in science and philosophy – and then, as now, seemed therefore to presage a loss of all values. In jurisprudence, as in philosophy, the new insights derived from the human capacity for war and atrocity had their own antecedents, not least in terms of cultural flux on each side of the Atlantic.

The contingent event of war – and the ideological strains leading up to war – drove theorists back to 'natural law' models, in part because of the altered picture of human nature and the associated need to review the credibility of man-made laws. This 'trauma' also drove individuals like Auden, and possibly the unconscious trends within the greater intellectual community, back to the natural law view – sometimes amounting to a reliance upon the divine as the only 'bearable' way to deal with the vertiginous reality of war and human suffering. Alongside Simmond's historical account of the natural-positivist divide as unnecessary bifurcation, we can still observe an unexplored parallel line. Auden's poem betrays a personal turning away from the philosophical journey of positivism (and indeed his attraction to Kierkegaard places him in almost exact

---

31 Whitehead's *Process and Reality* (1929) Cambridge: CUP, exemplifies this. On the one hand, his writing is so impenetrable as to obscure the rational appeal held out by his position. In addition, he claims to achieve a further, macroscopic synthesis, an 'organic' process, encompassing not only the time-space problematic, but also God – the 'vertigo' of freefalling space and time invites a compensatory organic metaphysics. It is likely that, at the very least, this undermined his claim to scientific objectivity and thus his credibility. For Davidson, it confirmed a psychologically sceptical positivism, though Davidson adapted Whitehead's notion of the event as moment.

32 To borrow directly from Whitehead's terms, which at times bear some resemblance to those of Gerard Manley Hopkins.

33 Whitehead's rationale would seem to point up the ethical challenge of incipient events – his view of a dynamic universe in which both man and God are implicated in the realms of possibility nevertheless places great focus upon the percipient intervention, the *action*. Though there is a kind of optimism inherent in the idea of 'process', it bears an uncertainty not present in conventional notions of teleology.

opposition to Comte) and it reflects the 'popular' account – quite apart from the
exchanges undertaken by scholars such as Fuller and Hart – of why the natural/
positivist divide became crystallised by war – as atrocity and human frailty drove
theory 'back' towards 'natural law' certainties and humilities.[34] Yet, the
continuing influence of positivism as an offshoot of an enlightenment project that
sought to explore intellectual possibility as an expression of human capability and
potential[35] – as a quest for an ethical legitimacy born of reason – remains vast. The
links between logical positivism and linguistics, as well as logical positivism and
legal positivism, are more than merely historical. They reflect a deliberate
resistance to emotivism and are sustained by a separability thesis of which a *sense*
arguably should be sustained, despite the caution voiced by the collapse of the
fact/value distinction.[36] The alteration to the actual course of theory is more
difficult to chart – with its strands of cross-fertilisation – but despite the small
shockwave of the war/natural law tremor, British positivism is still predominant
because of an 'incremental', sceptical intellectual tradition (a characteristic which
Whitehead deplored for obvious reasons). Yet, we cannot resist the iconic power
accorded to war in the minds of men as a *locus* of *ideological* reaction, even if we
understand it intellectually and physically as just another contingent event, or just
another collision of historical forces, as opposed to a predominantly *engineered* act
of aggression, of a controlled embodiment of 'evil'.[37] The event itself provides a
testing ground for possible conflicts between – and the credibility of natural and
positivist models of – notions of legality, *and* for arguments about whether, and to
what extent, each *contains* elements of the other, given the potential of 'the event'
in posing an opportunity for theory to be tested against a problem-centred
moment. Certainly, the 'contest' between positivist and natural law theories
seems writ large in the political rhetoric surrounding accounts of legality; the
embarrassment of religious faith *behind* the machine of secular law and politics an
interesting entity[38] threatening a potential collapse of the claimed distinctive
ideological integrity vis à vis the 'fundamentalism' of Eastern positions. On the
one hand, we may say that philosophy is now more fit to raise an analytical
account of potentially synthetic conceptual strands. On the other hand, any such
highly evolved positivism capable of rising from the ashes of a fragmented

---

34 Indeed, as has been noted, the event of war itself contributed to the fragmentation of
    the Vienna Circle as an unfolding centre of logical positivism.

35 In contradistinction to the infantilising mindset forced upon Man by an overweening
    metaphysical shadow. The position emerging here would tend therefore to 'lean'
    towards a positivist 'emphasis' *as an ethic*, in contrast to the analysis posed by Stephen
    Hall – see 'The persistent spectre: natural law, international order and the limits of legal
    positivism' (2001) 12(2) European Journal of International Law 269–307.

36 Albeit a collapse with more ancient roots than are often admitted, with 'Humean'
    restoration and with an added potency in current scientific and humanities theory.

37 The European split over whether military action in Iraq was legitimate, with a failure to
    comply with a multitude of resolutions on the one hand and a lack of consensus on the
    final resolution on the other, has certainly been an interesting lesson in international
    law and politics. The division of international lawyers regarding action on the status of
    Resolution 1441 is summarised by P Gould, in 'War with Iraq "could be illegal"', *BBC
    News Online*, http://news.bbc.co.uk/1/hi/uk/2826331.stm.

38 For a discussion of perceptions of the religious 'war', see 'Atlantic storms', *Time*:
    www.time.com.

international legal and political order is threatened, not just by that fragmentation, but by the clear seduction power of alternative principles which offer to *salve* as well as *assuage* the brute conditions of material existence – a real battleground between natural and positivist views of legality.

How then does this affect how we envision the natural law/positivist divide, or future models of law? How do currents of theory presently unfolding compare with those of the 1930s and 40s, remembering that, insofar as the disputes about relativity and its possible/probable impact on metaphysics were concerned, they were in place long before the war, and that the argument, that positivism can be a more conscientious, because conscious, basis for ethics, remains compelling. Legal positivism, in the 'macrocosmic', 'structural' sense, may be 'about' the source of law, but its adumbration of analytical positivism is a direct descendant of empirical method. The most difficult question is still the relation of sense data – including our articulation of it via semantic logic – to constructions of 'reality'. Looking back at Auden's crisis, his turning, like many of his generation, from positivist polity to fundamental faith can be characterised as a failure of rationalism, an inability to stem the tide of atavistic instinct in the face of ideological crisis. For Auden specifically, AN Whitehead proved a poor propagandist for rationalism, compared to Kierkegaard, partly because of Whitehead's impenetrability, but also, arguably, because of the *sentimentality* behind Whitehead's drive for an *organic* account of rationality and science – a process and reality which seem very much like an act of bad faith – which was a forced synthesis. Whilst noting the patent danger that *positivism's* own logical resistance to the annexation of a moving popular ideology may leave it vulnerable to being 'overrun' by mass ideological appetite; the failure of an 'organic' account linked to logical positivism at *that* time may provide a warning to us now. Though the collapse of the fact-value distinction is further verified in the scientific, as in the philosophical, realm with implications for logical and legal positivism, which may herald a necessary and natural flowering of synthetic theories, such as consideration of deontic logic, the need for a fundamental *sense* of a neutral positivist ethic should hold the centre together in time of crisis. Similarly, in Auden's poem, the 'leap' of 'we must love one another *or* die' looks very like a metaphysical knee-jerk, a 'thin' theory of the good, a natural lawyer's assertion of faith, with its promise, behind the apparent stake in utility ('if we don't create a workable polity, a workable international relations, we will kill ourselves') of immortality ('if we achieve universal love, we achieve a kind of immortality, a defeat of mortality itself'). The alteration to 'we must love one another *and* die' at least gives proper place to the knowable physics of our mortal imprimatur. The final stanza acts both as a warning and as a reclamation of this need for a centre. The collapse of rationality preceding it (which Auden himself could not control, yet subsequently found intellectual and artistically untenable), the insoluble paradox of 'the error bred in the bone' wishing not for 'universal love', but 'to be loved alone', so improbably juxtaposed with 'we must love one another or die' implies a centre that cannot hold. The final stanza reminds us that the focus of this debate lies not with attempts to produce rationalisations of compromise, but with attempts to concentrate on notions of justice; and it is significant that the 'little' points of light originally inscribed in the stanza signalling individual visions of justice are revised as 'ironic' points – a veering back toward sceptical rationality rather than toward the 'little' of sentimental individuals cathected from community, with their burden of impotent fatalism. The institution of 'ironic' points of light in the approach to justice (in the final stanza of Auden's poem) reasserts the sense of the sceptical, whilst the erasure of the 'little' points of light with this irony in place of littleness is a rejection of the vision of an impotent human agent and concomitant fatalism that tends to underlie the 'natural law' model, secular or otherwise, because in the thrall of a static, rather than dynamic metaphysics.

At the time of writing the poem, Auden was sceptical of political and philosophical discourse – he had witnessed its corruption in Europe and its contribution in the journey to war. Auden's poem bears witness to the contention that the complete fracture of individual and collective views of the polity, alongside the separation of 'positivist' from 'naturalist' accounts of philosophy, is an historically *and* logically questionable phenomenon. The section tracing a direct line 'from Luther to Linz', whilst daring scholars to produce an 'accurate' account of the pathway, is admirably met by Simmonds' analysis of the misunderstood journey from Protestantism to positivism. Furthermore, Dworkin's work is symptomatic of this mistaken history and, in utilising a cathected form of Protestant autonomy, runs the risk of suffering the selfsame tensile weakness exhibited in the irreconcilable aspects of Auden's poem. Auden was also at that time infused with a faith in American claims to philosophical and political neutrality, and this may well have imbued the poem with its sense of the masses sincerely hurrying towards their ethical life. His later rejection of the poem hints at his more characteristic intellectual scepticism and at his recognition of the tensile 'fracture' or 'seam' in the poem. As time went by, his realisation that the United States offered simply another flawed promise of a noble dream was corroborated by the political and popular colonisations endured by the poem itself. His reservation could reflect the reservation we should maintain regarding the roots of American jurisprudence, which claim a foothold in *both* natural and positivist traditions.[39]

The poem's tensile weakness, its conception and colonisation in the context of political cultures claiming neutrality, exemplifies the ease with which theoretical fracture is metabolised for sundry purposes. It also points up the need to consider the complex interaction between ideological rhetoric and intellectual cultures. In this regard, Dworkin may be seen against the backdrop of an American history of belief in the *possibility* of neutrality, in individual integrity quite divorced from the taint of the subjective. In his essay 'American jurisprudence through English eyes: the nightmare and the noble dream',[40] Hart clearly identifies the particularly American *locus* of this phenomenon – naming Dworkin, Posner and Pound as particular examples. Yet, Hart does *not* fully explore the political culture which

---

39 The maintenance of ongoing parallel strands is intriguing and complex, clearly linking to genuine influences in the American realist tradition.

40 HLA Hart (1977) 11 Georgia Law Review 969, reproduced in Hart, *Essays in Jurisprudence and Philosophy* (1983) Oxford: OUP, pp 123–44, to which pagination herein refers.

gives rise to this illusory path.[41] Is not this same rhetoric of neutrality, coupled with the culture of a constitutional rights 'shield', detectable in recent American political theory and international policy? Auden's initial poetic weakness may reflect a moment of seduction by this puritan political voice, with its apparent resolution of individual and collective – in a local politics of global aspirations – heralding intimations of immortality of a kind. The noble aspiration of neutrality and integrity had long characterised American jurisprudence and tended to colour the presentation, at least the rhetorical stance, of international political policy;[42] but the conclusion that:[43]

> ... rights theory has a long and honourable ancestry in the natural law tradition in America ... and has long been closely associated with less formal and more substantive modes of legal reasoning

betrays an innate fealty to a particular metaphysical framework, 'natural', pervasive and sometimes febrile in its expression. Though Fuller forwards a hypothesis concerning the source of law which draws upon the American model,[44] in the words of Atiyah and Summers he 'fails to develop, as has American legal theory generally, a synthesis reconciling natural law and positivism'.[45]

A more general conclusion may also be derived from these attempted conciliations. Whilst remembering the false footing of the 'separation thesis', there is a need to ensure that engagement between analytical and normative, natural and positivist, theories foster *meaningful* encounters that serve the semantic and conceptual possibilities whilst remaining alive to their own logical limits, resisting the attractions of a wish-driven synthesis, as exemplified by Whitehead and Auden, amongst others. Auden divined that, though eccentric, Whitehead made some attempt to sustain the link with 'sensory phenomena'[46] and thus his odd conjunction of physics and metaphysics holds both a caution and a lesson to

---

41 *Ibid*, p 127. Indeed, Hart identifies the decision in *Roe v Wade* 410 US 113 (1973) as an example of judicial partiality *simpliciter*. Yet the decision may be characterised altogether differently. For 'finding' a constitutional source through the indirect route of 'privacy' (as was the case in *Roe*), whilst fettering the freedom with inbuilt constraints, might be seen as a persuasive sop which, whilst appearing to bear the force of constitutional right, is nevertheless vulnerable to assault. On this same point, Dworkin himself is persuaded that the decision really does bestow a 'right' (see Dworkin, *Life's Dominion* (1994)). Thus, Hart and Dworkin are oddly in agreement in their understanding of the *significance* of the judgment, though differing in their accounts of the antecedents.

42 Though not, of course, domestic politics – Atiyah and Summers, *Form and Substance in Anglo-American Law* (1991) Oxford: Clarendon, p 248: 'In nineteenth century America ... the natural law heritage and positivist doctrines did not at this time significantly diverge: both led to the view that law was and in some sense had to be "neutral", and in this sense differed profoundly from politics, which depended upon diverse political ideologies.'

43 *Ibid*, p 266.

44 *Ibid*, p 261.

45 *Ibid*, p 262.

46 Mendelson – see fn 11, above.

current theorists.[47] Though collisions of space-time in terms of 'natural' disasters may be closer to the kind of examples Whitehead had in mind, the contribution of human cognition to the concatenation of events not always entirely derived from human activity, and ending in war, is an especially meaningful testing ground for the contest of the 'then and now' in the juristic evaluation of the natural/positivist nexus. A theory of how we apprehend the contingent world seems intimately bound to how we perceive the jurisprudential model of law;[48] and it is our inability to reconstitute destroyed matter, or the irrevocable alteration in our world that is 'history' (whether as death, murder, war, pre-event ignorance, or pre-discovery innocence), which makes the linear view of time and space *appear* the only tenable vision of reality – in other words, mortality, and the *permanent* effects of contingent events force us to order our world, both practically and morally, in a particular way. If we could grasp – howsoever it may be an illusion – that we are all obliged to share our physical condition as laws which appear to operate as linear event sequences with teleological implications, what impact would or could this have on our collective understanding of individual moral responsibility, and therefore on the shape of our institutional structures, such as law? Would our envisioning of the entire framework be altered, as well as that of the normative significance of the individual act, of individual agency?[49] Are we then better able to see the legal system, model the source of law, as a pragmatic response to a vertiginous situation, rather than the 'inevitable' outcome of an unfolding though disputed empirical narrative; are we better able to see or justify the 'multi-positional' nature of the contingent event, of legal and political discourse? In short, could such a view of the physical world affect our 'necessary' metaphysics?

If the 'error bred in the bone' of all humanity is our need 'to be loved alone' – if this habitual self concern is not only dominant, but normal, which form of legitimation for the legal order *logically* will have *imperium*? A vigorous qualification of purist assertions of natural law might recognise that a 'return' to natural law, provoked by contingent crisis, is a predictable return to the atavistic, or shamanistic, intellectual device at a time of peril – as seems to have been the

---

47 The vision of an 'absent' space and time, with a dynamic model of human and divine existence 'in process', may render his theory fundamentally frail, if not in terms of vulnerability to logical attack, then in terms of intellectual reception of the model. In addition, his ability to *transmit* his ideas may in part have suffered from his own transition across epistemologies at a time when the attendant vocabularies were not particularly receptive. Nevertheless – and this is a lesson – Whitehead's discussions of spatio-temporal coincidence had become more intelligible by the 1940s, the very time when Auden was undergoing his war-induced crisis. War could be described as the ultimate historical example of ideological fracture becoming 'visible' in a space-time collision as contingent event.

48 The focus of early 20th century physics and philosophy became the problem of relativity, and Whitehead's attempt to explain this in terms of the relationship between a non-linear space and time and the 'fixation' of space and time in the moment of the contingent event may provide the root of a contrasting ethical position to that posed by the concept of relativity.

49 This nods towards the original empirical concerns of the Logical Positivists. See, also, M Williams, *Empty Justice: One Hundred Years of Law, Literature and Philosophy* (2002) London: Cavendish Publishing, Conclusion.

case with Auden himself. Certainly account should be taken of the metaphysics of morals which, though in one sense questionable as so much incommensurable ephemera of the sentimental mind, nevertheless reflect an enduring and universal 'meta-' or 'supra-'physical reality for mankind. Modern scholars – for example, Simmonds, Coyle – are revisiting the intellectual and historical reasons for such synthesis, from the epistemological and conceptual bifurcations traced by Simmonds to the growing scepticism of the fact/value distinction;[50] but account should be taken, on the *other* hand, of the history, and intellectual *locus standi*, the intellectual robustness of the *logical* positivism that contributes to legal positivism.[51] Though some 'truce' may be desirable, though it may even be logically, rationally inevitable or incontrovertible, it is nevertheless the case that the natural/positivist nexus is itself a battlefield. This may be a natural,[52] as well as accidental or contrived, site of difference, more or less intellectually tenable than the 'opposition' theory might suggest – as with the atomistic world of physical positivism and grafting of any supra-physical 'natural' theory, so also with the 'molecular' structures of global politics. Just as the overt fundamentalism of some 'non-liberal' ideologies clearly pose the threat of primitivism, so too will the covert threat – disguised as an allegedly flexible, secular heterogenous polity – of undeclared fundamentalism posed by liberalism.[53] In the 'contest' between 'natural' and 'positivist' models of international law recently invoked, experts were divided as to which model prevailed in the analysis of international pacts and breaches leading to war, but political characterisation appeared to rely upon a prioritisation of naturalist arguments, with positivist justifications supplied in a rearguard, retrospective and defensive campaign.[54] Both natural and positive law theories are attempts to erect justifications for legitimacy and authority of law as systems of control and order – the tendency to be oppositional and essentialist is likely to be driven by this, by an underlying caution that authority will dissipate if either appear to compromise inherent claims to a coherent belief system – the one based on an internal/biblical 'moral' code, the other on a dispassionate rational code, neutral as to content. Auden's poem marks the crisis of ideas that such tension represents. In a collection of Auden's essays we are told that: [55]

---

50 Synthetic enquiries form an influential current in contemporary jurisprudence: see Coyle, 'The possibility of deontic logic' (2002) 15(3) Ratio Juris 294–318.

51 There is no escape from an element of subjectivism, yet the inherent location of positivism as an attempt to approach a value-neutral enquiry itself amounts to an ideological position. Resistance to asserting a *locus* on the ideological register, provided it adheres to a declared political integrity *through* resistance, is a potential ethical strength, and to some extent a precondition, of the positivist mode of reasoning. On either side of the 'divide', however, a loss of consciousness of such constraints renders theory vulnerable to the *visceral* attractions of an all-encompassing metaphysics.

52 There may even be a neurological, as well as historical and cultural, reason for the tendency to polarise belief, to adopt either a predominantly religious or metaphysical world view, or a more physical and empirically-driven account – VS Ramachandran at the University of California, San Diego, '... has found evidence of brain circuitry in the temporal lobe that has given rise to religious experience'; see www.internet-encyclopedia.org/wiki.phtml?title=Religion.

53 Dworkin's Protestantism might be characterised as the atomistic corollary of this.

54 See 'Iraq war product of neocon philosophy of intelligence' at http://rightweb.irc-online.org/analysis/2004/0402pi.php.

55 *Op cit*, Bucknell and Jenkins, fn 23, p 99.

[t]owards the end of the 1930s Auden began to question ... whether natural community ... could still be deemed to exist. At the root of this questioning was the rise of Fascism with its dependence on identity of feeling as a substitute for the quest for truth. Auden found it impossible to deny Fascism's socialist roots. At the same time he was unwilling to reject socialism simply because it had, like any political philosophy, a potential for distortion. Instead he laid the blame firmly on something he had always mistrusted – the imprecision of romanticism. He traced this back to Rousseau's desire for a return to nature and original community. While he recognised the earlier value of community, Auden now believed that society was progressing from Catholic community to Protestant individualism ... 'it will be only when they fully realize their "aloneness" and accept it, that men will be able to achieve a real unity through a common recognition of their diversity ...'.

To achieve such recognition of diversity, in a profoundly political sense, the debate must occur between individuals and communities authenticated as political actors in a world order of confessed absolutes and mixed motivation on all sides. Where fundamentalist belief declares war on autonomy, liberal myth perpetuates infantilised autonomy: both must be admitted. The amelioration of 'aloneness' can only occur when the status of individuals and interest groups is not ordained purely by a pre-emptive political, ideological or economic world stage, but by a willingness to adopt new mechanisms, capable of receptive and reflexive enhancement of alternative points of view and capable of fostering a mature engagement between individual autonomy and collective polity.

CHAPTER 2

NATIONHOOD AND IDENTITY –
RS THOMAS: MINISTERING OTHERNESS

INTRODUCTION

This chapter considers issues of identity and nationhood through the prism of politics and power as generated by the poetical work of RS Thomas in his relation to Wales. Though perhaps peripheral to more central political and social discourse concerning identity and nationhood, the messages and powers of poetry – whether as barometer of immanent sensibilities or idiosyncrasies – are strong and intriguing in the context of a country in the process of developing a new sense of self, with quite conscious structures of development in the wake of devolving powers.[1]

The seam of philosophical and legal commentary and scholarship regarding race and ethnicity continues to grow, and to grow more sensitive to the issues evinced by questions of identity, from the personal to the local and global levels. Individual interaction – with immediate environments, are neither fixed nor entirely volitional. Yet, in positing the past and emerging possibilities of culture and identity, focus upon flux and lack of volition identifies the subject as haplessly and helplessly overdetermined,[2] whilst focus upon the capacity for social interaction and integration may fail to capture the inadequacy of the subject facing the contingency and vertigo that is the human condition.

That said, it is useful to consider the pace of progress when thinking about the possibilities of local-to-global identity. Though a relatively small and economically stretched country, Wales is a fascinating instance of an emerging, partially devolved unit consciously struggling to evolve a new ethic of being. This status provides an interesting exemplum in terms of evolving questions of international, as well as local, polity and has begun to be the focus of some

---

1   For a fascinating discussion of links between art and nascent politics, see Ian Ward's review article (Ward, 2000), reflecting that: 'the ultimate failure of the republic lay in its inability to secure a credible public philosophy ... [an issue] which carries contemporary political weight'. Ward's discussion expounds upon the thesis that the failure was 'at root, an aesthetic one' and that this surfaced particularly in the writings of poets such as Marvell and Milton. A more subtly politicised poetry than that produced by the fiery RS Thomas might have proved more apposite to such developments. Since originally writing this account, the great poet RS Thomas, frail but indomitable, sadly has died; a retrospective scholarship on his work will gather pace.

2   Simon Clarke (2003, p 96) points out that key theorists in this field have posited models which describe current crises but create difficulties of their own: 'Horkheimer and Adorno's work places emphasis upon the massive irrationality that has accompanied the development of modern society ... There are several problems with their work ... perhaps the most worrying is the biological determinism emanating from the use of Freud's instinct theory.'

interesting parliamentary debate, ranging from discussion of how to imagine identity and nationhood, to how such factors link to broad economic, social and constitutional issues.[3] Though vulnerable as well as responsive to the demands of disparate claims, whether predominantly ethnic, linguistic, social or political in nature, the will to forge anew, with a cultivated awareness of global, historical pitfalls in such shapings, is clear.[4] Commentary upon the implications of identity in Wales and in the world becomes ever more reflective. As Graham Day asks:[5]

> ... how many concepts of Wales? And how many ways of being Welsh? [a] problematised Welshness ... One does not have to be a devotee of globalization, for example, to see how hard it is to assert nowadays that the land, livestock, water and even brains located inside Wales somehow belong to it and it alone; ... the history, far from being settled, has been reworked again and again, and remains in contention ... we are reminded of Raymond Williams's insistence that the actual Welsh cultural formation has been produced in a prolonged interaction between 'always diverse' native elements and the dominant and alternative effects of an occupying power ... The revival of various sorts of nationalist politics and the evident staying power of ethnicity as a phenomenon had made it necessary to reconsider some of the one dimensional predictions made be earlier modernizers ... Nationalism as an ideology is concerned with the structure of a nation as a 'people' and as such is oriented towards concealing differences rather than recognising them ... they rely upon the cultivation of beliefs and practices which draw a particular group together, while exaggerating the distance between it and those who are felt not to belong ...

This comment points up the false position created by overdetermined visions of nationhood – the risk that in protecting a perceived 'internal' identity, the perception falls far short of the potential for a healthy diversity occurring 'on the ground'. Yet what might be classed as 'underdetermined' visions can be damaging too. As Holohan and Featherstone remark in their discussion:[6]

---

3   See www.publications.parliament.uk/pa/ld200102/ldselect/ldconst/147/2052701.htm, which provides an account (dated May 2002) of questions taken in the United Kingdom parliament in relation to Welsh identity, devolution and legislative difficulties. In giving evidence to the Select Committee on Constitution, Mr John Osmond spoke of the technical legislative and political failings resulting from partial devolution, and went on to explain that, compared to Scotland, the picture in Wales was complicated by a desiccation of identity derived in part from the lack of historically secure institutions of state: '... we have not had those kinds of institutions. The sort of things which typify Welshness are a very strong sense of place, which relates to locality more than Wales as a whole, a strong sense of culture and the issue of the Welsh language. All those things are potentially divisive and they have been and continue to be so, so it is very hard to build a sense of unity around Welshness. That does not mean to say, however, that Welshness is not strongly felt; it is intensely felt. Sometimes I feel it is more intensely felt than Scottishness in actual fact, but it is much more difficult to put your finger on ... [but] there was a shift in generations and a younger generation emerged ... which did not have the same feelings of resentment and threat around the issues of Welsh nationality ... certainly in my lifetime, the language [has come to be] associated with ideas of modernity rather than things of the past ... you see emerging the infrastructure of a civic society here which I think is very positive ...'

4   The focus on health, education and especially upon children as a precious resource – presaging the creation of a Children's Commissioner for Wales – speaks of a conscientious construction.

5   Day, 2002, pp 231–41.

6   2003, pp 2–5.

Within many liberal democracies race is seen as characteristic of an earlier stage of humanity that must be denied or repressed in order to ensure the continuation of non-violent social relations ... [but] It is precisely through the attempt to deny racial identity that liberal democracy encourages the violence of racial antagonism. The destruction of racial categories, so that racial aliens conform to the dictates of liberal individualism ... incites an increase in violent attempts to re-assert subjective difference as racial superiority. Therefore, we want to argue that racial antagonism should be understood as the dark side of liberal individualism ... [on the other hand] the Macpherson report [resulting from the Stephen Lawrence case] advances an exemplary argument for the acceptance of the other as racialised subject ...

Nor is the issue simply one of 'balance', but it goes to the heart of how the individual is viewed within the metaphysics of the polity – there is an elemental philosophical interaction between visions of the personal and of social ethics of relevance to the very different visions transmitted by RS Thomas and by Raymond Williams. In considering how a discussion of 'racism' can be understood as an incident of innocent transmission of received identities and entrenched beliefs, Charles Mills[7] identifies the analysis of racism put forward (by, in this instance, Garcia):

> ... as a volitional, non-doxastic analysis ... racism [as] primarily a matter of ill-will. Thus the double significance of his title: the 'heart' – the essence – of racism is a matter of the heart, the traditional seat of the emotions. Whereas left-wing analyses of racism have traditionally favoured structural, and socially holistic accounts, for which power is crucial, Garcia sees this claim as an error ... Garcia's theoretical move is that he has shifted the framework of discussion from the socio-political to the ethical ... the ethical here is being made to drive the explanatory. Since it would be odd to speak of structures as being motivated by vice, the logic of structural exclusion has to be personalised. Since morality is central, and the wrongness of racism is located in the individual heart, the wrongness of institutional racism has to be explained in terms of an infection from this diseased heart to larger social structures ...

Interestingly, this juxtaposition of ideas and discourses again points up the 'double-edged' impact of the work of Thomas – that he writes with passion of the incursions upon an already (in his view) debilitated race, whilst disseminating a personalised view of racial and national purity, which is debilitating for all parties – reflecting not just upon the 'hearts' of his subjects, but his own heart too. Wedded to a mythically 'pure' past and individual subject, such personalised, immovable politics cannot embrace the wider picture, nor create a poetics of political transformation.[8] As Mills suggests (Mills, 2003, p 61): 'the individual heart cannot be the theoretical starting-point because this organ beats in the bloodstream, the systolic and diastolic flow, of the larger corpus of the body politic ...' Whilst all this might have been said without reference to poems and

---

7   2003, pp 30–59.
8   Though national identity remains a strong force in Welsh culture, it is many-faceted, vibrant and frequently outward-looking with a thriving popular music and arts culture, a diversity capable of inclusiveness, a distinctive sense of identity not necessarily linked to language, but to history and place also.

letters, the complex, half-said flow of myth, ideology and individual frailty that is poetry – and our dialogue with poetry – tells us much about our link to the wider body politic, of the nature of our own ministrations of otherness.

RS THOMAS AND OTHERNESS

The thoughts – and poem – discussed in this chapter were stimulated by 'collision' with the poetry and politics of RS Thomas, particularly the poem 'Those Others', discussed here though not reproduced.[9] RS Thomas is renowned for being a curious and contradictory mixture: a gifted and inspiring poet; a passionate advocate in support of the preservation of Welsh culture, who yet severely reprimands the Welsh for their perceived failings; an Anglican priest, who berates the notion of Anglican influence and does not see the contradiction; an advocate of Welsh language, who wrote poetry in English; a priest, who devoted his life and identity to God, and saw his poetry as a sacred gift, which must be treated with due reverence (contrast Gerard Manley Hopkins for whom the first vocation was the priesthood, and poetry a very troubling second) yet on the other hand railing against the 'untenanted' cross. Seeing no contradiction in being a priest who supported the torching of English homes, he famously remarked in 1998: 'what is one death against the death of the whole Welsh nation?'[10]

In another contradiction, Thomas speaks of being 'no-one', yet his autobiographical writing – entitled *No-one*,[11] is written in the third person, which seems to embody more a Messianic stance than a negation.

Often Thomas's poetry dealt with profoundly universal questions – the relation between body and spirit, between life and death, between beauty and ugliness of soul, between God and Nature, man and machine, personal and collective identity, and spirit and myth.

Yet, at other times, the poetry can seem intensely narrow and parochial – in his zeal to preserve Welshness there is an identity between nourishment and corruption in speech (clearly there are many links here to WB Yeats, Seamus Heaney, Derek Walcott, James Joyce).

---

9   The story behind development of this chapter is therefore somewhat personal. In one sense, any link to 'law' is tenuous – there is no overt discussion of legal principle, case or theory – but in another sense, the relevance to law is omnipresent, since issues of race, ethnicity, nationality and identity permeate legal thinking in many fields. One is struck forcefully by the 'double-edged' nature of the writings of RS Thomas. The first stanza quoted from 'It Hurts Him to Think' could as well be the spitting of a zealot bent upon extinction of the 'other', as the plea of a – in Thomas's case, putative – victim of racial and linguistic incursion; it could be found in the mouth of any zealot, whether Welsh-English, White-Black, anti-Semite, -Jew, -Arab, resentful son to abjured mother, mother tongue or mother earth.
10   The quotation can be found for example at http://en.wikipedia.org/wiki/Ronald_Stuart_Thomas.
11   See discussion by An Sonjae at www.sogang.ac.kr/~anthony/ThomasHill.htm.

In 'It Hurts Him to Think',[12] Thomas says of the English:

I was
Born into the squalor of
Their feeding and sucked their speech
In with my mother's
Infected milk, so that whatever
I throw up now is still theirs.

In his simultaneous conjunction of an idealised ancient Welsh literary tradition and a despised modern English presence (and lower class English at that) he does not mince words. In 'Border Blues', Thomas is accompanied[13] by the 6th century Celtic saint, Beuno, who fled Powys to escape the Saxon invaders, in the plea for cultural sympathy lies an unashamed racism:[14]

I was going up the road and Beuno beside me
Talking in Latin and old Welsh
When a volley of voices struck us; I turned,
But Beuno had vanished
In his place
There stood the ladies from the council houses
Blue eyes and Birmingham yellow
Hair, and the ritual murder of vowels.

RS Thomas has several poems dealing with 'otherness'.[15] A focus of interest in Thomas derives partly from the fact that as poet, as *politically charged* poet, he has the potential to be the focus of a nationalist, even racially fundamentalist, movement – imagine how his message *might* have been taken up in the current convergence of ethnic/religious tension elsewhere – his poetry a crucible for passionate anti-English feeling. Yet this seems not to have happened. He has the potential to incite radical politics, even racial violence, but the invitation is largely ignored. Despite its power and potential for mass appeal, the play of politics through poetry creates a diffusion of the message in this medium of contradictory acidity.[16]

---

12 Thomas, 1993, p 262.
13 The problem of colonialism, of racial and linguistic 'impurity' is of course shared by many other poets. Contrast Seamus Heaney's appraisal of Derek Walcott: Heaney, 1989, p 24): 'For those awakening to the nightmare of history, revenge – Walcott has conceded – can be a kind of vision, yet he himself is not vengeful. Nor is he simply a patient singer of the tears of things . . . He assumes that art is a power and to be visited by it is to be endangered, but he also knows that works of art endanger nobody else, that they are benign. From the beginning he has never simplified or sold short. Africa and England are in him. The humanist voices of his education and the voices from his home ground keep insisting on their full claims, pulling him in two different directions . . . he made a theme of the choice and the impossibility of choosing . . .' Whether it is incontrovertibly the case that art is always benign in its influence is a moot point.
14 Ward, 2000, p 69.
15 Those specifically *named* as such are to be found in RS Thomas (1993), comprising: 'Those Others' at p 111 – to which we will return; 'The Other' at p 410 dealing with ambivalence to self, to compromise, to the opposition between spirit and machine; 'The Other' at p 457 dealing with the omnipresence and omnipatience of God, and 'Other' at p 235, considering again the base and the divine, God and the machine, spirit against Mammon.
16 See fn 3 for brief political background.

A more measured political profile in Wales may be ascribed to cultivated developmental influences as well as pragmatic reasoning. The Welsh cultural revival has matured beyond alienation, skirting extremism. In addition, there are well-recognised internal splits in Wales, between different notions of ethnicity, identity and politics. Also, Thomas may have undermined his own political potential in that, in trying to champion the cause of a vulnerable culture and language, he often *berates* the Welsh for being less than wholly devoted to the cause. Indeed, as we shall see, his poetry betrays an ambivalence towards the Welsh.

POLITICAL THEORY: CONTRASTING RS THOMAS, CARADOC EVANS AND RAYMOND WILLIAMS

How does Thomas's idea of Welsh identity and ethnicity compare with that of other Welsh intellectuals? His writing is dominated by two influences – mediaeval Welsh literature and mythology, and God. Through mediaeval literature he hopes to echo and re-awaken in the Welsh their own ethnicity. Through God he hopes to inform, give conscience to that ethnicity. Yet his understanding of ethnic identity is dangerously romantic and ambivalent; and as a champion and as an expression of divinity he is similarly troubled. In Thomas, there is little place for redemption.

Compare this with the early 20th century writer Caradoc Evans who, in *My People* (Evans, 1987), and to the chagrin and anger of many Welsh people, 'exposed' the corrupting, repressive influence of the Church and the resultant cowed indignity of Welsh village life.[17] On publication, many Welsh people were so horrified by the representation of baseness that it contained that it was repulsed as 'pornography', showing 'the utmost contempt for his (Evans') countrymen' (quotes from John Harris' 'Introduction' to *My People*). Yet Evans hoped thereby to liberate the Welsh people from the joint stranglehold of poverty and religion, through socialism. That very combination of cultural tradition and religion advocated by Thomas was identified by Evans as itself the source of poison.

Raymond Williams, a more recent secular Messiah, has had a more open-textured politicised notion of the future for ethnicity:[18]

Many of the things that happened, over centuries, to the Welsh are now happening, in decades, to the English. The consequent confusion and struggle for identity, the search for new modes of effective autonomy within a powerfully extended and profoundly interacting para-national political and economic system, are now in

---

17 *My People*, at p 17 as explained by John Harris. In his 'Introduction' Harris explains: '*My People* portrays the culture of South Cardiganshire as dependent upon a rigid class system, itself legitimised by a debased form of religion. Though Evans came to regard the essence of that culture as residing in its religion he did not confine himself to the chapel and its corruptions. *My People* has a social dimension not always recognised; its challenge was political and it was politically persecuted . . .'

18 Quoted by Dai Smith, in his essay 'Relating to Wales' in Eagleton, 1989, p 36.

many parts of the world the central issues of social consciousness, struggling to come through against still powerful but residual ideas and institutions … at many levels, from the new communal nationalism and regionalisms to the new militant particularisms of contemporary industrial conflict, the flow of contemporary politics is going beyond the modes of all the incorporated ideologies and institutions. The Welsh, of course, have been inside these cross pressures for much longer than the English. And as a result we have had to learn that we need to solve the real contradictions between nationality and class, and between local well being and the imperatives of a large-scale system. Consequently, we may be further along the road to a relevant if inevitably painful contemporary social consciousness … what seemed a sectoral problem and impetus, to be dressed or dissolved in mere local colour, is now more and more evidently a focal problem and impetus: not particular to but to a significant extent particularised to Wales …

Most significantly, where RS Thomas looks to the mediaeval and mythological tradition for Welsh identity and berates and rejects vehemently what he sees as the incursion of machines, of industrialism, of Mammon, Williams sees this as a signal to the future. Whilst industry has undeniably 'exploited' Wales, Dai Smith explains how Williams's view is reconstructive:

> Wales is rediscovered through understanding the social process of its past … This is the only real exit from a timeless, mythical Wales which will otherwise suffocate the living Welsh. It embraces change rather than the dynamics of modernism, for it sees change as growth that is rooted, pruned and fostered by communities who strive to make choices for their culture in their own local and national terms. The vehicle for this route is working class struggle. The map is history … in *The Fight for Manod* [he] rejects the enforced, outworn separation of industrial/urban from agrarian/rural, since this is the burden of an actual history that has to be transcended … such a divide is the principal explanation for the splits (economic-social-political-cultural-linguistic) within his own native country … The shift from agriculture to industry … [has] been so subversive of traditions and national ideals that it has proved easier to shun them than to comprehend them. This, too, is a Welsh divorce that Williams would see as part of wider separations …[19]

It is also one in which we might see Thomas implicated.

Ultimately, for Williams, the *best* of Welsh heritage and identity is found in that cohesive *community* identity. Nevertheless, he recognises that 'community' is a troublesome word. Indeed, in relation to his writing on race and national community in Britain, Francis Mulhern notes that:[20]

> … whilst Williams is correct that appeals to abstract legal rights … are unequal to the social strains of Britain's changing ethnic composition … he seriously underestimates the critical value of such appeals for the people who actually suffer the strains … and in neglecting this, he mistakes the character of popular racism, which is not merely the xenophobia of settled neighbourhoods but part of the politico-cultural inheritance of the British 'national community' … The lesson to be learned from this political misjudgement bears on the idea of 'community'. Not an

---

19   *Ibid*, p 38.
20   'Towards 2000, or News from you-know-where' in Eagleton, 1989, p 88.

actual social reality but a polemical attribution (or 'interpellation'), 'community' is an untrustworthy category. It obscures the real object of socialist analysis, which is the existing order of collective identifications …

Nevertheless, Williams has recognised that, in Wales, identity in community has endured *despite* the incursions of industry, of poverty (and, we might suggest, of troublesome priests):

> Williams … argued that work like *Culture and Society*, which redressed an English literary and intellectual balance, derived its insights into culture-industry-democracy from the society which had been shot through with their assumptions and consequences – Wales. The latter term he now saw, in some ways, as a larger synonym for 'community' and a living rebuttal of vacuous universalisms in literature, politics or economics. Without endorsing the wishful thinking of the 'Small is Beautiful' school, Williams began to emphasise the necessity of community breakthroughs and local controls in order to face down both centralized and local power structures …[21]

As Messiah then, as political firebrand, Thomas finds himself less than effective and I think that the difficulty can be located in his ambivalence, his barely repressed contempt for the failings of others, as well as otherness, and his rigid insistence upon an idea of nationhood, which is both romanticised and destructive, and locked into a static relation to the past compared to the dynamic recovery of Williams. It is *because*, unlike Williams, Thomas cannot enter into Welsh identity that he cannot empathise. He is an *outsider* who believes he has the only key to the inner sanctum when all along the altar, and the congregation, have moved elsewhere. Most of all, his poetry is imbued – for all his claim to being 'no-one', with a heavy presence of his 'I'; and perhaps this is another reason for his less than Messianic impact. The 'I' is not merely a location of self but a negation of other. Though Thomas is without doubt a poet of great gifts, one may with relief conclude that the deeply troubled 'self' of Thomas, and of his message, undermines the Messianic potential.

My interest in RS Thomas began first, of course, with his poetry, powerful, melancholy, spare; but being married to a Welshman who himself feels ambivalent towards the 'meanings' ascribed to his roots, and having moved to Wales and with my children learning Welsh and each of them feeling a great sense of romanticism and passion for the Welsh heritage, yet sometimes encountering anti-English sentiment at school, my relation to the poetry, which is very concerned with 'Otherness', became more complex. Add to this my own hopeless romanticism and identification with Welshness – the 'connectedness' deriving from having Cornish mining ancestry on my father's side, and being part Irish and part English on my mother's – and you have a mongrel looking for an identity in a time when claiming identity in the British Isles is a contentious pastime.

---

21 Williams's vision of flexible, yet enduring, community has recently been borne out in a study of Cardiff's Tiger Bay history by Glenn Jordan, an American historian, demonstrating an exceptionally *inclusive* working culture, celebrating diversity whilst preserving identity; see *The Guardian*, 14 March 2001: '"Mixed Metaphor" – proving that racial harmony isn't just a dream'.

As a woman married to a Welshman, with children who are half Welsh and who speak Welsh, I wondered how such mongrel identity would strike Thomas. To his poem, 'Those Others', which again reveals his terrible ambivalence, his role of judge where his countryman is sullied with base coinage, a confused empathy for the impoverished hill farmer who yet keeps alive, in Thomas's eyes, the ancient mythological, still to be awakened Wales, I wrote a response, along with a letter (which I do not now have)[22] asking how any of us can lay claim to a sovereign racial identity which so outlaws otherness:

A Reply to 'Those Others', RS Thomas

So natural a poem begins Ego
appraising those others
miming the struggle in your soul
the brooding faces of your brothers
with their small dole
the earth-warmed eyes of shipwrecked farmers
the heart's doomed knell.

Though you feign hate
in little ironies, the frailest trace
of ruder creature clay
discovers your embrace.

> What of those others
> you would abjure
> seeking barest shelter
> on this wild shore?
> (orphaned, wandering
> Celts-of-the-heart.
> perfidious, lusty, pious
> lonely as you could wish
> half-Celt. Full-pelt
> pell-mell desecrated
> Uncelt).

Oh Man of God
blessed is the grace
whose clenched fist brands a brute earth
with the benediction
'My Place'.

(Melanie Williams)

---

22 The letter very earnestly explained my own 'coming to consciousness' from a simplistic search for a national identity – borne of my interest in family history, of the Cornish language and its links to Welsh – to a realisation that the exclusivity/inclusivity pattern set up by such a search compounds problems of racial exclusion. I explained that this lesson was particularly brought home to me by having to 'think through' the position of myself and my children as 'mixed race' insofar as none of us are simply 'Welsh' or 'English'. A very white middle-class luxury diversion, you might say – when the problems of 'race' encountered were minimal, and a rather self-indulgent form of coming to consciousness. But the dialogue in my head extended into a dialogue with Thomas and his poetry, where the austere, savage assertion of identity combines so seductively in poetry to appear as a kind of plangent 'truth'; hence the defensive poetic 'reply'.

Writing the poem forged part of a journey for me, away from the state of 'unbeing' that is 'emotional ethnicity'. Simply, I realised that there was no logical divide – *any* assertion of racial identity carries with it implications of a hierarchy of racial being – and with it, implicit racism; and whilst we might carry affections for place, for landscape, or whilst territorial divides might exist for pragmatic reasons, we should not confuse the two. The letter was conciliatory, supplicating: I explained the story behind the poem – the positive expectations, the school taunts, the determination to swallow pride, to 'understand'. Yet I knew the poem was provocative – especially in challenging the possible contradiction in a priest who rails against developing a 'brotherhood of man' – but I hoped to engender a dialogue with Thomas, a hint perhaps of how he might square the contradictions.

Characteristically, the reply I received was terse and – whilst adopting a direct *rhetorical* stance – evasive. It read:

Dear Mr Williams[23]

Thank you for your letter and the poem. I am used to being misquoted or misrepresented but dislike being portrayed as a fool or lunatic which is what the media do now and again. Because one has a vision of what an ideal Wales could be like it does not mean that one should become hysterical or indulge in paranoia.

Yours sincerely,

RS Thomas

---

23 I had signed the letter ML Williams and had referred to myself in gender-neutral terms; I had not wanted to contribute any gender assumptions to the anticipated dialogue. Given the subsequent reference to 'hysteria' and 'paranoia', this perhaps made little difference.

CHAPTER 3

ETHICS, LAW AND ASSISTED SUICIDE – RECLAIMING THE SANCTITY OF DEATH

INTRODUCTION

Since the writing of the article contained in this chapter, the 'euthanasia' debates have become more furiously event- and discourse-driven. In Britain, the case of Diane Pretty[1] – who deliberately subjected herself to public awareness in an attempt to rally understanding and support for the plight of those suffering from terminal, physically debasing conditions – created a forum for discursive exploration, whilst the more recent case of *Burke v GMC*[2] reminds us that too ready a move toward acceptance of the notion of euthanasia may indeed create a new type of victim. From another point of view, the *Pretty* and *Burke* cases have ground in common, in that both seek legal endorsement of an individual's rights (through the notions enshrined in the European Convention on Human Rights (ECHR)) to express their autonomy in directing what should happen to their bodies at the advent of total incapacity and perhaps incipient death. The emergence of this pattern of events permits new perspectives upon the euthanasia debates.

The *Pretty* case was exceptional in the forthright competence of the claimant. Pretty knew what awaited her and knew precisely how she wished to deal with it. Failing in the domestic courts, she might yet have drawn upon the enshrinement of the rights and autonomy culture reflected in the ECHR and the European Court of Human Rights; but rights are a disputed territory, their boundaries contested by disparate groups. The dispute crystallises in the academic opinions put forward by Keown and Pedain, respectively. In his case note on *Pretty*, Keown (2002) endorses the approach taken by the courts and reiterates Lord Bingham's assertion that Art 8, protecting the right to respect for private and family life:

> ... was expressed in terms directed to the protection of personal autonomy while individuals are living and there was nothing to suggest that it protected the choice to live no longer ... Indeed, the risks of the slippery slope were evident in the logic of the central argument deployed by Mrs Pretty's own counsel. If she had a 'right to self-determination in relation to issues of life and death' then, as Lord Bingham noted, this would extend to voluntary euthanasia for those too disabled to commit suicide. Indeed, why would the claimed right not extend to those who were neither disabled, dying nor suffering? (Keown, 2002, p 9)

---

1   *Pretty v UK* (2346/02) European Court of Human Rights, 29 April 2002; (2002) 35 EHRR 1.

2   See *R (on the Application of Burke) v General Medical Council* [2004] EWHC 1879, where the chronically sick Mr Burke sought to re-affirm the commitment of the medical profession to a presumption in favour of the sustaining of life, asserting that current General Medical Council (GMC) guidelines, in effect, permit doctors to withdraw nutrition and hydration upon subjective criteria.

Pedain (2003) on the other hand, suggests that the conception of autonomy derives from that of private life:

> ... a broad term not susceptible of exhaustive definition. It protects a right to personal development, and the right to establish and develop relationships with other human beings. It also recognises an inviolable sphere of privacy ... The period of dying forms part of life. To deny that a provision which prohibits interference with the way in which an individual leads his life relates to the manner in which he wishes to die seems to involve a fundamental misunderstanding of the conceptual connection between the right to personal autonomy and respect for human dignity, the preservation of which is the underlying objective of all human rights law ... (Pedain, 2003, pp 189–90)

Taken together, the glosses provided by Keown and Pedain highlight the fluidity of our understanding of rights and demonstrate that the identification of a right, even to the point of law, is culture- as much as logic-driven. Keown, a 'pro-life' rhetorician, could not reach any other conclusion. Reflecting tangible concerns about the dangers to vulnerable persons, which might ensue from an alteration in law, the stance endorsed by Keown nevertheless reflects a paralysis of law when nodding towards its Judeo-Christian roots. Such thought perpetuates a chilling combination of clinical regret at the tragic individual outcome alongside the legal hymnal to the (allegedly) inviolate house of moral certainty – as is generally the case with dogma-driven intellectual positions.

Although law should maintain its role as the protector of human interests and values, it is located in a realm of changing norms.[3] Over the last few decades, this realm has witnessed alterations in the location accorded to different ideological influences. Law's realisation of its religious roots must be placed in context with the belief systems, which cluster around the secular stance now central to the legal disposition; it is this very disposition that has permitted innovations in relation to other issues formerly proscribed by the Church, as well as law – abortion, homosexuality and so on. Though the dangers of the 'autonomy culture' must be borne in mind, they are least manifest in the desire of a competent, terminally ill woman to gain permission for an assisted death.

The factual backgrounds to the cases of *Pretty* and *Burke* clarify how the territory should operate. Both claimants have a sustainable claim to 'right'. Persons like Diane Pretty, competent, knowledgeable and facing appalling conditions, should be allowed to reclaim the power to end her life in more reasonable circumstances than those allowed by nature. This need not herald a change in our cultural reverence for life, nor threaten vulnerable individuals unable to give full expression to their desires, or those fearful of a knock-on change in attitude towards the disabled. Les Burke's case flags a means of charting such territory – that the presumption in all circumstances, unless there is evidence little short of overwhelming to displace it, should favour life. Both Pretty

---

3   In tandem with medical science and technology, creating alterations in the experiences which confront our mortal selves – for good and ill.

and Burke, and their champions and foes are not merely expressing opinions, they are expressing themselves and the beliefs and accounts of meaning which shape them.

For the champions and the foes however, the battle is merely academic, not mortal, and we should look with especial care at those rhetoricians who claim a legal and moral certitude which results in a stony indifference to the case in hand. Ready to give full expression to their own belief system, through the claimed ordinance of the law, they remain indifferent to the fully instantiated reality of the beliefs and values lived and embodied by the claimant. The essay which follows is an attempt to lead them into that reality – a reality which one day will become their own: the reality of loss from which there is no return and in which the touch of the divine may be starkly absent.

POETRY AND THE LAW AND ETHICS OF EUTHANASIA[4]

Law's relationship with the notion of physical death is characteristically hyperborean, for the most part wishing to identify, distantly yet accurately, a moment of decease. The busy 'life' of law – the civil concerns of property and probate, or the domain of criminal returns – can then hurry on. Thus, when asked to examine the minutiae of mortal human suffering and confer justice according to a calibration of that decline, the law is poorly equipped to meet the challenge. Voluntary euthanasia and physician assisted suicide are unpalatable topics, yet the compassion and the courage to give legislative support to those who have good reason to seek assistance in ending their lives may be the mark of true civilisation. Arguably, recognition of the sanctity of human life would respect first, individual integrity and autonomy, as demonstrated by the will to exercise control over the process of death, and, secondly, the fact that the sanctity of a unique life may be best celebrated by refusing to sustain that life under intolerable conditions.

The central section of this chapter uses poetry, and a literary essay, as core texts in the exploration of the ethical-legal dilemma of voluntary euthanasia, especially with regard to the desire for a controlled 'good death' – a physician assisted suicide – in the face of terminal illness. Poetry, both as an experience and as a source of ethical critique, can provide a rich and rigorous stimulus to current ethical models. Having journeyed through the moment in human history when intellectual progress was constrained by rigid disciplinary divisions, with law worshipping largely at a self-referential altar, we may have arrived at a more liberated place, where other forms of human discourse can be consulted to enrich our understanding. Many of the rational objections, which might be raised against art by traditional jurisprudence – that it is subjective and emotive, that art is not knowledge, but merely perception – can be levelled, more or less, at sciences,

---

4   An early version of this chapter appeared in the (1998) *Australian Feminist Law Journal* 10; and a later version in Manderson (ed), *Courting Death* (1999) London: Pluto.

humanities and law, with or without the benediction of Derrida; but greater than this debunking of claims to purer lineage is the fact that art can supply law with essential human insights lost to formal thought.

Historically, Church and state ideologies have militated against indulgence of certain aspects of autonomous control over our physical selves. Law, as the inheritor and instrument of these ideologies, has been slow to acquire the language of rights where there is conflict with institutional interest in the preservation of each human unit. So law perpetuates the plea that assisted suicide, euthanasia and, until recently, suicide itself, offend against a notion of sanctity that embraces both a view of life as the property of a deity and as the property of the community.[5] Self destruction sets an unfathomable and dangerously anarchic precedent.

Despite the rapid development of rights discourse, the ethical and legal debate surrounding voluntary euthanasia is enmeshed by this heavy inheritance, locked into endless shadow-boxing between the corners of sanctity and autonomy. Attempts to respond to the new culture of individual responsibility and rights, through legislative authorisation of assisted suicide, are vulnerable to attacks from these polar combatants. In addition, conducting the debate within the confines of such abstract regions feeds the continuous displacement of core issues, such as whether legislators, lawyers and ethicists have confronted fully the face of death and terminal illness, and whether society and medicine can develop, with no loss of integrity, revised conceptions of a good death.

The terminally ill may be subjected to an unwittingly ruthless medical culture committed to the prolongation of life. Yet we have become alienated from the processes of death and dying in terms of social and psychological practices: both are sanitised from view, banished from the hearth of our nuclear family. It is as much in ignorance and in fear that we recoil: the unknown is more instantly a spectre than a friend.

The relevance of poetry to the present discussion is predominantly as a *source* of moral and ethical discourse, and as a method of imposing upon the reader an authentic relationship with that discourse, of having a relationship with the *idea* of death and dying and consequently with its full ethical implications. A similarly authentic relationship with the full implications of ethical-legal decisions should be nurtured in judges and legislators. Law's forensic relationship with the moral or ethical problem – the tendency to promote a (somewhat illusory) image of detached, 'scientific' doctrinal analysis – fosters a 'static' view of a problem in law. It is dissected, anatomised and consigned to its doctrinal or legislative fate. Yet in the life of the legal subject the problem (and this does not apply only to the

---

5   'Sanctity' and 'autonomy' are identified as the core concepts in ethical debates on both abortion *and* euthanasia. Suicide was formerly criminalised not just because of the theological objections to self destruction, but also because it was an offence against the state, as the wanton removal of a unit belonging *to* the state, with all the potential for subversion of state interests that such self-determination implied. 'English law might be said to recognise a right to self-determination, inasmuch as suicide is no longer a crime ...' (Ashworth, 1995, p 285).

'problem' of voluntary euthanasia) is *experienced*; the subjective encounter is kinetic, interactive, progressive.

Since the words 'aesthetics' and 'ethics' can be appropriated in the service of diverse hypotheses and bestowed with variable meanings, philosophy alone may be the most stable source of definitions for present purposes.[6] Human dilemmas, such as abortion and euthanasia, are usually approached via the conceptions of *applied* ethics:[7] the 'rights and wrongs' of a 'practical' dilemma are explored through 'analytic activity in which the concepts, assumptions, beliefs, attitudes, emotions, reasons and arguments underlying ... decision making are examined critically'.[8] Yet historically and conceptually, *pure* ethics – the evaluation of what is meant by ideas underpinning moral debate (that is, the ideas of good, evil, beauty and virtue) – is intimately linked to aesthetics, to the *appreciation* of such concepts. In Scruton's words:

> The aesthetic interest ... always sees more in an object than its mere appearance ... For example, when I look at a painting, I do not see only colours lines and shapes. I see the world that is represented by them, the drama which animates that world, the emotion that is expressed through it. In short I see a meaning. (1994, p 445)

Similarly, for a legal subject, death, or a 'good death', is not a static concept, an 'object' with a 'mere appearance'. It is a process redolent with meaning, an intimate materiality *and* spirituality. The judge and the legislator engaged in evaluating the dilemma, has a moral duty to *appreciate* its meaning. Appreciation denotes immersion, experience of a process.

This paper attempts to provide such immersion through experience of the aesthetic. 'Reader experience'[9] of the aesthetic text – of the medium as well as the message – is a crucial step in critiquing the ethical viewpoint that it purveys. All too easily, judges, lawyers, legislators, make decisions which may have a crucial, perhaps devastating, impact upon the life of the individual. Having the power to make decisions, it is moral cowardice to shy away from the full implications of the decisions. Reader experience of the text confronts the reader, in microcosm, with the impact of the moral crisis. Murdoch points out that:

> ... the idea of 'objective reality' undergoes important modifications when it is to be understood, not in relation to 'the world described by science' but in relation to the

---

6   A most clear and accessible text is Scruton (1994).
7   Scruton (1994, pp 12–13) clarifies the conceptual foundations of philosophy. Of applied philosophy, he comments: 'There are as many branches of this as there are occasions for human folly.' The principal components howsoever characterised, are the philosophies of religion, of science, of language, political philosophy and applied ethics. In *pure* philosophy there are four central divisions: logic – the study of reasoning itself; epistemology – the theory of knowledge; metaphysics – the theory of being; ethics and aesthetics – theories of value.
8   See Gillon, 1994, p 2.
9   On the role of the reader, see references in Fish (1989). Postmodern theory has contributed an exercise in 'consciousness raising' regarding the interactive and subjective nature of the process of reading – see Hutcheon (1988). For a readily accessible survey, see Eagleton (1988), especially at pp 54–90: 'Phenomenology, hermeneutics, reception theory'.

progressing life of a person ... We have to learn the meaning [of moral words]; and since we are human historical individuals the movement of understanding is onward ... and not back towards a genesis in the rulings of an impersonal public language. (1970, p 26)

Through the poetic form the reader, the putative ethicist, witnesses the contingent and kinetic force of the subject's experience, just as war photography may capture the essence of a conflict more meaningfully than political conjecture. Such an approach could, of course, be accused of being an emotive tactic, of propagandism. Yet the excision of the emotive and contingent from a debate is itself a rhetorical tactic.

It may be said that Western civilisation has reached a crossroads. The ever increasing recognition of individual rights and emphasis upon an educated and *informed* autonomy for which the law is a crucial instrument, jostles with the more archaic influence of paternalism. The repeal of the Northern Territories legislation[10] on voluntary euthanasia allegedly was a result of lobbying by minority pressure groups: a flagrant abrogation of the democratic process. Allowing abstract and largely unrepresentative ideologies to hold sway over the hard-fought claims of the individual legal subject engaged in a mortal conflict, in which the outcome is the mode of death of the subject, indicates a serious breach of morality and of justice.

This chapter does *not* seek to be a survey of current ethical-legal theory; however, an introductory comment may be helpful. The tendency of ethicists to explore life and death issues through use of the key concepts of 'sanctity of life'[11] versus 'autonomy' holds the *potential* to convey the extremity and scope of the dilemma. Yet this potential is rarely realised. Just as the procedural and doctrinal abstractions of law may be blind to the subtleties of human life, so too, the use of these words may skirt or diminish the profound questions of human existence that they consider.

Practical ethics (the usual tool used in relation to medical ethics issues) is valuable in identifying and anatomising the factors within a particular practical dilemma and the relationship of those factors to moral codes. So, for example, practical ethics will remind us that the major issues in conflict, when considering abortion and euthanasia, are those of sanctity of life versus autonomy, with the moral value ascribed to each depending upon their context – so sanctity may 'trump' autonomy in the context of a predominantly 'religious' evaluation. The

---

10 Despite evidence from an opinion poll that 75% of Australian citizens supported the legislation, the Northern Territories Rights of the Terminally Ill Act was repealed in March 1997 following lobbying by religious and 'right to life' groups. This legislation imposed stringent safeguards to prevent abuse of its terms.

11 Arguably, the notion of sanctity is not the exclusive property of theologians. For a comprehensive collection of essays on the subject of euthanasia, see Keown (ed), *Euthanasia Examined* (1995) Cambridge: CUP. This includes a theological view – expressed in an essay by Anthony Fisher (at p 318 of Keown) as: 'Rationally we must recognise that were we to say yes to medical killing we would have to abandon the sanctity of life principle.'

analysis has been further addressed by reference to a theoretical frame – to deontology, or consequentialism.[12] Practical ethics will usually entail notating an index of the ethical criteria that should be included in order to survey properly the issues informing a particular dilemma. For example, when considering voluntary euthanasia – a source of intense debate in the United Kingdom, United States and Australia during the last year – a practical ethics summary of the issues is typified by Thiroux, essentially as a list of co-operative and competing moral considerations.[13] Whilst such a survey may be an invaluable resource in identifying central issues, it may also create a reductive closed circuit of reason, where the content of the survey is ultimately exhausted by its terms.

Dworkin (1995) reinvigorates the debate by conducting a critique that is both linguistically and conceptually liberated from such closed circuits. Such analysis departs from the tendency of ethical debate to express the issues in terms of irreconcilable polarities. Most profoundly, he recognises 'that death is special, a peculiarly significant event in the narrative of our lives'; that for most people the *manner* of their deaths is of 'special, symbolic importance' (1995, p 211). Yet even this refreshing use of the language of aesthetics, of 'narrative' and 'symbolism' as opposed to that of ethics – 'sanctity' and 'autonomy' – is detached from an active engagement with the world of aesthetics. A return to art, to ethics and aesthetics, may achieve such a goal.

ETHICS AND AESTHETICS: A POEM, AND AN ESSAY ON POETRY

The primary medium selected for the following discussion of the ethics of euthanasia may initially seem a strange choice. 'The Almond Tree',[14] by Jon Stallworthy, is a poem about the birth of a child suffering from Down's syndrome. The link with euthanasia is not directly suggested by the poem, but springs from the insights the poet provides into the experience of tragedy. The poem links to the issue of mortality in a larger sense, not just because it deals with the death of an idea, but because it is a poem of immense physicality and spirituality, of the material body, of journeys and of endings.

The poem opens with the narrator describing his journey to hospital as a typically excited expectant father. Experience is heightened by expectation; the narrator feels omnipotent – the 'lucky prince', 'summoning summer with my whistle' and wishes fervently for a son. For the narrator this is a profound moment in personal and human history:

---

12 There are many textbook sources. An excellent discussion of the application of theory to medical ethics is provided by Gillon, 1994.
13 See the summary in Thiroux, 1980, pp 204–05.
14 Reproduced with the kind permission of the poet Jon Stallworthy. The text can be found in Allison, 1983, p 1366.

> I was aware that blood was running
> down through the delta of my wrist
> and under arches
> of bright bone. Centuries,
> continents it had crossed;
> from an undisclosed beginning
> spiraling to an unmapped end.

The unborn child heralds an apotheosis, a synthesis and perfection:

> New
> minted my bright farthing!
> Coined by our love, stamped with
> our images, how you
> enrich us! Both
> you make one. Welcome
> to your white sheet,
> my best poem!

Yet the birth heralds not joy, but tragedy. The narrator-father is told that his son is 'a mongol', engendering not synthesis, but a form of death – of hopes, expectations, ambitions; death of his 'old' self. Ultimately, however, this death heralds a rebirth. Indeed the 'old' self, his obsession with worldly achievements, omnipotent control of his surroundings, the blessing of the college bells, the desire for *a son* as the crowning glory to his masculine, collegiate persona, now, in the light of tragedy, appears shallow and impoverished. The love engendered by the imperfect child cannot be calibrated by worldly, material criteria, nor is it conditional upon conventional expectations, but allows the narrator to be released from the myopia of a thirty-year gestation:

> wrenched from the caul of my thirty
> years growing, fathered by my son
> unkindly in a kind season
> by love shattered and set free.

Throughout, the narrator's experience is represented and charted with reference to the symbolic power of a tree, the almond tree of the title. The flowering tree most profoundly provides a commentary and context to the events of the poem:

> my son sailed from me; never to come
> ashore into my kindom
> speaking my language …
> The almond tree
> was beautiful in labor. Blood
> dark, quickening, bud after bud
> split, flower after flower shook free.

These two utterly divergent images, the poignant, isolated son, adrift in an alien existence and the vibrant, fertile life-giving tree, budding and blossoming, are brought together dramatically in a stanza which purposely merges the two:

> on the darkening wind a pale
> face floated. Out of reach. Only when
> the buds, all the buds, were broken
> would the tree be in full sail.

This merger is achieved not simply by the containment of the two issues within one stanza, but also by the form – short breathless phrases, running together – and the convergence of images in the final line, where the tree *is* a ship.

This extraordinary convergence donates a powerfully expressed refinement to the frequently condensed 'sanctity of life' argument. The fecund tree, like humanity, is budding its offspring in a process, which is both beautiful and violent, blood-dark and splitting. Though the pale face of imperfection floats out of reach, it is only when the buds, *all* the buds, are broken, that the tree would be in full sail. So, perhaps, a society can only embark upon its voyage, balanced and complete – in full sail – when it accepts its full complement of humanity, not just some buds, but *all* the buds – the perfect and the imperfect, the halt and the lame.

It is significant that this poem, concerned as it is with cycles of life, death, wisdom and rebirth, is focused upon the image of the tree – itself a powerful icon in the symbolic and mythological representations of life, birth, wisdom and rebirth.[15] It is perhaps this power of the tree as icon which enhances the universality of an essay based upon the memory of a tree. The essay is a critique, by Seamus Heaney, of the poetry of Kavanagh, and not only the image of the tree, but shared concerns provide a notional link to 'The Almond Tree'.[16]

Heaney's essay, 'The placeless heaven, another look at Kavanagh',[17] begins anecdotally with Heaney recounting how his aunt planted a chestnut tree in the garden, in the year of his birth. As the tree grew, Heaney grew, and he came to identify himself with the tree. After some years, the family moved away, the tree was cut down and thoughts of the place and the tree diminished. In maturity, Heaney's thoughts returned to the tree, or rather to the space where the tree had been, and he came to identify himself with the space, just as before he had identified with the tree, except, says Heaney:

> … this time it was not so much a matter of attaching oneself to a living symbol of being rooted in the native ground; it was more a matter of preparing to be unrooted … [to] a placeless heaven, rather than a heavenly place. (1989, p 4)

The spiritual significance of this transition, from tree to space, is exemplified by Heaney's critique of the poetry of Kavanagh. The early Kavanagh poem:

---

15 For example, Evans (1981, p 1133) notes the tree of Buddha or wisdom, the tree of knowledge, the tree of life, the tree of liberty, to name but a few. According to Hastings (1921) the almond has a symbolic, Biblical connotation of 'to waken or watch'.

16 The essay is contained in a collection of literary essays (Heaney, 1989), which provides lively intellectual critiques of the texts explored. Moral and political issues are central to Heaney's understanding of the *purpose* of art: 'The "poet as witness" … represents poetry's solidarity with the doomed, the deprived, the victimised, the under-privileged. The witness is any figure in whom the truth-telling urge and the compulsion to identify with the oppressed becomes necessarily integral with the act of writing itself.' (1989, p xvi)

17 Essay in Heaney, 1989, pp 3–14.

... starts up like my childhood tree in its home ground; it is supplied with a strong physical presence and is full of the recognitions which existed between the poet and his place ... an imagination which is not yet weaned from its origin.[18]

In contrast, Kavanagh's later poetry includes place:

... within the horizon of Kavanagh's mind rather than the other way around. The country he visits is inside himself ... at the edge of consciousness in a late poem ... we encounter the white light of meditation; in the early poems, the familiar world stretches reliably away.

This analysis resonates with the initial comments on 'The Almond Tree'. The 'early' self of the poem, like the early Kavanagh, or the early Heaney, identifies with the incidents and artefacts of his surroundings: he is 'not yet weaned' from the furniture of an immature identity – the enchanted wood, Magdalen Bridge, the college bells, the wish, not for a healthy child, but for *a son, a son*. At the end of the poem, the self has been transformed, 'wrenched from the caul' – the trappings which maintained the former, foetal self.[19]

The analysis is relevant to a discussion of ethics because it resurrects a profound aspect of the euthanasia debate touched upon by Dworkin. Dworkin dares to recognise that the prospect of death, like the experience of tragedy, can have a narrative and spiritual significance for the individual and that institutional, or legislative, thwarting of the decision to die in an appointed way and place may thwart or fracture that narrative and spiritual vision, thereby inflicting greater suffering upon the individual. Heaney's essay on Kavanagh suggests a further gloss to this issue, in two ways. First, it narrates and legitimates the fact of spiritual growth – that the individual subject is not the static infant of a paternalistic state, but is engaged upon a kinetic spiritual and ethical journey. Secondly, it reminds us, with a forceful aesthetic vision, that the narrator, the subject, the 'I', who has traversed the precipice, from egocentric foetus to heath-blasted soul, has been forced to stare unblinkingly into the void, the treeless space, yet maintains a vision of the self – of the placeless heaven rather than the heavenly place.[20] The terminally ill patient who chooses to control death is not an infant in need of protection from self, but a remarkable individual who deserves support in this stage of an inevitable journey. A society which denies that support, whether

---

18 *Ibid.*

19 This accords with existential viewpoints: 'it does not follow that the Existentialist is reduced to silence, unable to offer anything describable as an ethic. For there is, one might say, a "super-directive" which he can consistently promulgate: to live *authentically*' (emphasis added, Cooper, 1990, p 171). In psychoanalytic terms, the infantile integration of self with incidental externalities is realised through the 'fort-da' scenario: 'Everything begins when several signifiers can present themselves to the subject at the same time ... It is at this level that *Fort* is the correlative of *Da*' (Miller, 1992, p 65)

20 The notion of a placeless heaven disrupts orthodoxies surrounding both the notion of 'heaven' and 'place'.

under the guise of paternalism, sanctity, the 'slippery slope'[21] or whatever, is itself still in the foetal position.[22]

We have seen that one reading of 'The Almond Tree' lends support to the notion of sanctity of life, with the fused images of all the buds breaking and the tree in full sail. A case can be made for a different interpretation however, one which is prompted both by the Heaney analysis of Kavanagh and by the realisation that the poem, for all its compassion, is surely not intended purely as a 'pro-life' manifesto. Whilst the narrator-father has learned love through adversity and cherishes his son, the transformative *locus* of the poem *is* the narrator-father. No longer the blind and naive egocentric of the beginning, he now surveys the landscape of personal tragedy with an enlightened wisdom. Like Heaney and Kavanagh, the imagination has been 'weaned from its origin' and can contemplate the empty space with equanimity. The fusion of ideas – the pale face floating out of reach, the tree in full sail once all the buds are broken – may speak of the acceptance residing in true autonomy rather than the acceptance demanded by the classical notion of sanctity. In accepting that his son will never come:

ashore into my kingdom
speaking my language[,]

the narrator-father bears witness to his own growth through pain. Whilst a pale face floats out of reach, the father approaches completion and balance – full sail – only after the buds, *all* the buds, of his pain are broken. Though this poem shows compassion for the son, it also bears compassion for the self; it is not about '*fathering* my son' but the humble realisation of being '*fathered* by my son'. Although the almond tree maintains its presence throughout and is not cut down, the narrator-father confronts the death, the darkness, the space:

In labor the tree was becoming
itself. I, too, rooted in earth
and ringed by darkness, from the death
of myself saw myself blossoming.

Dworkin's acknowledgement of narrative, of the symbolic importance of life and death, asserts the central importance of individual autonomy, an autonomy in wisdom. This linkage, between narrative, symbolism and autonomy, is enriched

---

21 Discussion of the ethics of euthanasia, as demonstrated in the debate surrounding the Australian repeal of the Northern Territories legislation, is haunted by fear of 'the slippery slope' – that legalising assisted suicide will lead slowly to a *policy* of *involuntary* euthanasia. The Australian legislation seemed well tailored to resist such corruption. Further, the claim that legalising assisted suicide undermines social morality, sending the message that life is not sacred, is arguably misleading. It may be said that the sacred value placed upon life can be upheld by supporting individual assertions of autonomy, which rarely may be reflected in the right of the terminally ill to end life.

22 Not merely medicine and law, but neither psychoanalytic theory nor anthropology are particularly helpful in theorising the individual assertion of autonomy in death. Anthropology tends to observe and record death rituals and beliefs as the realisation of collective, social goals (see, for example, Barley, 1995), whilst psychoanalytic theory has been very much dominated by Freud's 'death instinct'. Modern medical anthropology has come close to addressing the issue in exploring the narratives of illness. For an interesting discussion see Good, 1994. Yet even here, death is significantly absent.

by the vision of 'The Almond Tree'; by the space contemplated by Heaney and Kavanagh. In addition, the aesthetic vision demonstrates that sanctity and autonomy need not be the polar opposites of ethical theory, but co-equal actors in the formation of personal narrative. The exercise of autonomy, the art we make of our lives, is itself an assertion of a right to sanctity, not in a religious context of holiness, but in the sense of pure inviolability. Further, that the addition of the words 'narrative' and 'symbolism' to the vocabulary of ethics can perhaps encompass some other words, such as 'authenticity'[23] and 'compassion'. Individual decisions in the face of adversity should be respected as integral to identity, to the narrative and symbolic view of the self. To deny this autonomy is also to deny the authenticity of the experience and the decision; it is a failure of compassion on the part of society. As Heaney says of Kavanagh:

> ... when he had consumed the roughage of his early Monaghan experience, he had cleared a space ... the rewards of it were a number of poems so full of pure self-possession in the face of death and waste that they prompt the deepest of responses.[24]

The utilisation of 'The Almond Tree' and Heaney's essay on Kavanagh as a *locus* for exploring the major poles of argument in the euthanasia debate may be subject to the following major objection. According to the first reading of the poem, the experience of suffering provides a gateway to spiritual enlightenment and growth. This being the case, the alternate proposition is already well on the way to being undermined – if suffering brings spiritual growth, how can we assert the moral rectitude of support for deliberately ending life and suffering; how can we identify a moment when torment outweighs growth? At one level the question is unanswerable, except perhaps by a deity (and reliance upon that source of enlightenment predicates belief or faith). Yet, surely, we must accept as *integral* to the autonomy of the individual the right to assess and assert the arrival of such a moment even if, in practical or metaphysical terms, continued spiritual growth is still possible. We are ready to intervene and arrest suffering at other levels, but shrink from the finality of death. Our analysis is beset with difficulties – the imprecision of language, the seductive spectre, whether religious or not, of winter flowering.

The use of the term 'narrative' to consolidate the 'spiritual growth culminating in autonomous control' model of the dilemma which is human suffering may invoke an additional criticism.[25] Both the model and the term presuppose a level of conscious intervention, of planning and control in the apparent 'pattern' of our lives, which corresponds to the notion of 'authorship'. Yet, arguably, this simply indulges the *desire* for control, promoting an over-idealised vision both of

---

23 Of course, authenticity is a key concept both to existential theory and to art itself. Heaney summarises Kavanagh's poetry in maturity as 'an example of self-conquest, a style discovered to express this poet's unique response to his universal ordinariness, a way of re-establishing the authenticity of personal experience and surviving as a credible being' (Heaney, 1989, p 14).

24 *Ibid.*

25 My thanks to Dr Nigel Simmonds of Corpus Christi College, Cambridge for clarifying this point.

individual subjecthood vis à vis the community and of the brutally random facts and chances steering our biological existence. Thus it may be said that a more accurate analogy is that of 'readership' – a process by which we attempt to interpret and impose coherence upon events essentially beyond our control. Nevertheless, even in the act of reading, we are dis/empowered by the inevitably personal significance that the text holds for us. Occasionally we must return to a standard text – that of mortality. To shrink from its imperious gaze, to gloss the challenge via a retreat into entirely dehumanised abstractions may, with no little irony, concede to a nihilistic passivity.

Yet another broadside may be levelled at the approach adopted in this chapter. Clearly, Heaney's essay on Kavanagh provides a framework for exploring the entire dialectic, from the ethics of passive acceptance to those of active integration and synthesis through the notion of narrative growth and narrative control. Why then play the arguably 'redundant'[26] card that is 'The Almond Tree'? The sceptic may maintain that it is an emotive indulgence, designed to satisfy emotional appetites whilst masquerading as a plea to the cerebral. This presupposes that the cerebral and emotional exist not only in separation, but that one is inferior to the other. Use of the Heaney-Kavanagh framework alone might permit the discussion to take place within a purely abstract context. Despite the reservations of my notional sceptic, I would assert that reading extracts from the poem, stage by stage, is not merely an aid to interpretation, but is itself an exercise in ethics, forcing the reader to submit to the charge between the emotive and the purely cerebral, whilst experiencing the profound disequilibrium of tragedy lived in the moment. This is significant because legislators and theorists commonly omit this vital stage of instantiation, thus feeding the more tolerable retreat into the abstract and impersonal. Simmonds (1993, p 68) explores this detachment of moral precepts from the particular, recognising the resultant dangers:

> ... a ... sublimation of law occurs whenever juridical metaphors are employed to clarify the fundamental features and sources of our moral life. The complex, and potentially tragic, character of morality requires us to cope with a disorderly and conflictual array of values and commitments. This cannot be reduced to the thin gruel of rights and principles.

The legal subject, the single unit of the community, can all too easily be sacrificed – not simply to the interests of the community, which may or may not be justified on utilitarian grounds – but to a blindly mechanistic legal system, in which the legitimate claims of the legal subject can be marginalised or ignored. Pashukanis, quoted in Simmonds,[27] argued that:

> ... within the developed legal systems of bourgeois society, the legal person becomes an abstract bearer of rights, with no more substance than a geometrical point employed in the construction of a drawing ... Precisely in so far as it reflects

---

26 By this I mean that the purely analytical framework of this chapter arguably could be conveyed simply by reliance upon Heaney's essay, which provides a basis for exploring the key issues. This view would render the use of 'The Almond Tree' 'redundant' if the experiential lesson that the poem provides is disregarded.

27 Simmonds, 1993, p 67.

the fluid and atomistic nature of a market society, law ceases to embody the hierarchical structures of social life, but takes on a fetishist quality, becoming an illusory heaven of equal principles and abstract subjects.

Reduction to a 'geometrical point' is a disturbing context for individual experience of rights adjudication, particularly when the individual is claiming the right to choose the time and manner of death in a society sufficiently informed and advanced for such rights to be debated.

CONCLUSION

The philosophies of law, and of medicine, are intimately bound to the mechanics of living, to preserving and enhancing our stake in the world. The issue of death remains peripheral to these processes. The approach taken in this chapter provides a fresh basis for exploring the ethical positions raised by the subject of death. Two points in particular may be asserted. First, that the medium of art *can* provide a rigorous framework for the examination of moral questions; great artists, such as Seamus Heaney, have not been afraid to respond to the philosophical, political or moral questions raised by their work. Regarding themselves as preserving a 'hard' theoretical domain, many disciplines, including the law, have distanced themselves from artistic endeavour as a field lacking theoretical rigour.[28] Latterly, literary theory has produced some staunch and vigorous arguments that are capable of ready application elsewhere.[29] Yet, ironically, literary texts themselves are frequently irretrievably metabolised – often at the altar of theory – or skirted with caution. It is hoped that this chapter demonstrates that aesthetics – literary texts – are a serious site and source of ethics discourse. Secondly, that the full impact of that discourse can only be conveyed through contemporaneous experience of the text, or parts of the text, by the reader. In other words, telling the reader what a theory, a case, a painting, a text, is 'about' (fraught with difficulty, since all texts are vulnerable to the inevitable subjectivity of readings) is not the same as providing the reader with sufficient extracts from the text to experience its message and its power virtually 'first hand'. Some will be quick to argue that the 'power' of a literary text derives from its emotive content and is thus unreliable. One response is that many legal authorities derive at least some of *their* power from 'emotive' rhetoric. The main point, however, is that the power of many texts of quality – aesthetic, scientific or legal – is composed of rational, deductive, rhetorical and emotive elements.

Heaney's essay appears in an anthology of essays entitled *The Government of the Tongue*. It is a masterfully provocative title, juxtaposing two disparate ideas, the notion of government, the constitutional body, and the tongue, surely at once an entirely powerful and entirely vulnerable bodily constituent. Thus we are

---

28 An excellent note on this 'alienation' of art is given in Douzinas, Warrington and McVeigh, 1991, p 162.

29 Of the many texts that could be mentioned, Fish (1989) is seminal to the transposition of reflection via the field of literary and legal studies.

reminded of the violation that unwieldy government, unwieldy law, can impose upon our inner being, and perhaps of the ultimate ungovernability of a cry for justice – the ungovernable tongue. The least governable tongue would seem to be the voice of art, with its discomfiting, disorienting and invigorating subversive power. The poignant experience of the suffering subject, the enlightening messages of art, can teach society much. Yet fear or scepticism may nourish the relegation of both to a deserted ante-room, drowned out by the voice of the bigot or the whirr of the legal machine. If we are to ensure the dignity of citizens who, like Kavanagh, display 'pure self-possession in the face of death and waste', we must ensure that *all* tongues are properly governed.

An interesting twist in the philosophical tale of this discussion realises a most compelling argument 'against' such use of 'The Almond Tree'. Demonstrating the integral role of point of view in the debate, this counter-reading provides a moot illustration of how a practical ethics source can be turned on its head.

At the time of writing this chapter, copyright permission was sought from Jon Stallworthy for the reproduction of his poem. The very process of approaching the poet brought a new sensibility to the poem,[30] which was sharpened upon receipt of the poet's reply. No *reservation* was expressed on his part; nevertheless the substance of his answer gave pause for thought.[31] Though the version of 'The Almond Tree' referred to above was the version made available in prominent collections, Professor Stallworthy had originally written a final set of verses, verses which he initially omitted but re-instated in later collections;[32] they are as follows:

> You turn to the window for the first time.
> I am called to the cot
> to see your focus shift,
> take tendril-hold on a shaft
> of sun, explore its dusty surface, climb
> to an eye you cannot
>
> meet. You have a sickness they cannot heal,
> the doctors say: locked in
> your body you will remain.
> Well, I have been locked in mine.
> We will tunnel each other out. You seal
> the covenant with a grin.

---

30 Indeed, had the necessity of writing to the poet been uppermost at the time of writing the Stallworthy-Heaney discussion, the detachment gained might not have been achieved, since of course the poem is not simply 'about' a spiritual journey, but a journey undertaken in relation to a birth. The use of a poem as a 'practical ethics analogue' in relation to an argument concerning assisted suicide is instructive; the use of a poem exploring the issue of the birth of a disabled child in conjunction with such a topic might well be seen as insensitive, crude or sadly ironic – a central issue for 'pro-life' supporters crudely harnessed to the use of 'the opposition'.

31 Professor Stallworthy has kindly given permission, a second time, for use of the poem, and an explanation of the additional stanza.

32 Professor Stallworthy explains: 'the verses originally appeared in the collection *Root and Branch* which carried the section of "The Almond Tree" that I subsequently dropped – but eventually included in *Rounding the Horn: Collected Poems*, as a separate poem called "Firstborn".'

> In the days we have known one another,
> my little mongol love,
> I have learnt more from your lips
> than you will from mine perhaps:
> I have learnt that to live is to suffer,
> to suffer is to live.

Though the intrinsic message of the poem is unaltered – the poet in both versions ultimately:

> from the death
> of myself saw myself blossoming,

> Wrenched from the caul of my thirty
> years' growing, fathered by my son,
> unkindly in a kind season
> by love shattered and set free.

Marking the role of personal identity, narrative and spiritual growth in the experience of pain, the ambit of the message alters dramatically with the addition. On the one hand, it can be argued that the message concerning the importance of narrative coherence to personal spiritual growth and identity remains unaltered – the focus is still upon the lessons learned by the poet, the advances in his understanding afforded by the experience. Yet the most powerful argument *against* any use of the poem in service of a discussion of the ethics of physician assisted suicide resides in the alteration, not only the focus upon the uniqueness of life lived in the moment – the sensual response to the sun's light – but the final lines: 'to live is to suffer/to suffer is to live.' Choosing the domain of poetic discourse, set apart from entry into the fray of ethical argument, the poet encapsulates the powerful argument in opposition – that life and suffering are inseparable, at least in the narrative account that gives meaning and sense to life as he has come to understand it. The question of whether to impose that view, as a sentence, upon the suffering of another who would choose to separate their suffering from life, through death, holds a moral status of newly unfolding complexity.

PART II

LAW AND POPULAR CULTURE

CHAPTER 4

CHOICES AND CENSORSHIP –
THE PLAY OF FAME AND INFAMY: JOHN VAN DRUTEN,
PLAYWRIGHT AND LAWYER

INTRODUCTION

Though emerging popular media create new worlds of normative challenge, the need to challenge norms is well illustrated by the worlds falling away from us. This chapter presents a brief biography[1] of a life from just a few decades ago – that of John van Druten, who worked when the law of censorship was easily harnessed to individual authoritarian whim, supported by the self-serving repressions of paternalism and prejudice. An idiosyncratic snapshot of the era, van Druten's life pans from the prosaic and mundane to the glittering and sublime – a jobbing playwright adept in the steady production of entertainment, touching upon social conscience of moderate gravitas. Somewhat less well remembered in recent years, van Druten is best recalled as the dramatist creator of *I Am a Camera*, now popularised in the hit musical and film *Cabaret*. Generated originally by the work of Christopher Isherwood's *Berlin Stories*, the play came to being through the drive and creativity of van Druten, for whom British disquiet at the moral issues raised by the play typified those very characteristics he sought to escape in his journey to California in the late 1920s.

Though *I Am a Camera* appeared to enthusiastic acclaim in New York in 1951 – only six years before van Druten's death and in a decade much removed from the controversial cultural events which had shaped him – the 1950s in Britain proved conservative and austere, not least in its attitude towards risqué theatre. Charting the tale of 'Sally Bowles', a woman of liberal affections ('loose morals' or 'depravity' would have been the terms used in former years) who becomes involved in unsuitable relationships with different men, and lives a somewhat wild existence and has an abortion, the play also reflects upon the complexities of Berlin social and political life in the 1930s and comments upon the real moral failure that is anti-Semitism. In 1952, Lawrence Olivier Productions put the play before the Lord Chamberlain's office for scrutiny with a view to eventual production on the London stage. The reservations and moral concerns expressed by the Lord Chamberlain's office, and subsequent debates surrounding the play and discussions of its potential for film, are fruitfully explored by Aldgate (1999).

---

1   The chapter concentrates upon those little events tracing van Druten's journey from minor academic in Wales – via brief censorship scrutiny – to major playwright on Broadway. An earlier version of this chapter was written for the centenary celebration of the department of law, University of Wales, Aberystwyth. The Centenary Collection appears in the *Cambrian Law Review* (2004) and the editor of the *Review*, Richard W Ireland, has given kind permission for the reproduction of that portion of the original contained in this chapter.

Aldgate recounts that three areas of concern were identified by the reader for the Lord Chamberlain's Office: the references to 'whores' throughout the play; the line 'Throw her on a couch and ravish her'; and the opportunity given to Sally to give reasons for securing her abortion – 'I imagined how it would grow up and how after I'd put it to bed at nights I'd go out and make love to filthy old men to get money to pay for its clothes and food'.[2] In submitting to pressure to supply suitable alterations, van Druten substituted 'tart' for many of the references to 'whore', changed the 'Throw her on a couch' line to 'Knock her down. Throw her on a couch or something', and changed the other questioned line to 'I'd go out with filthy old men to get money to pay for its clothes and food', and removing the words 'ravish' and 'make love', all to the satisfaction of the Lord Chamberlain. Still a daring social commentary, this watering-down may well have contributed to the mixed reviews received by the play.[3] Though some representatives of a moral austerity in the 1950s would have reviled the play in any event,[4] it had a moderately successful run for ten months in 1954. Crucially, however, the reservations concerning the play returned when consideration was given to making it into a film. Though moral debate might be properly undertaken within the realm of the theatre – the place of intellect and 'high art' – talk of a film version immediately drew concerns that the 'mass' audience of the cinema might not exercise sufficient moral discrimination. Talks therefore focused upon the imposition of an 'X' rating. As Aldgate recounts, members of the British Board of Film Censors undertook extensive correspondence regarding the suitability of the film. These exchanges reveal just how partisan were the moral politics of the day, and the consequent difficulties created for playwrights in trying to undertake expositions of 'social realism'. Mary C Glasgow, for example, commented :

> We have no hesitation in saying that we regard this material as unsuitable for a film. Apart from the dialogue, which is appallingly vulgar but could presumably be pruned at the script stage, we consider the whole subject unacceptable. It may be argued that this account of a decadent section of society, without standards of any kind, moral, social or sexual, is interesting historically – although we did not find it so in the play. As a film, we cannot see how it could be other than harmfully degrading to the cinemagoing public ... (Aldgate, 1999, p 432)

Thus, the 'cinemagoing public' was not only to be protected from those depictions, which might prove 'harmfully degrading' (though not necessarily 'untrue' in providing an accurate depiction of how lives were – and are – lived), but such lifestyles were safely to be regarded by the 1950s as of 'historical interest' only – this in the decade preceding revelations concerning backstreet abortions and the subsequent passage of the Abortion Act. Another commentator, Audrey Field, maintained that:

---

2   Aldgate, 1999, p 426.
3   Aldgate (1999, p 428) recounts that the critic Ivor Brown wrote: 'I have, in my dour, Platonic way, a strong conviction that this piece (or at least this production) might have been an honest gin-and-bitters; but has had a strawberry ice cream sloshed over the top of it.'
4   The Public Morality Council, for example, as mentioned by Aldgate, 1999, p 429.

> I agree that there are a number of 'shock' lines and, for a film, a great many of them would have to go ... As to the story, admittedly Sally does not get her just deserts by, eg, being raped by her brother-in-law and going mad; nor, on the other hand, does she reform and qualify for a good man's love.[5]

Gerald Sharpe reported that:

> My wife and I are by no means prudes but she was deeply shocked in particular by the references (a) to Fraulein Schneider's bosom, (b) to Sally's preference for going into the man's bed, and (c) to syphilis. For myself, I would like to see the last of the unwanted baby and the abortion arrangements and aftermath ...[6]

Almost amusing in the simultaneous denial and promulgation of prudery, the comments demonstrate the prevailing mindset, which not only preferred a denial of issues, but which, in the case of the comment invoking 'just deserts', reflected an absolutely rabid hostility to those who overstepped the conventional line in their lifestyle choices or life events. An initial reworking for the film, which allowed Sally to emerge as a successful older woman reflecting upon her colourful life was not allowed; 'We could not have Sally coming back prosperous and successful – a living advertisement for a shiftless and promiscuous way of life', and consequently the screenplay was altered so that '[t]he principal difference of course is that it is now made perfectly clear that Sally is poor and completely unsuccessful'. With the excision of the tragic, 'social realism' aspects and with a new perspective, which lightened the tale into one of mere farce, the annihilation was complete. The film was a failure and critically denounced.

It is little wonder that in the work produced by van Druten throughout the 1930s and 40s, the 'moral challenge' was undertaken with a notably light touch – only in the adaptation of Isherwood's work is such extreme controversy to be found. As the ensuing account demonstrates, van Druten was consistent in producing work that generated a steady touch of social commentary, and was cleverly tailored to the contrasting nuances of political sensibilities and audience interests; the vision of that old master – law – provided with sufficiently dense pebble glasses, until further notice.

Links between the fields of 'law' and 'literature' can emerge from endless permutations; tracing 'the lawyer' in 'the writer' is a frequent and sometimes fruitful pursuit in 'law and literature' studies;[7] and just as 'greatness' may be

---

5   Aldgate, 1999, p 432.

6   *Ibid*.

7   An exhaustive discussion of the field of 'law and literature' need not be undertaken here: texts – both books and journals – engaging with this interdisciplinary link are various and readily found – in Europe, for example, Maria Aristodemou, Adam Gearey, Richard Ireland, Professor Ian Ward, Willem Witteveen and the present writer (Melanie Williams) all hold an ongoing interest in the field. In the United States and Canada, studies are particularly flourishing with the work of Professors William A Davis, Gary Boire, Lawrence Douglas, Jill Tomasson Goodwin, Anne McGillivray, Mary Polito, James Boyd White, Richard Weisberg – no doubt many worthy names have been omitted from this list. Examples of writers with 'direct' links to the legal profession include John Buchan, William Faulkner, Henry Fielding, Henry James, George Borrow, Franz Kafka, Herman Melville – but again, the list is an example only, by no means exhaustive and capable of great expansion once the notion of 'direct' is queried.

systemic or imposed, so, with texts and writers of texts, it might be said that some are born to law, some grow into law and some have law thrust upon them.[8] Some have a tangential but profound relation to 'legal' issues, yet others, claiming crucial jurisprudential significance, may prove profoundly tangential in their contribution to debate. Writers such as Dickens, Shakespeare and Hardy undertake learned and critical reflections on the conventions of society and law, yet hold tenuous and complex juristic antecedents themselves, whilst others, such as Fielding, Kafka and Henry James, can trace direct lineage in juristic training and this is readily detectable, as theme or trauma, in their work.[9] Rarely can it be said, however, that a writer with such antecedents has had direct experience of learning, thinking and teaching law yet chooses to mount the fictive assault upon conventions via the frailties of intimate life rather than the intimate frailties of law. Such is the case with John van Druten however: a man who chose the subtly subversive medium of tragi-farce, leaning to vaudeville, over that of epic authority, yet posed an engaging and popular challenge to establishment values.

Discovery of the unexpected is one of the delights of history. Looking back to the gay,[10] café-society literati of the 1930s, the names of Auden and Isherwood spring readily to mind, whilst 'van Druten' is less recognisable. Yet in the time of Auden and Isherwood, John van Druten – the novelist and playwright whose work gave rise to *Cabaret*[11] – was a major star in the heady constellation that formed their circle, a daring comet in the orbits of Berlin and Broadway. That 'Johnny' van Druten began his professional life as an academic in the law department at Aberystwyth University is even less well known, yet the recurring themes of many of his plays – questioning sexual inequality and prejudice, corruption and intrigue – reflect *not* simply the daily preoccupations of any provincial law school! but adversarial skills and ethical concerns, which in modern times would have been amply rewarded in the celebrity accorded to prominent advocates, whether champions of human rights or imbibers of high-society intoxicants. Somewhat ironically, the challenge to values invoked by his earliest success came close to giving him 'legal trouble' – in the great tradition of literary texts that question social convention, his work was subject to censorship.

---

8 With apologies for this somewhat tawdry colonisation of the saying, occurring in original form and elegance in Shakespeare's *Twelfth Night*.

9 The examples are taken as discursive markers only. A survey of the similarities and differences in approaches taken by those with a 'direct' legal training as compared to the 'barefoot' jurist (so to speak) would be interesting in itself. The distinction between the two groups may itself be somewhat questionable, but perhaps affords a novel starting point. The tangential links to the law in the lives and works of Dickens, Shakespeare and Hardy are well known. Dickens, in particular, may be regarded as having a more than tangential claim to the title of jurist, having intimate experience of the field, both from work as clerk in a law office and as Parliamentary reporter. Fielding, Kafka and Henry James are prominent examples of that substantial group of writers with direct, personal experience of professional legal training.

10 The reader may place their own construction upon this word. In the context 'either' meaning is apt.

11 The musical hit *Cabaret* was first staged in 1972 and was derived from the play *I Am a Camera* by John van Druten.

STUMBLING TO LAW: FROM BRITISH MUSEUM STEPS TO ABERYSTWYTH SEA …

Frankly, John van Druten (1901–57) did not so much seek 'lawyerdom' as stumble into it. In his autobiography, *The Way to the Present*[12] he recounts the haphazard journey to the law, undertaken against his inclination for the theatre and largely to meet the expectations of his parents:

> The real world meant the office and the Law and dining with relations, all the things that Father had called duty. Once again I was glad that he was no longer there; had he been alive, my turning to the theatre would have brought us into battle, in which he would have stormed and exercised his authority to forbid this [other] kind of life for me.[13]

This 'real world' of the office was indeed likely to have been dreary – van Druten entered the law by way of articles, assigned to draw up endless abstracts of title in the stolid, British, Dickensian tradition. In contrast to this, he recognised that academic life – always perhaps a slightly less than 'real world' – would at least promise the satisfactions of teaching, whilst at the same time promising the possibility of emulating an admired scholar:[14]

> If I had to stay in the Law in some capacity, it seemed to me that the least unattractive one would be that of a teacher. To begin with, I should have leisure for my own pursuits, and good vacations;[15] the theoretical side of the Law I had always been able to enjoy as an intellectual exercise; and in lecturing, at least, I would have some chance to express myself and my personality, employing, in however attenuated a form, what talents I might have as actor or as writer. Moreover, I believed that I could make the study of the Law a little less unappetizing to students than the majority of my teachers had enabled it to be for me, and if I could achieve a fraction only of the qualities of skill in exposition and personal magnetism which I so much admired in Dr Burgin[16] as a lecturer, I would, I felt, be doing something in which I could take pride and pleasure.

---

12 J van Druten, *The Way to the Present: A Personal Record* (1938) London: Michael Joseph. The second stage of his autobiography, *The Widening Circle*, appeared in 1957, the year of his death.

13 *Ibid*, van Druten, p 230.

14 *Ibid*, p 233.

15 This being the days when vacations were not under pressure from the demands of conference circuits and research papers. Though van Druten *was* 'invited' to pursue LLM study and/or work on producing research papers, his autobiography candidly records his unwillingness to do so, preferring instead to take luxurious holidays with his mother when not engaged in the development of his creative writing skills.

16 Presumably a lecturer for the Law Society Examinations at the University of London, where van Druten took his LLB – to date brisk enquiry has not confirmed this presumption.

A possible post emerged at Aberystwyth, this being in the groundbreaking days of Professor Levi's reign.[17] In suitably surreal mode – for an incipient junior lecturer at Aberystwyth who would one day take Broadway by storm – van Druten's first meeting with his new head of department reads like a stage direction for a classic musical and reveals a weakness for stereotypes:[18]

> My meeting with Professor Levi ... took place, at his suggestion and for reasons I have never understood, on the steps of the British Museum, and he told me in his second letter that I should recognize him by the instrument he wore as an aid to deafness. From his name I imagined him to be a patriarchal person with a beard and a hooked nose, possibly even a skull cap; to my surprise, the man with the ear appliance who greeted me outside the Museum was a spruce, dapper, smartly dressed man of fifty, with a springy step and a bright, attractive face. He had an oddly pitched voice and a curious accent, unlike that of any other Welshman I have known. He greeted me with great friendliness, and took me to the Palace Hotel where he was staying, while I wondered why he had not asked me to call upon him there in the first instance. I am still wondering today. At tea, he chatted amiably about his Oxford days, slurring over all discussion of work, and waving aside my questions as to what would be expected of me ...

Though sometimes depressed by the wintry evenings, van Druten for the most part enjoyed his experience of teaching, and there is reason to believe he must

---

17 The Alumni website (www.prom-aber.com/feature/law.html) on the history of the Department of Law – *100 years of passing laws* – written by Richard Ireland, comments:

> Two vivid and contrary personalities dominated the first years of the Law School: Professor TA Levi and Professor Jethro Brown ... Levi was a radically different man, no less the intellect but more eccentric, characterful, maverick even. He was the son of Rev Thomas Levi, a tough Minister of the Presbyterian Church of Wales. He brought to the youthful School energy and dynamism ...

Thanks to Dr Ian Salmon, who reports that the annual reports for the University record that: 'John van Druten (LLB London) was a lecturer in Law from 1923 to 1926. He ran the North Wales Law School in Rhyl for articled clerks, and also lectured in College on the History of English Law'. Van Druten's autobiography (*The Way to the Present: A Personal Record*, 1938, p 237) comments:

> Professor Levi ... suggested that I should prepare ... a course of lectures for the degree classes at the college on the History of English Law, which I had given him to understand was my special province. This was not strictly true. For the Honours examination for my LLB I had had to choose one extra subject beyond those required for the Pass examination, and, from a number of alternatives, I had selected Legal History; but the knowledge required for the single three-hour paper on the subject was hardly sufficient for it to be regarded as my speciality. However, I had given Professor Levi that impression and I had to live up to it, and for the three years that I remained a teacher of law, I maintained and almost justified the deception that I was a specialist in its history ...

18 The *penchant* for stereotyping may be a natural concomitant of the 'placing' of characters, beloved of the dramatist. Van Druten, in fact, held a personal sensitivity concerning anti-Semitism; the *Diaries of Christopher Isherwood, Vol One: 1939–60*, Katherine Bucknell (ed) (1996) London: Vintage, p 649, record:

> *September 1956:* Johnnie came to lunch with me at the studio three days ago. He says he asks himself what he shall write about next – it must be something he knows really well. He decided it must be half-Jews, and Jews who 'pass'. He, himself, is half Jewish. I never realized this – always thought it was only a quarter, at most. He is *far* less Jewish than Stephen or John Lehmann, not to mention the Reinhardts. Has he anything Jewish about him? Yes – a certain *gemutlichkeit* and a certain furtiveness.

have been a refreshing teacher. His record of this time provides an interesting insight into the life he created – and encountered – in the classroom:[19]

> I tried to treat the students as the lecturers of the Law Society had treated us, with some degree of formality, addressing them as Mister instead of by their surnames, which I think, contributed a flattering elegance to their classes with me. The legal rhymes and limericks that I had written in my hours of inattention at the Law Society came in useful now as diversions for the students, and, by way of mnemonics, I turned Leading Cases into doggerel for them to learn, thereby introducing an unfamiliar note of lightness into the proceedings ... The tradition of the College, handed down from the oldest professors, was for lecturers to dictate at the end of each hour a brief summary of what they had been teaching, which summary the students afterwards learned by heart and expected to be able to use in their examinations. Many of them, it was said, had come to the college with their fathers' note-books, sitting under the same professors, and had been able to dispense with note-taking altogether ...

Nevertheless, Van Druten enjoyed teaching the 'eager, likeable and enthusiastic' students cramming in the law school at Rhyl, as well as Aberystwyth, and clearly found the working conditions conducive to the development of his creative ideas beyond the lecture room, drafting versions of plays, poems and parodies, with occasional small successes in terms of publication. Primarily in love with the theatre, van Druten set himself a challenge:[20]

> ... the sea, as I walked along the front on my way to a ten o'clock lecture, was bright and cheering, but my problems had not left me, and I made a solemn promise to myself that, if by the end of the year I had achieved nothing of my ambition, I would take it as a sign that I had been mistaken in it, and make the permanent surrender to an academic career that I had thought the night before was the right thing for me.

By the end of that summer, *The Return Half*,[21] an 'innocuous comedy with a conventional plot', was produced in London. Though successful on a modest scale, the play was clearly the work of an apprentice cutting his teeth, rather than testing his capabilities. It took the guidance of an inspiring agent, JL Campbell, 'the most important man in my playwriting career'[22] to move van Druten forward: 'If you have really *got* to write, because the idea fascinates you and you can't leave it alone, then you must write it, however slight or bad it is, but not because you "think it will go down well".'[23]

Working through several more ideas, the writer finally hit upon a combination of ideas which appealed to this more profound level of creativity:[24]

---

19 *The Way to the Present: A Personal Record* (1938) London: Michael Joseph, p 247.

20 *Ibid*, p 252.

21 *The Return Half* is referred to in van Druten's autobiography as a play which apparently toured the smaller theatres of London. It does not, however, appear on the lists of significant works by van Druten.

22 *The Way to the Present: A Personal Record* (1938) London: Michael Joseph, p 256. Van Druten notes that Campbell was a native of Virginia and later became known as a novelist in his own right.

23 *Ibid*, pp 256–57.

24 *Ibid*, p 260.

I went back to Aberystwyth ... I had seen Douglas in *Fata Morgana*[25] and, while I had not cared a great deal for the play, I had been impressed and moved by the bruised simplicity and youthful hurt and puzzlement of his performance. For the next few weeks I pondered on those qualities, trying to evolve a play which should interpret them. The first plot that occurred to me was a highly melodramatic one, with a first act taking place on a boy's last day at school, in which he looks forward to getting out into the world with all its freedom and excitement. The rest of the play was to show his disintegration, his involvement in a night club shooting, and a final sobbing disillusionment. But when I came to plan it in more detail, all that I found attractive about it was its first act setting, so that I jettisoned the rest and began to build again from that, keeping the action wholly in the school. Within two weeks I had the plot of *Young Woodley,* and within another three I had finished the play. Much of it was written in the train, going to Rhyl; in the character of Simmons, the housemaster, I released my strong dislike for two members of the staff at Aberystwyth, as well as that which lingered in my memory for a [school]master and in Mr Woodley I made one more attempt to present an apology to my father ...

We can gain a sense of the timing of this writing – around 1925 – and of the significant tensions hanging over van Druten in terms of the responsibilities impacting upon him from the law on the one hand and the theatre on the other, when he confesses that, whilst waiting for a verdict upon the marketability of this new play, he is forced to meet the demands of revolutionary changes in land law:[26]

> The new law, abrogating the entire system of real property which had existed in England since the Norman conquest, was shortly to come into force, and it was necessary that I should teach its intricate provisions in the coming year, so that much of my time was spent in mastering them and in preparing a new set of lectures, a task involving all my powers of concentration, exactly as though I were back in my examination days again ...

It would seem, then, that though the detail does not appear on the official record for the University Annual Report, van Druten had been drafted to teach the revolutionary new changes associated with the Law of Property Act 1925. Not for the first time in the history of academic law, a junior member of staff no doubt seemed the most appropriate choice (we will not say 'easily collared') for such a task; and, no doubt, not for the first time we might surmise that the embrace of land law signalled the demise of the lawyer, though rarely can such demise have heralded a journey from Aberystwyth to Broadway.

---

25 The *Fata Morgana* was reputed to be a mirage, often seen in the Strait of Messina and traditionally attributed to the sorcery of Morgan le Fay. She was believed to reside in Calabria, a region of southern Italy (source: Hutchinson Multimedia Encyclopaedia, available at www.hme.co.uk). The story has undergone a number of metamorphoses, including a work fiction by Leo Frankowski and a poem by Christina Rossetti.

26 *The Way to the Present: A Personal Record* (1938) London: Michael Joseph, p 264.

THE LORD CHAMBERLAIN'S ROLE IN AN AMERICAN DREAM

Young Woodley[27] was to be the first significant success of van Druten's career. Significant in being sought by Mr Basil Dean[28] of St Martin's Theatre, and in being the first of van Druten's many plays to be staged in America, it was also significant in attracting the notice of the censor. Just as life was becoming suitably glamorous, with van Druten lunching with Basil Dean at the Ivy Restaurant, the Lord Chamberlain refused the play a licence, interpreting it, as van Druten recounts, as 'an attack upon the public school system, liable to cause offence to scholastic bodies and pain to parents and guardians'.[29]

Reading the play today, one might surmise that the most potentially explosive aspect of the plot is to be found in the attraction between a young schoolmaster's wife and an eighteen-year-old prefect. Such breaking of taboos would have been shocking for the time, though the play provides spirited mitigation: 'a boy is not supposed to be a man until he leaves school at the age of eighteen, but nature has reached her goal some years earlier than the schoolmaster.'[30] An article in *The New Statesman*,[31] both attacking the censorship and reviewing the play, provides an insight into the play's more subtle challenges to convention, as well as to its perceived strengths:

> … now and then the Lord Chamberlain makes such an alarming blunder that it raises the whole question once again; and never in the history of the censorship during the last fifty years has the Lord Chamberlain and his official reader of plays made such a bad, such a wholly inexcusable, blunder as in the banning of Mr John van Druten's play *Young Woodley* … The success of this play was as striking as it was deserved; so much so that for the whole of the present week it has been playing at the Arts Theatre Club every night to crowded audiences whose enthusiasm has been quite unprecedented … The slightest attempt at exposing any of the weaknesses of our public school system is regarded as a Bolshevistic attack on the British Empire, and we are immediately treated to nauseating humbug about the Battle of Waterloo and the playing fields of Eton … The vices or virtues of homosexuality are undoubtedly stimulated by our public school system, and whether we like homosexuality or dislike it, surely it is futile to pretend to ignore the notorious fact that the segregation of hundreds of boys between the ages of fourteen and eighteen conduces to this practice … Mr van Druten is not concerned with homosexuality in *Young Woodley*, he has wisely left this dangerous theme

---

27 *Young Woodley: A Play in Three Acts* (1928) London: Victor Gollancz.
28 Basil Dean was a hugely influential figure. The Basil Dean archive is held at the University of Manchester. Basil Dean (1888–1978), theatre impresario, was the Director of ENSA – the Entertainments National Service Association – and pioneer of British filmmaking.
29 *The Way to the Present: A Personal Record* (1938) London: Michael Joseph, p 266.
30 Quoted in *The New Statesman* in 1928, this line appears in the play *Young Woodley* in the context of a frank discussion of burgeoning sexuality: 'What do they think we are … Celibate monks? Good Lord, it's human nature isn't it? I was over in France last year; met a lot of French fellows. Things are pretty different over there, I can tell you. Why, practically every boy has got his *petite amie…*' (*Young Woodley: A Play in Three Acts* (1928) London: Victor Gollancz, p 15).
31 18 February 1928, pp 593–94.

alone. It is, however, lurking in the background as an alternative danger to the dangers he illuminates ... [yet in the depiction of the love between schoolboy and housemaster's wife] van Druten is to be most congratulated. He has given us a remarkable and a profoundly moving study of young love, and his insight into the nature of young Woodley and of his attitude towards love is so penetrating and delicate that the last scene of parting between Woodley and Laura is one of the finest and most deeply felt creations in modern drama ... That such a play should be under the censor's ban is simply ludicrous and the ban should be lifted at once ... Let nobody talk of the degeneration of modern life when such a play and such actors can be found in London!

In one stroke, van Druten had reached that enviable position of touching the moral quick of social norms, so that the selfsame material could attract the notice of the censor for being 'degenerate'[32] whilst being lauded by the literary world for its 'nobility'. Perhaps unsurprisingly, a 'highly coloured' account of the banning of the play appeared in *The Western Mail*: '... hinting at improprieties in the play so that when I returned to Wales I found Professor Levi in a state of indignation, urging me to bring suit for libel, and I had to calm him down.'[33] Nor in the long term did the debacle do him any lasting damage – on the contrary; as with modern times, such notoriety raised the temperature of debate and promised healthy sales in America, where the play quickly re-emerged free of the censor. In an interesting example of a well-trodden phenomenon in Anglo-American cultural history, America, so often the stated guardian of puritan values, proved the more liberal forum for this impassioned play; but then, unlike England, America was not confronted with a challenge to its own age-old bastions: the public schools of England were but little more than a quaint artefact of distant shores. By the time of the Christmas vacation, van Druten realised, from press cuttings and from letters from America, that the play 'was one of the big successes of the Broadway season'.[34] Within months, van Druten had witnessed the drawn-out and heart-rending death of his mother, whilst at the same time receiving 'dizzying' amounts of money into his usually modest bank account. Everything seemed to point to change:[35]

> Of one thing I was certain, and that was that I would not return to Aberystwyth for more than the remainder of that term. I was going back the next day, determined to hand in my resignation immediately, allowing the three months of the summer vacation for the prescribed period of notice. Even in making this decision I experienced a momentary conflict and hesitation, hearing an echo of my mother's voice doubting the wisdom of throwing up a regular occupation. But I knew that I could not remain in Wales without the background of my home ... It was an actor friend who suggested what I ought to do, which was to go to America and find what I was seeking there ... in Aberystwyth, my statement that I wanted to go to America served merely to give further colour to the idea [that] it was only moneyed, idle

---

32 An excellent discussion of the history of the Lord Chamberlain's power of 'pre-publication censorship', and of the wider issues and notorious cases concerned with censorship, is provided by Rolph, *Books in the Dock* (1969) London: André Deutsch.

33 *The Way to the Present: A Personal Record* (1938) London: Michael Joseph, p 268.

34 *Ibid*.

35 *Ibid*, pp 275–77.

people who went for pleasure to the States. This, at least, was the point of view of the older and more academic faction; my friends among the junior staff rejoiced with me in my good fortune …

Though treated 'courteously' and 'kindly' by the senior academics, it is not surprising that they were out of sympathy with this no doubt seemingly wild switch from the law, unaware as they must have been of the extent to which van Druten's heart had always been elsewhere.

As the title to this chapter suggests, it is for his later work, leading to *Cabaret*, that van Druten is most likely to be known and remembered, and there is a story to be told, too, in the conception of this still hugely successful play. As the *cognoscenti* may know, *Cabaret* was actually developed from van Druten's play *I Am a Camera*, written in 1951 and itself a skilful adaptation from Christopher Isherwood's *Berlin Stories*.[36] By now the 'elder statesman', van Druten was clearly still an energetic and willing dupe in the machinations of his theatrical circle; as Finney recounts,[37] impoverished and somewhat languorous, Isherwood and his coterie found it difficult to harness their material, whilst van Druten proved both a willing workhorse and a masterly craftsman:

> With Lesser Samuels, Speed Lamkin and Isherwood started collaborating on a dramatisation of 'Sally Bowles'. When this attempt to raise money failed, Dodie Smith and her husband Alec hatched a successful plot to interest John van Druten in undertaking the dramatisation, secure in the knowledge that if he did, his reputation would be sufficient to ensure that it reached the stage. One day that spring at van Druten's desert ranch, after leading the talk round to adaptations of novels for the theatre, Alec Beesley casually said to van Druten, 'I bet you can't write a play about Sally Bowles.' Van Druten took the bait and sat down the same day to block out the first part of what became *I am a Camera* … 'Almost everything in the play is his', Isherwood has said, apart from an autobiographical line or two. Van Druten invented the character of Sally's mother, made up the Fritz-Natasha sub-plot, supplied Frl Schnieder with an anti-semitic streak (which made Isherwood feel bad) and gave the material its dramatic shape. By early June he had completed it. By September he had obtained financial backing to cast it and direct it himself …

---

36 The *Cabaret* 'press kit' website at http://networksontour.com notes:

> John van Druten was best known for his two skilful adaptations, 'I Remember Mama' (1944), based on Kathryn Forbes' autobiographical novel *Mama's Bank Account* and 'I am a Camera' (1951) from Christopher Isherwood's *Berlin Stories*. Otherwise, his reputation rests largely on the successful comedies *The Voice of the Turtle* (1943) and *Bell, Book and Candle* (1950). Many of his plays later became successful films … He was also a well-known stage director … in 1951 van Druten directed the Rodgers and Hammerstein musical 'The King and I' on Broadway … As an adult he would spend half the year in New York and half near Los Angeles on the AJC Ranch which he owned with Carter Lodge and – before his death – the British actress and theatre director Auriol Lee. A fall from a horse in Mexico in 1936 left van Druten with a permanently crippled arm despite numerous operations. He was a contributor to Christopher Isherwood's *Vedanta for the Western World*.

37 Finney, *Christopher Isherwood: A Critical Biography* (1979) London: Faber & Faber, p 209.

SOCIO-LEGAL COMMENTARY IN THE GUISE OF POPULAR THEATRE

Though van Druten's links – to *Cabaret*, Isherwood, Auden and Broadway – have proved to be the most durable and visible indicators of his celebrity, he was a prolific and hugely successful playwright, becoming a kindly, somewhat avuncular, figure in the lives of less organised characters, such as Isherwood. Isherwood's *Diaries*[38] provide rich insights into the glamorous, yet demanding, life of the Hollywood/Broadway 'set', in which van Druten played so prominent a part, providing lavish parties and dinners at his desert ranch. Though the diaries reveal aspects of van Druten's character in some detail, he nevertheless remains somewhat elusive overall. He was a Christian Scientist[39] and a pacifist, revealing lawyerly skill in framing the pacifist agenda. At the same time, he proved worldly and skilful in his handling of the 'incipient' *prima donna*. As Isherwood recounts:[40]

> Pacifism was also the basis of my newly formed friendship with John van Druten. I met him, for the first time, at the Gotham Hotel, where he was recovering from an operation on his arm. He was easy and funny and charming, very much in his theatrical element. Ruth Chatterton, the actress, came in. John told her he had started on the new play (*Leave Her to Heaven*) in which she was to star. I have never seen anyone put on such an act. '*Johnny* – !' she tearfully, joyfully gasped, 'Oh – Johnny, *darling!* Oh – I'm so *glad!*' John handled her perfectly – he was cool and pleasant, submitting to her kisses without a sign of disgust. I admired him as one admires an expert animal trainer.

> … After some discussion, John and I formulated the following questions, and John sent them to Rudolf Messel, Runham Brown (secretary of the War Resister's International) and George Lansbury.[41] They were:
> (1) What is a pacifist to do in wartime (apart from merely refusing to fight) and what activities are permissible to him, by way of defence or otherwise, if he is (a) in England, or (b) in a non-combatant country?
> (2) What permissible alternative is there to war in opposing an aggressor whose pledge cannot be relied upon?
> (3) If none, does one open all doors to the aggressor and let him take everything he wants?

Unlike Isherwood and Auden, van Druten seems not to have been overt about his sexuality, was generous and inventive, yet deeply responsible. Take, for example, this July 1940 extract from Isherwood's *Diaries*:[42]

> *July 17.* John van Druten and I are working together on an episode for the British War Relief film. Murder of an old lady by her housekeepers, with slow poison, in the Dickens style. It is all Johnny's idea, and I can hardly contribute anything to it. Johnny is so inventive, anyway. He's always three jumps ahead of me. His mind is agile and graceful, like a nimble monkey. It takes naturally to parody and pastiche. Johnny really loves to write: there seems to be absolutely no struggle, no effort

---

38 *Op cit*, fn 18.
39 *Op cit*, fn 18, p 112.
40 *Op cit*, fn 18, p 14.
41 The *Diaries* record that these were prominent British pacifists.
42 *Op cit*, fn 18, p 107.

involved. It is all play, and he approaches it without inhibitions, like a child. Yet, at the same time, he is the shrewd, experienced professional, deliberately creating theatrical effects and very conscious of how his audience will react to them. He is charming and polite to me, but I don't feel that I'm being of the slightest use to him …

What comes across is an extremely able and witty man, for whom the discipline of legal training may well at least have contributed some solid grounding in the discipline needed for effective writing. For the world of the law, however, it is interesting to ponder for a moment on the prominent themes of his work, especially in the context of a time when social realism in the literary text often provoked disquiet. Extensive coverage of his many works is not the purpose of this study[43] – rather, it is to provide a sense of the man, and of the clear links between his theatrical and innate juristic identities. For example, in *Behold, We Live* (1932)[44] the hypocrisies of social values are examined. The story traces the growing affection between a couple, trapped in loveless marriage to others and to whom divorce is denied. Respectable, conscientious and sincere, both are made to suffer for their love. Evers, a successful lawyer, is 'passed over' for the Bench because of the perceived 'impropriety' of the relationship, whilst his lover Sarah suffers interminable guilt at this damage to his career. Evers dies young, of a terminal disease, under the vengeful eye of his wife, who forcibly keeps Sarah from the deathbed. Though somewhat melodramatic, the themes clearly challenge conventions upheld as watchwords for respectability, which yet foster the mean, the base and ignoble. In the next year, van Druten wrote *The Distaff Side*,[45] a play similarly concerned with the problems created by overzealous divorce law and extramarital relationships, yet concentrating, with more humour, upon the complex, intuitive feminine understanding of relationships that exist between grandmothers, daughters and granddaughters. Van Druten, whose autobiography reveals a touching devotion to his mother and uncanny understanding of women generally, clearly appreciated the subtleties of the feminine mind. He also understood the appalling suffering to which women were made subject in a world and time promoting double standards. In *The Voice of the Turtle*[46] (1943), a couple are 'thrown together' by circumstance. More boldly this time, van Druten explores the territory of sincere, healthy relationships 'outside' marriage and includes a female character who, as a result as much of 'nature' as of 'nurture', is a 'free spirit', recognising the possible *infidelities* lurking in the conventional ceremonials of monogamy – a kind of Sue Bridehead[47] of Broadway.

In 'Double-marking', a poem by Dorothy Parker,[48] the character, Sally, is resistant to the claims of monogamous commitment, not – as is conventionally claimed – for fear of being betrayed, but because *she herself* cannot be sure that

---

43 An exhaustive list is not provided, but see fn 36, above, for a flavour of this output.
44 *Behold, We Live* (1932) London: Victor Gollancz.
45 *The Distaff Side* (1933) London: Victor Gollancz.
46 *The Voice of the Turtle* (1943) London: Michael Joseph.
47 The similarity to Hardy's tragic heroine in *Jude the Obscure* is partial, but notable.
48 *The Voice of the Turtle* (1943) London: Michael Joseph, p 152.

such commitment, even to one for whom she holds genuine affection, is for her:

> I will not make you songs of hearts denied
> And you, being man, would have no tears of me,
> And should I offer you fidelity
> You'd be, I think, a little terrified

Most shockingly, in response to 'Bill' anticipating that Sally might not wish him to stay overnight because she might 'rouse the beast' in him, Sally confesses 'Bill … there's a beast in me too!'[49] – an expression of feminine libido couched in daringly frank terms. In terms of cultural history, this is relatively radical, social realism and social challenge, clearly paving the way toward the social and political commentary of *I Am a Camera* and *Cabaret*, and appearing decades before overt discussions of female libido and feminine autonomy became the norm.

In short, then, there is more to John van Druten than meets the eye. As a somewhat fleeting visitor to the shores of west Wales, those shores gave him pause to begin the construction of a notable theatrical career. Though appreciated today as a genuine and significant player in the heady world of 1930s stardom,[50] he remains somewhat eclipsed in the popular mind by names such as Isherwood, a man perhaps more wilfully schooled in 'backing into the limelight'. Even when brought fully into view, as the instigator of the still hugely successful and endlessly re-made[51] *Cabaret*, van Druten's more subtle identity, as proto-feminist, as social commentator and as sparkling mind, suggests a world of opportunities strangely missed. Famous he was, and no doubt suffered no regret at his transient engagement with the legal academy. Perhaps in modern times he would still have been drawn inexorably towards the theatre and its heady constellations, as other lawyer-playwrights of today are drawn. Yet, had he lived today, one senses that his range of skills might have made a justly dramatic contribution to socio-legal discourse and legal change. Realistically perhaps, he would not have wished his life to be any other way. Though, to be sure, the world of the law can offer some startling characters and dramas, an overlong sojourn in Aberystwyth would have denied encounters such as these:[52]

> *December 9, 1942*: Dinner with Huxley and van Druten at Romanoff's. The choice of restaurant was Johnny's idea. He wanted to meet Aldous again, and I suppose he felt that only the best was good enough: he admires Aldous enormously. Johnny seemed very young: an admiring boy in his teens. One of his nicest qualities is his entire humility in the presence of someone he considers his superior: he assumes, as a matter of course, that all his plays and his success are just so much junk in comparison with Aldous's least word, and yet he never once flattered him or said anything embarrassing …

No, on reflection, 'Johnny' van Druten doesn't sound at all like a lawyer.

---

49   *The Voice of the Turtle* (1943) London: Michael Joseph, p 110.
50   Websites referring to the work of van Druten abound, and there is a clear resurgence of interest in his work in the United States particularly.
51   Remakes of *Cabaret*, both in stage and film versions, are testament to the continuing relevance of its themes, combining political with cultural upheaval.
52   *The Diaries of Christopher Isherwood*, fn 18 above, p 260.

CHAPTER 5

A MEDIA HIJACK – RAPE, HOUSEHOLDER DEFENCE – LEGAL DEBATES TAKEN HOSTAGE BY *STRAW DOGS*

INTRODUCTION

Straw Dogs, released uncut on video for the first time in 2002, is known most notoriously for two issues of legal note – its controversial rape scene (with resultant feminist response) and the censorship reaction which ensued. The depiction provoked questions of interest for current policy debates, not least in critical points still undetected in relation to the offence of rape. More dramatically overlooked were some wholly different juristic issues raised prior to the making of the film and overshadowed by the film debate. Gordon M Williams's book *The Siege of Trencher's Farm,* which forms the basis for the film, deals with a range of juristic issues, which also hold pressing contemporary relevance, issues taken hostage and buried in the furore and fascination which followed the release of *Straw Dogs.*[1] This chapter sets out to tell the story of these hijacked debates – occluded not only by scenes remoulded for the purposes of film, but by righteous indignation and reactive repressions.

This chapter will therefore chart two issues. The first, raised by the film, is that of rape, and discussion will show how, in taking issue with the sensationalist aspects of rape, commentators have overlooked less visible, but perhaps more significant, points. The second issue is raised by the book and largely overshadowed in the film – the theme of self defence in relation to householders. Thus, as topics are hijacked by diverse interest groups – by debate as well as movie moguls – the inherent *potential* debates shift and erode, so that aside from revealing a tale of media hijack, of social and directorial motives muddying debates, such shifts betray something of the sands that are ourselves.

---

1   Gordon M Williams, *The Siege of Trencher's Farm*: all page references in this chapter are to the 1969 edition, New York: Dell Publishing. The book is now republished by Bloomsbury (2003), with the title *Straw Dogs*. This seems particularly sad given that past critical commentary on the book has been wholly unfair; so dazzled are the film critics by their icon. Weddle (1995, p 20) says of the book that it is 'pure exploitation melodrama with a plot as old as movies: the meek bookworm pushed too far … Melnick (the producer) thought the tissue-thin narrative and characters could be turned into something of substance'. Weddle's review (and Peckinpah himself) credits the Peckinpah/Goodman rewriting of the book into screenplay with much of the ingenuity and substance that in fact appears in Williams's book. By contrast, the film does seem (as some British critics reported at the time) 'cardboard' in characterisation, a degradation of women and a depraved celebration of violence.

THE FILM: *STRAW DOGS* – RAPE DEBATES

When it was produced in 1971, the film *Straw Dogs* was at the heart of a censorship furore. Oddly, though it has maintained a reputation for having attracted violent feminist disapproval, such feminist commentary is today thin on the ground, a defiantly anti-feminist stance being much more evident in current commentaries.[2] The film is a pared-down and strategically altered version of the book[3] and was regarded as disturbing not so much for the indication of extreme violence, but for the explicit sexuality of the rape scene – an event which is not even hinted at in the book. Insofar as 'classic' elements of doubt are raised in sexual assault cases, the event in the film is carefully crafted – the woman *knows* her first assailant (he is a former boyfriend, a factor which creates ambiguity as to the nature of the act):[4] she acts provocatively; she invites him into the house; she is somewhat estranged from her husband, a man whose sexual potency is in doubt. All such factors are built into the scenario, rightly anticipating their contribution to ambiguity in sexual assault, an ambiguity reflected and often exploited in the courtroom and which could have given rise to more incisive feminist critique of the film.[5]

Indeed, the ambiguities of behaviour and response (in relation to the first sexual assault) can easily lead one to conclude that rape would be an entirely *inappropriate* label for such a case. One review[6] makes a persuasive case, providing an apparently forensic 'list' of factors which surely could damn the putative victim:

---

2   A brief 'Google' search of 'feminism' with '*Straw Dogs*' confirms this point.
3   In the film an American professor and his English wife rent an isolated farmhouse in the West Country. The professor lacks masculinity, is pernickety and restrained. His wife is in rebellion, bored with such domestic constraint. The locals are surly, secretive, distant, but she is friendly with one who was a former boyfriend. She admits him to the house, whereupon he quickly becomes violent, knocking her to the floor, slapping her and forcing her to have intercourse with him. He then holds her down while a second man has violent anal intercourse with her. Thereafter, the baiting gang create a siege at the farm, culminating in a violent and protracted debacle where the professor kills or horribly maims the attackers – despite the attackers' possession of a shotgun – and his manhood is restored.
4   Reflecting a key aspect of the recent debate over the evidential role of prior sexual history, s 41 of the Youth Justice and Criminal Evidence Act 1999 was enacted to restrict 'inappropriate' questioning, given that enquiry into prior relations had been used tactically by defence counsel during cross examination.
5   The feminist perspective deepens when one knows that the video release was, in part, the result of psychological analysis. A *Guardian* report (http://film.guardian.co.uk/censorship/news/0,11729,747454,00.html) noted:

> Psychologists who specialise in work with sex offenders were consulted about the film and they concluded it was not likely to encourage interest in rape or abusive behaviour … 'the [British Board of Film Censors] maintains a strict position on depictions of sexual violence that endorse or eroticise harmful behaviour, and will continue to do so. The board does not believe that the present version of Straw Dogs is in breach of that policy'. In the film Amy is raped first by an ex-boyfriend and then by another man. The psychologists said the first rape, which included a certain amount of ambiguity, was a realistic depiction of the complexities of such a situation.

6   '*Straw Dogs* (1971) from Johnny Web and Tuna': www.fakes.net/strawdogs.htm.

Let's look at them one at a time. The first 'rape' was with her ex-boyfriend, Charlie. Was it rape? Here are the facts:

- She stood in front of the window naked, so he could see her. She stared at him while she was standing there.
- She showed her body to the ex-boyfriend because she was mad at her husband.
- When the boyfriend came to the door, he asked if he should leave. She asked him to come in, and offered him a drink.
- As he was undressing her, she did say 'no' a few times. She also kissed him and stroked his face gently, and made sounds of pleasure.
- She never told her husband about the incident.
- Later, during the siege and after the 'rape', as she was being attacked by another guy, instead of calling for her husband for help, she called out for Charlie, the 'rapist' …[7]

But these 'facts' can be assayed again – though the film crafts such factors into the screenplay, they are less straightforward than the above account would suggest. The victim inviting the attacker into the home is not consent to intercourse – at this stage he is playing the helpful local with a fond affection rooted in the past. The fact that he had been a boyfriend of sorts is also treated with caution in the film – there are scripted comments to the effect that he has exaggerated the extent of that relationship. Thus the implication behind 'he asked if he should leave. She asked him to come in, and offered him a drink', is meant to be read as her preparing the way for a consensual event when, in fact, it seems indicative of quite *opposing* readings – that he portrays himself as hesitant and super-polite to gain her confidence, which indeed he does. Even her provocative behaviour – though a matter frequently raised by defence counsel in rape cases to discredit the victim's claim of rape – is not the same as consent to intercourse. In the film she does not 'stand in front of the window naked' (etc); she is preparing for a bath upstairs and *passes* a window (this is in a remote country house) with her upper body exposed; as she realises that she has been seen, she hesitates defiantly before moving on. Most misleading is the point: 'As he was undressing her, she did say "no" a few times. She also kissed him and stroked his face gently and made sounds of pleasure.' The scene does not depict a gentle 'undressing', following by half-hearted 'no's' and so on. It depicts real violence and intimidation, the threat of further violence if she does not submit, forcible penetration that is clearly without consent, and some minimal ambivalence on her part toward the end of the attack. Nor is failure to tell the husband evidence of compliance in the act, but can indicate shame and confusion springing from the entire course of events.[8]

---

7   In an interview with Susan George, the actress (who played the woman in the film), released with the DVD version of *Straw Dogs*, George recounts that:

Sam wasn't prepared to give me a definition of what was required … He wanted it to be the best rape scene ever shot … since I would be re-enacting this scene, he would have to trust my ideals and trust the fear and the threat [would be] conveyed in my eyes … There has been endless controversy about the fact that Amy at one point found it pleasurable – I agreed to make that interpretation … there was still conflict in her mind … the attacker had been a protector … for a moment it was nasty and unkind and for a moment she was lost in the man.

George herself demonstrates real ambivalence here – she refers to the 'rape', but also to arousal provoked by confusion and a powerful man.

8   Lack of physical resistance and failure to report – either to spouses or to authorities – are both known common factors in genuine rape cases.

Such point by point response to the review may itself seem a waste of time – a second reading of an already dubious source; but it is helpful to ponder first, how canny the screenplay was in mirroring the clearly already accepted elements of a rape scene, which would render it ambiguous as well as eroticised and, secondly, to realise just how readily such factors can be harnessed to create a 'case' that this was not rape. The account gains further credibility from the fact that the website bullet-pointed assay of this 'first' assault in the film, concluding 'this was not rape', is followed by a frank admission that the second assault by the second man in the film 'was rape – brutal and violent'.

Critical commentary on the film exemplifies these interpretative points. Weddle (1995, pp 20–25) asserts:

> He invites himself in, there is some bittersweet banter about the old days, then he forces himself on her. She resists, he slaps her around, she gives in, reluctantly at first, then passionately – all the pent-up frustrations, anger and unmet needs of her soured marriage released in a frenzied coupling. It starts out as a rape scene, turns into a sad and tender love scene, then veers hideously back into rape ... when Scutt shows up, shotgun in hand, Venner's loyalties shift in an instant from his old girlfriend to his tribal comrade. He holds Amy down while Scutt brutally rapes her ...

Scrutiny of the film reveals that the 'bittersweet banter' is, in fact, awkward and one-sided. The phrase 'he slaps her around' minimises the violence, conveying a symbolic rather than real assault. This description contrasts with that of Linda Ruth Williams (1995, p 26):

> Amy recoils from Charlie's hand as he beats her up before the rape ... All the time she screams 'No, no, no' as her actions are saying 'yes, yes, yes' – fear is turned into arousal. Its an image of the complicit rape victim that's as old as misogyny ... An act which starts as rape ends as lovemaking ... The second [rape] is incredibly disturbing, not only because of what it is in itself, but also because of what it implies about the earlier act. If this is 'bad' rape, then the first rape must have been 'good'. In the *Straw Dogs* discourse, rape is not necessarily negative – it all depends who's doing it to you ...

By contrast, Weddle (1995, p 25) reports:

> In a New York Times article that attacked the MPAA's rating system, Stephen Farber used *Straw Dogs* as a classic example of the agency's prudish ineptitude. 'The second rape, a sodomistic rape, was almost completely eliminated. Some critics have complained that the version in release expresses a male chauvinist fantasy, implying that women want to be overpowered and brutalised. Peckinpah's original version meant to contrast Susan George's responses to the two rapes. The second rape was as frightening and revolting as the first was erotic ...'

Comparing these two very similar, yet radically different, accounts of the events demonstrates just how persuasive 'accounting' can be, with Linda Ruth Williams alive to the *construction* of the semiotic event;[9] most telling is the quote referred to

---

9   Williams (p 26) also critiques the general construction of female figures in the film, noting:
     [the] straightness carved from warped materials, reinforcing the notion that straight
     women are always figures of perversity. The only other female we really get to know
     is Janice, an 'oversexed' young woman ... *Every time* Amy or Janice appear, their
     sexuality, excessive, disobedient, twisted, is foregrounded, through voyeurism,
     aggression, exhibitionism, paedophilia or generalised lusty waywardness ...

in the last extract from Weddle – 'The second rape was as frightening and revolting as the first was erotic' – a revealingly clear identity created between the concept of eroticism and that of rape.

For feminist theorists at the time, the first assault was particularly offensive in the depiction of a woman who begins by objecting to intercourse, but is apparently seduced by the mastery of her assailant to the extent that she clearly experiences pleasure in the latter stages of the event.[10] This even partial corroboration – of the notion that a woman's 'no' really could mean 'yes' – understandably enraged feminists. In purely mechanical terms, a lawyer would note that the act began with some vocal expressions of non-consent – 'no'. At the outset then, the act is rape – an act of penetration in the absence of consent. The offence of rape obtains for as long as such non-consensual activity takes place. Thus, the persuasive review summary – 'she did say "no" a few times' – would not prevent this being rape, since 'no' is overt evidence, crucial given the usual physical inequalities between man and woman.

Feminist outrage at the depiction, for consumer motives, of a compliant and willing victim is quite proper.[11] Russell[12] demonstrates just how such portrayal feeds into 'classic' rape appetites and myths, citing that:

Malamuth [1985] reports:
(1) about 10% of the population of [interviewed] male students are sexually aroused by 'very extreme violence' with 'a great deal of blood and gore' that 'has very little of the sexual element';
(2) about 20% to 30% show substantial sexual arousal by depictions of rape in which the woman never shows signs of arousal, only abhorrence;
(3) *about 50% to 60% show some degree of sexual arousal by a rape depiction in which the victim is portrayed as becoming sexually aroused at the end.*[13]

The film, therefore, plays shrewdly into already entrenched appetites in relation to *desired* victim behaviour and rape.

However, this justifiable concern masks a perhaps more apposite question regarding the depiction in the film, a question which has only come to light relatively recently, and is sharpened with the recognition of the concept of male rape. As the act continues, real ambiguity springs from the 'pain-pleasure'

---

10 Though the British Board of Film Censors (BBFC) said: 'The ambiguity of the first rape is given context by the second rape, which now makes it quite clear that sexual assault is not something that Amy ultimately welcomes' (http://film.guardian.co.uk/ censorship/news/0,11729,747454,00.html).

11 As is well known, the terror invoked by the situation of rape commonly produces a 'freeze' mechanism where the victim is practically paralysed and the forcible and non-voluntary nature of the act is likely to render it painful even in the absence of overt additional violence.

12 Diana Russell, 'Males' propensity to rape' at www.dianarussell.com/menrape.html. Russell's article is concerned to convey the degree to which portrayals of rape in the media may 'feed' predilections to commit rape. Her statistical evidence suggests that the number of men who would carry out such assaults on an opportunist basis is quite staggering.

13 Emphasis added. It is reported that this last statistic was recovered in 1986 and had not appeared in the 1985 report.

response; and this leads one to ask whether a woman who protests whilst discomfort moves to apparent pleasure would have any credibility in a court of law – her 'no' seeming truly a 'yes'.[14] Yet cases of what is now known as 'male rape' provide a quite different insight, with parallels in the more subtle territory of feminine physiology. As Rumney (2001)[15] explains:

> Research evidence suggests that some male rape victims experience involuntary physical responses during rape, including erection and ejaculation. Whilst this might be seen by many as an indication of consent, there is evidence that men can suffer such involuntary physical responses in a range of circumstances. Such responses can be used by the defence in two ways: first, as evidence of the complainant's consent and secondly, as the basis upon which it could be argued that the defendant had an honest belief in the complainant's consent and thereby does not have the *mens rea* for rape in accordance with the decision in *DPP v Morgan* …[16]

Nevertheless, the physically *extrinsic* nature of male arousal is capable, literally, of bringing the debate 'into the open'. Female arousal, in comparison, is not only more subtle and less starkly visible, it has also already been acculturated to the point where it would be even more difficult for those 'judging' the event to separate their 'cultural' knowledge of female arousal – the 'bodice-ripper' depiction of woman objecting then melting and finally gasping as she is overmastered – from any physiological account. Defence counsel play into this semiotic register, yet, just as male victims may show inadvertent signs of arousal – an image less readily eroticised, at least for mainstream markets – so too may women. As Lees (1996, pp 118–19) comments, having observed many rape trials:

> Defence counsel resort to all sorts of arguments to suggest that the woman really consented … Sexual arousal may cause the vagina to lubricate, but this does not mean that a moist vagina necessarily implies sexual arousal. There is great variability among women as to the changing state of the vagina at different points of the menstrual cycle and lubrication does not necessarily have anything to do with sexual arousal. Fear could affect lubrication, as could alcohol. Additionally, it is quite possible to be sexually aroused by being raped, which does not make the assault any less serious … The assumption … is that a woman could want sex without even knowing herself. It reduces the whole issue of consent to absurdity, in which the woman is denied any subjectivity … A physiological reaction to sexual assault therefore means nothing about whether or not the woman consented. Similarly with male rape, victims sometimes have erections and even ejaculate, which can undermine the victim's feelings of self-worth as he feels he is in some way colluding with his assailant …

---

14   An inversion which has an apocryphal reputation in the annals of rape cases.

15   (Quoted from p 2 of the e-journal version.) Rumney's discussion concludes that there are significant similarities in the stereotypes haunting male and female victims of rape in the courtroom, and suggests that juries may need to be educated in the variation of post-rape responses exhibited by victims.

16   The new Sexual Offences Act 2003 modifies the 'mistaken belief' defence, which derived from the case of *Morgan v DPP* [1976] AC 182. The Act defines the *mens rea* of rape as one where 'A does not reasonably believe that B consents' (s 1(1)(c) of the Sexual Offences Act 2003). For discussion, see Nicole Westmarland, 'Rape law reform in England and Wales', School for Policy Studies Working Paper Series, Paper Number 7 (April 2004). The introduction of 'reasonableness' situates the test within a more objective framework than previously obtained.

In a very direct sense therefore, *Straw Dogs* is only tapping into an established currency which is also recognisable in law. Yet, whatever the neurological or physiological oddity of the response to rape, the key question for a society claiming to stand for respect for the individual remains: did the victim consent to this invasion? Research on rape, whether of male or female victims, still provides an incomplete picture. Indeed, though one might expect greater judicial or juristic sympathy for the male victim – given the 'naturalisation' of rape in female victims[17] and an expected empathy with the male – this picture too is complex. The case of *Armstrong*,[18] as Rumney recounts, did not secure a conviction; the evidence of involuntary arousal led the judge to direct the jury to acquit on the grounds that there was 'not sufficient evidence' of the complainant's non-consent, the assumption being that, far from the victim finding the assault traumatic or unpleasant, it was pleasurable *and therefore* volitional (volition and consent of course being the key point of resistance to a charge of rape). Armstrong was a prison inmate who attacked a remand prisoner. Current research suggests that the court assays the social acceptability of the victim – reactions favour the 'conventional', 'respectable' victim. Wakelin and Long (2003, p 484)[19] note that societies are more or less 'rape supportive':

> People endorse such rape myths as victims want or enjoy rape … that people hold positive perceptions of and display positive behaviour towards in-group members and men … generally had more negative attitudes towards rape victims than did female participants … Men allocated more blame to the victim and less responsibility to the perpetrator … men blamed male rape victims more than women did. This could be because men fail to identify with men who have been raped, as they believe, in agreement with rape myths, that men cannot be raped because they have the physical strength to prevent it …

The background to the amendment of the definitions of sexual offences to include male victims in the definition of rape has not been widely discussed.[20] Yet an intriguing aspect of this legal change should be noted: the emotive power carried

---

17   It has been suggested, for example, that vaginal rape is less traumatic than anal rape because it is a 'natural' use of the female body; such 'naturalisation' of the body as object of use was of course imbricated into the law until 1991 in the United Kingdom, with the exception accorded to 'marital' rape.

18   Unreported, 10 April 1995, Weymouth and Dorset County Court, as cited by Rumney (2001). The case fell under the 'old' offence of non-consensual buggery, though Rumney recognises the relevance to the re-inscribed notion of rape.

19   This study provides a particularly acute recent comparison and statistical analysis of reactions to differing rape victims.

20   Formerly, forcible penetration of a man per anus was known as buggery. There were some publicised cases of such assaults in the City of London in the 1990s, which disturbed the population, which suggested a possible 'shift' from a murky underworld that could be easily avoided, to a bold pattern of assault in 'respectable' areas. Lobby by Stonewall was apparently effective in influencing legislators. We may note that, in the anxiety to dissolve inequalities between the sexes, giving male victims the redress of equally punitive sentencing tariffs alongside female victims of rape, the *lack* of correspondence is overlooked. Men do not become pregnant and suffer the violent protracted trauma of fear of pregnancy or either unwanted birth or termination, nor the pattern of sexually transmitted disease (STD) risks imposed upon women. The feminist lobby has been surprisingly silent on this point.

by the word 'rape' itself – the word denotes victimhood and effacement of individual autonomy more effectively than the semiotic allusions created by the earlier name for the offence.[21] The discussion as to whether an act is 'really' rape carries ideological, as well as practical (tariff) freight.

The serious point thrown up by such developments however, and utterly overlooked in the reaction to *Straw Dogs*, is the recognition that physiological responses do not necessarily accurately reflect volition and consent. Supported by unfolding scientific evidence, the rights and autonomy-driven trajectory of law provides increasing recognition of the special integrity achieved by the human mind, sometimes quite separable from the existence rooted in physical reaction. The physically *visible* nature of a response in male victims may allow this additional point to be debated more rigorously in relation to all victims. The body is driven by complex chemical and neurological[22] processes, which may diverge dramatically from the will, intellectual projects and desires of the subject.[23] Such is the pain and misery associated with rape that such a pain-pleasure response is extremely unlikely, but not impossible. It is quite clear, however, that such a conclusion is not readily reached in relation to the female victim. As in *Straw Dogs*, the outward signs of such divergent, 'mind-body' reactions are subtle and difficult to read, whilst the overt and visible nature of male arousal at least provides a provocative means to engender debate.[24] Indeed, whether such a proposition could be given credence in relation to the female victim *without* the precedent masculine example is doubtful.[25]

Let us be clear – depiction of a rape victim 'enjoying' the assault plays into the most predictable appetites and beliefs. Not only is such a portrayal common to

---

21 Though indeed the film *Straw Dogs* quite clearly indicates that anal assault can be at least as violent as vaginal assault.

22 Of course, arguments that one 'can't help oneself' have to be treated with caution in criminal law, given the opportunities this creates for perpetrator defences.

23 Note the case concerning Diane Blood's husband, whose ejaculate was collected even though he was in a coma (*R v Human Fertilisation and Embryology Authority ex p Blood* [1999] Fam 151).

24 Section 4 of the Sexual Offences Act 2003 creates a new offence of 'causing a person to engage in sexual activity without consent'. This is 'intended to make a clear statement that compelling others to do sexual acts against their will is an offence', and may cover, for example, those activities where a person is forced to masturbate, to some extent meeting the scenario of an involuntary 'pleasure-pain' response, though not one which extends to an event identifiable as rape. Oddly however, 'it was also intended to deal with women who compel men to penetrate them' – a scenario much less evident, and potentially even more evidentially and descriptively problematic, than those usually discussed. See Temkin and Ashworth, 'The Sexual Offences Act 2003: rape, sexual assaults and the problems of consent' [2004] Crim LR, May, 328–46.

25 In a recent Court of Appeal case, *R v Michael Patrick O'Brien* [2003] WL 1823034, a conviction for rape was overturned where a key question was the credibility of the rape complaint, where the complainant gave evidence that she 'pretended to have an orgasm' apparently in order to hasten the conclusion of the assault. The conviction was overturned in part because of the classic conflict of accounts, but also because the account raised doubt as to the absence of consent. Nevertheless, the victim's account was extremely detailed and harrowing and the claimed simulation of orgasm quite consistent with an appreciation of classic patterns of masculine sexual expectation used by the victim in an attempt to hasten the conclusion of the assault.

pornography, it also feeds general drives which seek to make an object of another – paedophiles, too, will frequently argue that children 'enjoy' their assaults. Nevertheless, since the film raises the issue, the opportunity for debate can be grasped in full. In recognising that rapes are traumatic and appalling events for the victims, and that such portrayals are in no way representative of the reality that is rape (but instead simply reproduce and feed misogynistic mores), the rare question of involuntary arousal should be met.

This account of stories within stories is not complete without reference to the testimony of Susan George, the actress who played Amy (the putative victim) in *Straw Dogs*. George recounts that Peckinpah's refusal to reveal details of his planned rape scene was so complete and protracted that it forced her to walk off set; only strategic brokering brought her back again, with a compromise that she would be allowed to convey the violence and fear primarily 'with her eyes'.[26] Thus, it may be argued, the feminist debate in relation to *Straw Dogs* itself suffered more than one kind of hijack. The general 'backlash' response circumscribed the feminist insights within the narrow parameters of stereotypes easily dismissed and deposed by the powerful lobbies of freedom of expression and media exposition. The incipient debate concerning volition and criminal jurisprudence deriving from *Straw Dogs* never occurred, though the potential to provoke such debate is a reminder that censorship would *not* necessarily assist in the path to enlightenment. This sidelining of a potential debate concerning particular aspects of rape in *Straw Dogs*, is attended by another dramatic 'hijack' of debates in criminal jurisprudence however, for *Straw Dogs* itself is based upon a book where no rape event occurs at all.

THE BOOK: *THE SIEGE OF TRENCHER'S FARM* – SELF-DEFENCE AND THE HOUSEHOLDER

The book is dedicated to the exploration of the problem thrown up by the need and capacity to defend oneself against violent attack and the 'story' of the book, the film and the media is not complete until this remaining element is told. The author, Gordon M Williams, recounts that he was stimulated by personal events to write *The Siege of Trencher's Farm*.[27] Obliged by business to spend some time away from his then home on Dartmoor (a beautiful, desolate and ancient moor land in the West Country of England), he returned to his wife, who had been anxious given that a fugitive prisoner – axe-wielding 'Mad' Frank Mitchell – was on the run from the grim, Victorian high-security Dartmoor Prison.[28] This led Williams to wonder what he *would* do in such circumstances – indeed, whether he would be

---

26 Though, in fact, the scene is quite explicit, the original planned scene apparently involved a much greater register of violence; Susan George regretted seeing the result of her request that Peckinpah set down his ideas on paper.

27 Gordon M Williams, *The Siege of Trencher's Farm* (1969) New York: Dell Publishing.

28 See interview with Gordon Williams, 'Gordon who?', at http://books.guardian.co.uk/departments/generalfiction/story/0,6000,1068063,00.html.

able to do anything effective at all.[29] Though primarily a pacy and gripping tale, *The Siege* deals sometimes reflectively with the key controversies thrown up by this dilemma.[30] In *The Siege*, Williams takes his original anxiety regarding how one would deal with an escaped psychopath, and rotates the focus so that an equal – if not greater – danger is posed by 'ordinary' citizens. Williams picks up on the penal policy debates concerning incarceration of the mentally ill:

> He was learning a lot about the English ... one of the impressions he had gathered was of an unsuspected brutality ... He could never believe that a people who had split the atom and produced Robert Graves could be primitive enough to put their mentally sick in a place like Two Water Institution for the Criminally Insane ... Quite apart from the fact that no building erected during the reign of Queen Victoria could possibly be suitable for the treatment of extreme forms of mental illness ... (1969, p 24)

Recognising not only the diagnostic difficulties posed by such cases, Williams further explores the ideological battle represented by such persons:

29　The writer has benefited from an extensive telephone conversation with Gordon Williams in September 2004. Mr Williams, recalling the very real threat posed by 'Mad' Frank Mitchell, remembers the deployment of a detachment of fully armed marines to the moor. Mitchell was reputed to be able to lift two men by the throat at arms length, and to lift the vast stones forming ancient bridges on the moor normally moveable only with the efforts of seven or eight men. When escaped prisoners were on the loose, farmers on the moor would leave a jacket, sandwiches and money on the doorstep in order to provide the escapees with sufficient means such that burglary might be avoided. Mr Williams considered the difficulties posed by such a man – how would one even begin to resist him – with a wooden club? How elemental such a situation is – so very akin to the fundamental stories of survival told by classic American Western films. For Gordon Williams, the insertion of the rape scene is crude and utterly gratuitous, though he has a theory about Sam Peckinpah's deep identification fantasy with the sexual dilemma played out by Susan George, a theory which for Williams accounts for the particulars of the scene. In the magazine *Playboy* (1972), Sam Peckinpah, depicting himself as the arch creator, said of Gordon Williams's book that it was so bad 'you could have drowned in your own puke'. Gordon Williams arranged for this quote to be on the cover of the recent Bloomsbury re-publication of the book (thanks to Gordon Williams for the details supplied herein).

30　Though holding basic elements of the ensuing film *Straw Dogs*, the book has crucial differences. As in *Straw Dogs*, in *The Siege* an American professor, George Magruder and his disaffected and bored wife Louise, rent a remote West Country farm. In the book however, the couple have a child, Karen. (One can easily understand why this detail was removed from the film, since the presence of a young child in the house would have compromised the depiction of violence and especially that of rape, rendering it a less readily marketable 'adult' film.) The locals seem surly and distant, contemptuous of the soft, well-heeled American. Local sheep have been found mutilated, the farm cat is found dead in the farmyard with rope around its neck. (In the film, this is *inside* the bedroom, symbolising an impending intimate assault.) As in the film, a mentally defective child-murderer escapes in a snowstorm onto the moor and in a weakened state is run down in the dark by George Magruder, whose only option in the storm is to take the injured and insensible man – Henry Niles – into the farmhouse. That night, cut off by the weather, the farm is attacked by a group of men, one of them wielding a shotgun; men who, knowing Niles is at the farm, mistakenly believe that he is implicated in the disappearance of a young mentally defective girl. (In the film the girl is sexually provocative and actually killed by Niles.) With these men baying for the blood of Niles, the farm is subject to a horrifying series of forays, culminating in the injury, and in some cases death, of the assailants. There is no rape scene.

Brought to trial for this murder, Niles became less a man than a battleground over which the forces of 'progress' and 'retribution' fought another of their grimly impersonal campaigns. The public wanted him put to death. Psychiatrists were found who would say that Niles was, in fact, sane enough to be hanged. Those who maintained that he was *still* a mental defective were unpopular. The way George had seen it, the English classed Niles with all the other ogres of the time. To them he was like the Nazis, a malignant excrescence to be quickly destroyed. For a time it had seemed that the counter argument – that Niles would have been obliterated *by* the Nazis – was too sophisticated an exercise in abstract legalism. But an English jury had once again found him not responsible for his actions ... To George this had been one of the most civilised public actions he had ever known. What had his own country to show in the way of parallels? The refined mediaeval horror of the Chessman case? The British had not hanged Niles, for whom nobody could say a good word ... a human agent of all the blind forces of evil that surrounded mankind. Words seemed to mean nothing. What you looked for was some sign. Bafflingly, there was no sign ... (1969, p 84)

Williams's concluding comments appreciate the relative insolubility, the inherent moral failure facing society:

This pathetic little man, who could hardly walk by himself to the foot of the stairs, was *he* the symbol of the age, the personification of blind, unthinking evil? ... how could you say he was perverted when you knew he had the mind of a child. You couldn't punish him – that was what progress and civilization meant, if it meant anything at all ... a hundred million people had been killed this century – by normal men ... (1969, p 107)

Such debate provides context for the even more intractable problem at the heart of the book. In shifting the threat away from the notorious psychopath, replacing him with the everyday villain and near-villain, the relatively tangible difficulty posed by overt psychopathy is effaced by the more pervasive and insidious problem of opportunist violence and of the feasible response to it. More or less 'ordinary' citizens, the men attacking the farm nurse a sense of grievance, a weakness rendering each man vulnerable to an *incipient* capability for evil.[31] More centrally, the householder, Professor Magruder, a law-abiding, somewhat fastidious and timid man, finds his belief system – his entire normative structure – challenged and altered by events. In this the book *The Siege* anticipates the controversy recently invoked by a real life case: the 'siege' at Bleak House, an isolated farmhouse occupied by Tony Martin.[32] Martin had apparently adapted to 'siege' conditions in his home to such an extent that his house was almost entirely boarded up, adding to the already decrepit and truly bleak appearance of the house. When Martin finally 'snapped', shooting at his fleeing attackers, killing

---

31 *The Siege*: 'Tom Hedden – *they didn't care ... it wasn't their daughters that had been took, only a Hedden brat* [emphasis added] ... Norman Scutt, the burglar and petty thief, had come there because Niles took him back to a world where he was somebody, the world of prison. Men like Niles were the lowest of the low. He made a thief feel like a judge ... Chris Cawsey liked to touch his own body with the knife ... he liked to cut into things ... Bert Voizey liked to poison rats because it made him the man who poisoned rats ... Phillip Riddaway just liked being with Norman. Norman was his pal ...' (1969, p 112).

32 *R v Martin (Anthony Edward)* [2001] EWCA Crim 2245; [2002] Crim LR 136 (CA, Crim Div).

one and injuring the other, the disproportionate level of this response displaced the notion of self-defence and, it was reasoned, corresponded more fittingly to the concepts of premeditation and malice inherent to murder, for which Martin was convicted. On appeal, the conviction was reduced to manslaughter on the basis of fresh medical evidence suggesting that Martin was suffering from a paranoid personality disorder classified as a mental abnormality within s 2 of the Homicide Act 1957; depression exacerbated this disorder, and:

> The fresh medical evidence established that breaking into his house would be perceived by M as being a greater threat to his safety than it would be in the case of a normal person ... and that M when firing the shot was suffering from diminished responsibility ...[33]

Academic discussion in this area recognises the broad inconsistencies in the law,[34] but in the concern to render principles refined and coherent such tests may still remain *less* sensitive to the fundamental questions explored by *The Siege* – how *would* one deal with such trauma, and how *should* one deal with it. The proper concern of the law of course is that legal sympathy should extend only to actions and reactions that are reasonable and not malicious. Though other jurisdictions, most notably Germany and the USA, are wholly sympathetic to 'fatal' protection of property,[35] the British approach has been more circumspect to the point where, in cases such as that of Martin, some have felt that the householder becomes a 'double' victim – of his initial attacker, and of legal principle.[36] The threat posed by burglarious activity is not a simple, predictable, 'mechanical' threat to inanimate property, but an invasion of being and – quite apart from the actual magnitude of violence – a negation of a key component of individual security, which cannot easily be calibrated according to an objective register.[37] Nor is it necessarily ethically correct to support a reduction of the murder conviction to manslaughter

---

33   See Rees and Smith, 'Homicide: murder – excessive force in self defence' (2002) Crim LR, Feb 136–39, Case Comment.

34   *Ibid*, at 139:

> The jury must have regard not only to the circumstances as D believed them to be but also to the consequent danger as he believed it to be. If that is right, evidence of the kind in issue in *Martin* is directly relevant and there is no obvious ground for excluding it at a trial in which private defence is raised ... There is an urgent need for some rationalisation of the law of necessity, private defence, duress, and provocation, all of which raise questions of the relevance of the defendant's personal characteristics but lack any consistent principle.

35   See Rigby, 'Reform call over Martin case', at http://news.bbc.co.uk/1/hi/england/norfolk/3098131.stm.

36   This is reflected in the presentation of the 'Tony Martin' Bill by Roger Gale MP in 2004, the thrust of which suggests that the (new) law:

> ... should be designed so that when an intruder/burglar breaks into a private residence (owned/rented/guest of owner, etc), that intruder forfeits his protection under the law. The presumption of innocence should be in favour of the homeowner who should be permitted to take whatever means he considers fit to protect himself/possessions/family and that the offender should not subsequently have any recourse in the Courts to sue his victim.

> See Bennion, 'Home defence: the Tony Martin Bill' at www.francisbennion.com.

37   In the case of Martin, it is tragic that a young man lost his life. There is also tragedy in the reduction of an elderly and isolated man to siege conditions with boarded windows and uprooted stairs, so severe was his apprehension.

on the basis of a depiction of Martin as a psychiatric case, when paranoia in such circumstances might be an entirely understandable, 'normal', reactive state and indeed – with persistent and dark intrusion – an extreme action might be a para-rational rather than paranoid response.

Though Gordon Williams's book explores the threat of extreme violence, it also explores the ambiguities inherent in all such situations for the stance of the householder. Martin, like Magruder, was a somewhat reclusive but hitherto law-abiding citizen, driven, by events, to homicide. As with Professor Magruder's educated early 'inner' voice, the jurisprudence of self-defence, applied to cases such as Martin, assumes an 'artificial' physical environment in situations of burglary and assault – one where the victim can effectively choreograph his resistance to attack. This presumption demonstrates an imaginative failure on the part of jurists – assuming a kind of *actual* 'filmic' quality to events, where a notionally predictable and slow motion of intrusion can be met by an equally staged response. The book reflects this: at the outset of the attack on the farm, George Magruder is a man of firm principles, a 'true' liberal.[38] He cannot imagine breaking his code, even when the attack is underway he reflects that:

> There was nothing he could do to this twisting head. He was a civilized man, refined to a point where physical violence was impossible, even in self-defence. If defending himself meant breaking this kid's skull then he couldn't defend himself. He was a modern man, he needed locks and doors and bolted windows and policemen. Objects defended him. He had lost the ability to stand alone and fight …
> (1969, p 124)

As the violence of events escalate, an almost imperceptible modification of those values is forced upon the Professor[39] and in the final *debacle*, survival is all that matters, as the constant reflection and rationalisation[40] is replaced with the only feasible defence – that of action:

> Now he knew the truth. All that nonsense about thresholds and civilization. He had won! That mattered, nothing else … He didn't have room in his head for *thoughts*. He had won. The man who had won. The man who *knew*. (1969, pp 176–88)

Discussion of the significance of the rape scene in the film and of the diminution of Gordon Williams's discussion in the book may be given some attention by feminist theory, quite apart from focus upon the technical details therein. From the point of view of feminist theory, the insertion of a rape scene – and especially *such a rape scene* – plays a clear part in a much greater fabric of ideological substrates,

---

38 The notion of the liberal is treated anyway with some irony. In the book, the American liberal academic Magruder states his position: 'When you people were thinking of hanging him back there I was one of twelve professors who signed a letter to *The Times*' (1969, p 83).

39 'He knew she was right. He was a civilized man and there was nothing he could do but open the door and let them drag Niles out of the house' (p 132).

40 Described as 'the shift of … inner conflict from "a worn-out liberal struggling to overcome a sense of moral impotency to that of an apolitical intellectual who struggles to repress his passions"' – a comment made by David Weddle in *Sight and Sound* and reproduced in *The Edge* review at www.theedge.abelgratis.co.uk/filmssz/strawdogs.htm.

with woman as cipher for the disputed territories of property and power. Indeed, though the film is trumpeted as the film that outraged feminists, there is a degree of mythologisation at work here too. Whilst it is true that feminist objections occurred, remaining comment – especially that dominating critical film commentary – was able to maintain a stance either 'playfully' or aggressively anti-feminist in the avowal of the film's triumphs; this, too, may tell us something of how influences unfold.

Insights may also be gained from psychoanalytic theory. Recognising the parallels in unregulated libido between film and book, rape and burglary, a politicised psychoanalytic approach might consider juristic disavowal (of the besieged householder or the unconventional rape victim) as symptomatic of cultural – and perhaps state – controls upon the libidinous individual subject. Law itself becomes complicit, not only in the regulation, but in the repression, of the subject in a relation of violence that is wholly original.[41] Such a focus disregards the rather more prosaic story of media hijack, which forms the practical basis for the link, as well as the practical reasons for legal caution towards such events – caution in relation to excessive householder response, and to false accusations of rape. Though crime statistics and conviction rates in relation to rape and burglary suggest that this caution must be tempered with concern for the victim, the stranglehold is real – in both cases a truly elemental battle of individual forces. The wrongful conviction of *one* falsely accused rapist, the risk to life of *one* burglar – both weigh heavily in the liberal scales, which are yet deadweight on the side of attrition rates in rape and burglary convictions.

At first sight, the two topics – of rape, and of householder self-defence – have little in common and are spuriously linked by producer and market mores. Both victims are driven to atypical behaviours invoked by third parties. Both self-defence and rape carry within them the doctrinal implication of a proper revulsion for excess, a measured response which reflects that revulsion; but in both there may be a failure to empathise with the maelstrom set up between the rational and the neurological. Any notion of 'diminished' responsibility in *either* case would insult the subject's ordeal, for such diminution begins with the perpetrator crashing in upon the place of the subject's integrity. Just as a physiologically 'perverse' response in the rape victim plays into the mores of a 'rape supportive' culture, so too the perhaps sociologically perverse notion of 'proper' responses by besieged householders threatens to create a 'siege supportive' culture. The filmic eroticisation of what began as a tale of identity crisis arising from one man's exposure to threat is unsurprising, a literal 'sexing up' of narrative[42] of no doubt profit-boosting,[43] as well as tantalising, interest to

---

41 See Jodi Dean's article (Dean, 2004) for a survey of Zizek's intriguing – and pertinent – discussion of the links between law's founding violence and the violence of relations between state, self and Other, superego and *jouissance*.

42 The potential was inherent: in a crudely unrepresentative marketing move, the original book cover shows a nubile woman peering from a darkened window as a man lurks outside.

43 If the desire to maximise profits *had* been a motivating force, it backfired, since the combination of sex and violence limited the classification and distribution potential of the film (as Gordon Williams himself commented to the writer).

the prospective audience and the film-maker, Sam Peckinpah.[44] Such eroticisation should invite us to ask questions beyond the simply reactive ones – indeed the *legal* issues raised by the scenes may do just that. In addition, Peckinpah himself may have had other than merely prosaic reasons for his choice – to shock is also to challenge. One might hazard that rape is added to housebreaking not only to maximise the market appeal of sex *and* violence, but also to maximise the impact of *utter* invasion; but the transposition of social questions represented by this change *itself* alters the discursive landscape – the media hijack creating unforeseen hostages of its own, whilst the germinal screed – the discourse that was not – languishes in other fevered cells.

In *The Siege*, Williams deliberately inverts the questions flowing naturally from his own initial event stimulus – how he might cope with a 'madman' on the loose – asking the more subtle question about the incipient violence in all communities, and the relationship between cultivated action and necessary action pursued by the victim. This is a serious and complex question, not properly met by a householder's charter. Similarly, the rape scene in *Straw Dogs* invites an inverted response from feminists, too – alongside the clearly indicated rebellion at the crass insertion of rape, and conversion of 'no' into 'yes'. The inverted question still persists – can the 'apparent' yes still count as no? Strangely correspondent, both points were hijacked by different bids for very differently construed notions of freedom.

---

44 In interview, Gordon Williams remains contemptuous – see 'Gordon who?' (fn 28):
    The original idea was for Polanski to direct. In the end they got Peckinpah. 'The man was sick,' Williams opines, reprising his encounter with an early version of a script that began with a page-long description of the female lead's tightly trousered rear ...

POPULAR MEDIA, SEX AND VIOLENCE: NATURE OR NURTURE? – SAVAGE OR CITIZEN? THE *CRASH* OF THE MORAL MIRROR[1]

INTRODUCTION

The portrait that emerged during Meiwes's eight-week trial was of a disturbed individual who had been obsessed since puberty with eating another man to become 'one with him' ... Meiwes claimed he was trying to fill a void left by his father Dieter, who abandoned the family when he was 12 ... [he] quickly confessed, but pointed out that Brandes had wanted to be eaten. Cannibalism is not a crime in Germany and Meiwes claimed he was guilty only of assisting in another man's death ... At the trial Meiwes opened his soul to the world and everyone knew that what he was saying was the absolute truth ... He would never have eaten his victim against his wishes, and when he has served his time he will indeed have plenty to look forward to ...

'The "caring cannibal" set to make a media killing'
The Sunday Times, 1 February 2004

Recent human history in the developed world may be seen as a reaction to release from feudalism – the actual feudalism of pre-modern culture being followed by the transformed feudalisms of modernity.[2] Our recent past saw the majority of persons living subjected to poverty and ignorance, as well as to the draconian decrees of state and Church – the society of thinkers, artists and entrepreneurs comprising our present world implicitly silenced, our own 20th century shadowed by one of repressions. Little wonder that recent decades have seen a pattern of libidinous excess, a veritable gorging in the sweetshop of possibility. The years have seen taboo after taboo uncovered, with the accelerating support of mass media and with the final velocity provided by the information superhighway.

Stumbling through the world of hard-won freedoms – to express, witness and feel, to test the outer limits of expression, witness and sensation – modern personhood is an unfolding experiment in a form of autonomy, an existential *Dasein*, patching new horizons for the island of the self. The presumption in favour of freedom of speech, of civil liberties (sustained, unless a compelling reason – by way of a tangible harm – can be found for their curtailment) was hard won and properly cherished. By and large, we may suppose that freedom of

---

1 An earlier version of this chapter appears in Freeman, M (ed), *Law and Popular Culture: Current Legal Issues Series* (2005) Oxford: OUP.
2 Supplied primarily, of course, through the ideologies of religion and politics.

access to information, representations and ideas, positively empowers the individual in dealing with the complex challenges of life and broadens creativity. With erstwhile taboos and prohibitions exposed as so much power exerted by worn ideologies and organs of the state, the person is now free to explore the existential enigma that is modern life and present reality. In the world of art, film and the text, this vision presages daring experimentation, whilst at the outer edges of activities proclaimed as generically linked freedoms, such licence is invoked to justify the continuation of access to activities of exploitative tenor. Oddly placed between these worlds – of 'high' art on the one hand, and margins of the obscene and pornographic on the other – is a popular culture of films and consumer images where sexuality melds routinely with violence.

Whilst it is a too-ready conclusion that current mass culture is symptomatic, as well as productive, of certain ills, the preponderance of materials concerned with sexual, violent and sex-and-violence conjunctions (albeit assisted by the generative forces of mass marketing) is surely a window, or mirror, to ourselves. Where our myriad freedoms might have heralded countless different possibilities in terms of the civic and social dialogue that is mass culture, we find a precipitation of common interests and concerns, a precipitation revealing primal proclivities. Encountering this culture, a passing Martian might be justified in assuming little progress, perhaps even a regression, in the human moral and intellectual story. What augurs ill, however, is not necessarily this preponderance of images and interests, but the passivity of our relation to them. As Huxley and Orwell both foresaw, weakness lies in the life suborned to the mere pursuit of appetites; and as legal history will attest, where denial may sharpen appetites, responsible, informed management can provide a more enlightening path to integrity and integration. In a review essay considering the inception of moral responsibility for legal purposes, Glannon (1999, p 212) recalls that our capacity for practical and theoretical reasoning and for rational and moral agency 'distinguishes persons from other animals', noting that:

> ... the psychopath's problem is not in recognizing reasons for or against certain actions, but instead in not reacting to, or not being motivated to act on, these reasons. This suggests that, while the psychopath does not lack the requisite cognitive and volitional capacities altogether, he seems to possess them to a reduced degree, which would justify at most holding him only partly morally responsible ...

In the works of JG Ballard, however, the reduction of 'requisite cognitive and volitional capacities' is a likely incident of everyday modern life, where extreme and multiple stimuli are available to a more or less disengaged and alienated population with poor emotional attachments and few, if any, guiding principles. From this standpoint, we are all vulnerable to a deadening of reactivity, whilst hypothesising the motivating forces in the psychopath – already arguably problematic bearing in mind the ambiguity resultant upon the possession of such capacities to a 'reduced degree' (how do we begin to quantify and locate the requisite degree?) – pathologises an artefact of social construction. Michelfelder (2000, p 147) asks whether there is justification for calling for a new ethics of responsibility, 'based on the reasoning that modern technology dramatically divorces our moral condition from the assumptions under which standard ethical theories were first conceived', and whether this question should be extended to the technologies of cyberspace. She concludes that the challenges 'do not stem from living in cyberspace but rather from living with cyberspace', though she acknowledges the possibility that:

> [i]n a world increasingly saturated by visual representations one comes to trust these representations more than one's own thinking or the direct evidence of one's own senses ... (2000, p 151–52)

However, the elegance of such cautious discrimination does not capture the violence of the rupture presented by the speed and distance of our current selves from our historically construed ethical selves.

The discussion which follows charts the reception of a film deliberately contiguous to the sex-violence conjunction. Two factors emerge as especially significant to the concerns of moral and legal philosophy. First, the film (and the text upon which it is based) asserts a morally neutral stance in relation to its revelation of human proclivities – akin to anthropological study. Secondly, the film depicts not 'merely' the conjunction of sex and violence, but the shift of appetites for such conjunction from the imaginary to the real, depicting characters whose appetites are met only when the deadening stimuli of mass culture is overborne by a subculture of heightened stimuli – where sex and violence meet – in the 'real'. Both factors are characteristic of Ballard's writing; for Ballard the real has ordinarily been surreal. Nevertheless, his artistic vision extends any understanding of the subcultural possibilities posed by mass culture, anticipating developments where empirical data but desperately treads. Our tiny global community of shared information and revelation bears witness to the disturbed subcultures arising from freedoms – from the clear opportunities presented for the cultivation of new appetites[3] to the replenishing of the old – and this surely invokes the need to cultivate a community of thought, of ethical sensibility in the midst of a world of glutted persons.

CRASH AND THE MORAL MIRROR

> Is this harnessing of our innate perversity conceivably of benefit to us? Is there some deviant logic unfolding more powerful than that provided by reason? (Ballard, 1995 – Introduction to *Crash*)[4]

---

3   No doubt 'new' appetites are derivations of age-old types, from paedophilia to pornography. The development of new menus and tools in the elaboration of such appetites does, perhaps, take us into new territories. The case of the 'caring cannibal' for example (indicated in the opening quotation), reveals a willing subjecthood in the victim and efficient conjunction of such rare victimhood with his perpetrator through the offices of the internet. See, also, the case of Graham Coutts, 'Killer was obsessed by porn websites', *The Guardian*, 5 February 2004.

4   Ballard, *Crash*, first published in 1973. All references are to the 1995 (London) edition. A brief chronology of events and facts relevant to this chapter may be of use at this point. The film version of *Crash* appeared in 1996, though lobbyists were still working to have it banned in 1998. Bernard Williams' *Shame and Necessity* (fn 37 below) was first published in 1994, though the lectures upon which the book is based were first delivered in 1989. The Report of the Committee on Obscenity and Film Censorship appeared in 1979. The Obscene Publications Act dates from 1959, with electronic transmission of pornographic material now covered under the Criminal Justice and Public Order Act 1996.

This quotation, from the introductory text of *Crash* by JG Ballard, poses a crucial but unacknowledged question facing secular liberalism: to what extent can, or should, society unleash, explore and experiment with the 'pathological' aspects of human interest in the unmediated context that is 'mass' culture? Despite passing media comment regarding the banal combination of sex and violence, which forms the everyday diet of popular culture, the diet itself has become staple. Already subject to little scrutiny, the sex-violence nexus – the intimate linkage of the two factors – is queried even less. Though the text of *Crash* has an erotic, violent, even 'pornographic'[5] content, the text disturbs rather than facilitates the process of erotic 'consumption' *simpliciter*, providing a consciously disruptive perspective upon elements of human culture and nature, elements of crucial importance to the law, but remaining curiously unexamined. Furthermore, the movement from text to film, from word to image, creates an additional aspect to the variables confronting self-understanding in this age of rapid cultural change, with its emphasis upon consumption of the visual.

At present, our culture tends to proceed on the premise that the autonomy of adulthood corresponds to a developed, discriminatory power over stimuli encountered, both by accident and design. Any argument that material might be potentially 'harmful' or 'altering' – either in terms of direct or oblique effects – tends to collapse under the weight of a presumption in favour of what is termed 'freedom': unless direct change can be proved, suppression of information is potentially and actually more harmful than exposition. It is a complex argument at the heart of the law of censorship and of how we determine the 'pornographic' as opposed to 'erotic'.

Crash is a story – originally a novel, later a film – tracking the erotic potential and social consequences of a consumer-led culture, in which the potential intimacy between sexual and violent impulses, specifically, the car crash as an erotic stimulus, is fostered. The importance of this text will be discussed later; for the moment, it creates a useful introductory reminder of the varied and growing popular culture impacting upon, and producing insights for, formal institutional cultures. Recent caselaw demonstrates the process of logic to which law has traditionally subscribed when dealing with such issues of freedom and moral character. The juristic process exhibits symptoms of a hermeneutic trap, an underlying stasis deriving from the image of mankind permitted to the law by current culture. Law must subscribe to, and protect, notions of autonomy, of rights, of individual judgment and personal freedom, notions nourished by a loosely hypothesised, average, legal subject, who is oddly separated from community in terms of the journey from right and responsibility, yet modelled as thoroughly integrated in terms of conscience.

---

5   'There is no settled definition of pornography either in the United Kingdom itself or especially in a multi-national environment such as the Internet where cultural, moral and legal variations all around the world make it difficult to define "pornographic content" in a global society' (Akdeniz, 1997, p 2).

The case of *R v Stephane Laurent Perrin*[6] demonstrates the difficulty created by such piecemeal modelling of the legal subject. The case reviewed the legality of an internet site advertising its pornographic wares by way of a 'preview', available free of charge to anyone with access to the internet.[7] The facts clearly indicated that a rejection of the appellant's case would be appropriate since the preview could be accessed by anyone, including children.[8] The risk to children rather overshadowed the residual question raised in the case – of how we might understand such 'harm' in relation to adults, though it was acknowledged obliquely, as an issue of relevance. Discussion considered jurisdictional issues in the light of the global availability of internet sites – a key consideration in terms, not just of the internet, but of a great deal of popular media. The central legal – and moral – questions, however, focused upon understanding the implications of English domestic law – the 'tendency' to 'deprave and corrupt' as cited in the Obscene Publications Act 1959, and the implications of Arts 7 (requiring that the conduct in question be demonstrably proscribed by law) and 10 (the right to freedom of expression) of the European Convention on Human Rights (ECHR). The case thus manifests an interesting tension between morally grounded prohibitions, the assertion of civil liberties 'rights' to freedom, and the formal positivist expectation of certainty in maintaining the rule of law. The court concluded that Art 10 provides for state proscription of activities that threaten the interests of democratic society, and that, in this case, such concerns outweighed the notional assertion of freedom within it. Given the risk to children posed by the site, this outcome seems unavoidable.

The broad normative question, raised by juristic consideration of material tending to deprave and corrupt in relation to the general population, however, remains largely unexplored. In reviewing precedent, it was acknowledged that a 'risk' of corruption to only a small proportion of the population did not necessarily justify the risk.[9] Even when understanding of the risk quotient was expressed – as later caselaw suggests it should be – in terms of a 'significant risk', it was acknowledged that the magnitude of such 'significance' would remain

---

6   *R v Stephane Laurent Perrin* (2002) WL 347127 (CA (Crim Div)); [2002] EWCA Crim 747, No: 2000/6463/Y2. All references use Westlaw pagination.

7   The notional 'screening' process derived from access available only by entering credit card details (proving a traceable, positive act on the part of the user, a traceable identity, and accession to adulthood denoted by such financial status) was therefore absent, thus creating a possibility that 'vulnerable' and 'young' people might view the preview, which involved scenes of coprophilia and fellatio. Given this risk, the outcome of the case was relatively predictable, with the website perpetrator failing in his appeal against conviction.

8   There is a clear juristic awareness that protection of children from harm is a paramount – and separate – concern from possible 'harm' posed to adults by the availability of pornographic materials. As the article by Adkeniz (fn 4 above) makes clear: 'the regulation of *harmful* content such as pornography and regulation of *illegal* content such as child pornography ... are issues different in nature and should not be confused' (emphasis added).

9   WL 347127, p 4, especially when that proportion may include children.

proportional to the circumstances in question; in other words, a risk might be significant even if the 'pool' of persons likely to be affected proved relatively small.[10] The court was reminded[11] of a *ratio* from the House of Lords to the effect that the Obscene Publications Act 1959 '... was not merely concerned with the once and for all corruption of the wholly innocent, it equally protected the less innocent from further corruption and the addict from feeding or increasing his addiction'. Later,[12] the court cited the observation made by Salmon LJ (in the 1968 *Last Exit to Brooklyn* case):[13]

> The Legislature can hardly have contemplated that a book which tended to corrupt and deprave the average reader or majority of those likely to read it could be justified as being for the public good on any ground ... What is a significant proportion is a matter entirely for the jury to decide.

The present case conceded that the concern to refrain from an overly 'draconian' interpretation of statutory constraints in the case of a book already in circulation (where, 'if the word "persons" was given the widest possible meaning, injustice might [have been] be done to the defendant because, as Salmon LJ said "there are individuals who may be corrupted by almost anything"') differed where a web page was concerned.[14] Furthermore, Lord Wilberforce[15] was quoted as stating that 'The tendency to deprave and corrupt is not to be estimated in relation to some assumed standard of purity of some reasonable average man. It is the likely reader. And to apply different tests to teenagers, members of men's clubs or men in various occupations or localities would be a matter of common sense'.

The play of logic – cautioning against invocation of notions of the 'average' and the 'reasonable' and acknowledging the difficulty posed by such concepts – of an empirically ascertainable core, which yet eludes proportionality arguments beyond those of the most general kind – demonstrates the hermeneutic paralysis gripping the field. In part, this is due to juristic concern to produce a *ratio* sufficiently flexible to be of use to the infinitely variable cases to come. Yet, additional unease is detectable, a shrinking from the task, rendered by something less tangible than conscientious unwillingness to produce a censorious normative ruling on matters of taste.

---

10 *Ibid*.
11 WL 347127, p 5.
12 WL 347127, p 9.
13 *R v Calder and Boyars Ltd* (1968) 52 Cr App R 706.
14 WL 347127, p 9. As already noted, the case rightly drew this conclusion bearing in mind the increased risk to children posed by the internet, and indeed the 'interactive' nature of the medium poses great challenges to the law in relation to different groups and categories of harm.
15 In *DPP v Whyte* [1972] AC 849, quoted at WL 347127, p 10.

Though the concepts giving rise to the Obscene Publications Act now have a substantial history, heavily debated in the popular and legal domains,[16] resistance to real examination of the image reflected back at humanity through the refractory mirror that is popular appetite seems almost perverse in itself. Jurisdictional issues, the variability of proportionality arguments, the tension between matters of corruptibility, freedom, certainty and the rule of law are all in themselves matters both of fact and value, the formal and the substantive. When elucidation of what is meant by a 'tendency to deprave and corrupt' remains patently unexplored, the concentration upon these more practical aspects of the problem simply compounds the state of paralysis. Expounding upon the statutory provision, the implicit aura of the caselaw exhibits a commitment to the maintenance of an invisible bulwark against corruption. Yet 'corruption' itself, though given the weight of proportionality arguments, is never discussed. Is it simply the lessening, by degree, of formerly held moral certitude? The loss of a never-to-be-defined innocence? An individual, leading imperceptibly to collective, decline? Certainly, such miasmic concerns seem to underpin the play of arguments, whilst at the same time undermining them, since the role of law – and the rule of law – must avoid overt forays into censorious leading positions; and the more 'solidly' legal ground – of demonstrating a direct link between controlling 'deviant' tendencies and thus inhibiting activities proscribed by the criminal law – is hotly disputed and empirically debateable.[17] Though caselaw faces a direct confrontation between socially deviant and criminalised behaviour, juristic debate is muted by consciousness of its uncertain 'supporting' role in the constant reinvention of cultures. Even where practical outcomes are inevitable in terms of mediating excesses, such outcomes cannot be traced by tracking a developing juristic rationale.

Crash has been discussed by academics and others largely in terms of ongoing debates about pornography and erotica, and much of the critical appraisal remains somewhat superficial because conducted at this level of 'appetites' without more searching enquiry as to what this implies. One recent book – *The Crash Controversy: Censorship Campaigns and Film Reception*[18] – undertakes an empirical study of audience responses to the film and thus might seem to promise

---

16 Though there has been a rich history of landmark cases on censorship in English law, an interesting phenomenon in itself is the relative *lack* of published academic discussion of censorship, certainly in Britain, from the 1970s to the present day (though occasional texts arose, for example Tribe (1974)). Recent texts include Lewis (2001b) and Akdeniz *et al* (2000). For a comprehensive and useful review of current law and debate concerning the specific issues raised by the availability of pornography on the internet, see Akdeniz (1997). Tangentially of course, the 'Hart-Devlin debate' produced a fruitful series of exchanges in relation to putative links between perceived deviations from public morality and tangible, and less tangible, harms to society. The millennium seems to have heralded a revival of the debate; such revival may be for a multitude of reasons. The tendency of lobbying groups to identify themselves either with the 'civil liberties' tag, or with 'family protection', can be predictably misleading, given the 'bandwagon' nature of popular debating polemic.

17 See discussion and references to various materials on this topic in 'The year 2000 – the empty city', in Williams, 2002, especially at pp 10–16.

18 Barker *et al*, 2001.

tangible material for the notionally empirical 'proportionality' and 'reasonable' versus 'average' caselaw discussions. The book provides statistical analysis of questionnaire answers, with tabulated outcomes in terms of 'positive' and 'negative' reactions. The study asserts a neutral stance in relation to research findings. It surveys the film's link to social and legal debates regarding censorship and recognises the difficulty of the terrain in the task of empiricism – the popular preconceptions, institutional assertions, the sensational and the mundane.

Yet, perhaps not surprisingly, the overall composition of the study – undertaken by senior academics within film and media scholarship – cannot but betray a predilection for particular views. The researchers portray themselves as social scientists in search of big game – chapters are headed 'One big controversy, several large research tasks', 'Reviewing the press', 'Expecting the worst', 'Talking about sex', 'The shape of positive responses', 'Four men's positive responses to *Crash*'. Despite boldly framed assertions concerning the role of the study in exploring the unexplored, of its embedded critique of the popular and the political, the text fails to transcend the level of prosaic and anecdotal. Those who responded 'positively' to the film (that is, 'liked' or 'enjoyed' it) are labelled 'positives' for the purposes of the study, whilst those reacting with reserve or hostility are the 'negatives', with 'neutrals' in between. The resultant critique is simplistic in the extreme:

> Centrally, we learned that there were only small differences in what people found memorable; the differences were in how they evaluated these. But the evaluations were complicated. While the Negatives were almost uniformly hostile to the kinds of characters in the film, the Positives were mixed – suggesting that positivity does not have to mean simple liking. More detailed comparison of the most frequently mentioned items showed that for the Negatives these were (absence of effective) storyline, and their (hostile) responses to characters; while for Positives they were general aesthetic appreciation of the film, along with a positive recognition of its themes linking cars, bodies and sex. The quantitative information on cinema and video-viewing habits supported the general notion that those with greater cinematic 'literacy' were generally more likely to be favourable to *Crash* – but the association was not very strong ...[19]

This philosophically, rationally and empirically flimsy 'finding' – that discerning people will respond favourably to the film – is corroborated by researcher conjecture concerning the likely impact of the popular press, particularly the contribution of the *Daily Mail* to the debate.[20] The location of the *Daily Mail* as an assumed 'universal' promotes the linkages forged by the text – conjecturally

---

19 Barker *et al*, 2001, p 164.
20 The *Daily Mail* did, in fact, pursue a campaign against 'moral corruption' centring upon films such as *Crash* and this campaign would form an understandable feature of the popular topography for the researchers. The location of the *Mail* in the midst of *empirical* findings rather oversimplifies the possible role played by such media however, despite the *Mail*'s clear associations with certain polemical positions. For a succinct discussion of the *Mail* campaign, and its attempts to influence the British Board of Film Classification, see 'They know what's good for you' at http://film.guardian.co.uk/censorship/news/0,11729,661823,00.html. For a note on the current position, see Munro, 2003.

locating 'negatives' or proto-negatives as probable *Mail* readers, with 'positives' as 'anti'-*Mail* and therefore liberal, freethinking and enlightened individuals:

> ... there was a strong tendency for those with positive orientations to *Crash* to engage in talk about their prior orientation to the film. This was truer of those who liked the film than of those who approved of it. We believe this arises mainly from the discrepancy [between] the nervousness induced in many viewers by the Mail's campaign, and their realisation that they enjoyed the film. Those most strongly registering approval were more suspicious, we suspect, of the Mail, therefore less fearful in advance of the film. There was a smaller, but still noticeable tendency for Negatives, and especially Disapprovers, to want to talk about intended/implied audiences – which fits well with our perception that those who disapprove a film such as *Crash* will tend to work with a 'figure' of some other audience who might be affected by it ... Positives were considerably more keen to speak their minds on censorship than Negatives ...

> A more puzzling finding was that Likers and Approvers were much more likely to want to talk about characters; while in the opposite direction it was especially the Disapprovers who avoided such talk. These tendencies are sufficiently strong to provoke some speculation. Might it be that the Disapprovers tended to be so strongly hostile to the film per se that they declined to discuss the characters as such, since to do so would be to allow their fictional status and the defences that that might introduce?

> To us, though, the most striking tendency came with Modality Talk, that is, with talk concerning the relations between the film and the filmic world, and the world beyond the film ... to our surprise, in both cases it emerged that Positivity was strongly associated with a propensity to such talk ... What is interesting about this ... was that the Disapprovers of *Crash* are evidently the least likely to want to discuss it in modality terms. This is surprising, and counter-intuitive. One might expect that those who reject the film on moral grounds might have been expected to want to raise questions of censorship, and of the possible impact of the film on the world, or to worry about a breakdown of the fiction/reality boundary. None of these appears to have been the case. Instead it is the Positives who want to talk about modal issues ...[21]

What is 'counter-intuitive' for the researchers, 'true' and 'more' true are not necessarily grounded in universals as the language suggests. The broad message of the research – supported by the nomenclature – is that 'positives' emerge as free-thinking individuals, open to experience and more reflective. They are prepared to look 'beyond' the erotic and talk about 'characters' and are clearly enlightened intellectuals engaged with the scientific media discourse that is 'modality talk'.[22] Yet the research does not consider the host of issues which such

---

21 Barker *et al*, 2001, p 171.
22 Whilst it would not be suggested that any member of the sample audience was either insincere, or had 'criminal', 'deviant' or any other socially disapproved tendencies, it is well known that paedophiles, for example, are highly skilled in 'emotive' sensitivities, taking great interest in characters, personalities, motivations and so on. Such ability or interest in itself does not 'prove' anything.

assumptions might ignore. Aside from the clear predisposition of the researchers towards those responding as 'positives', what does it really mean, to be 'a' positive? The research simply mirrors the same ethically distorted simplicity satirised in Huxley's *Brave New World*. Does 'liking' the film – even to the extent of thinking about characters and entering into modality talk – necessarily tell us anything about the issues underlying the censorship and civil liberties debate? We are meant to be persuaded that the research produces incontrovertible evidence of the innate moral superiority of audiences who 'like' films on the edge of the censorship debate – that they are more empathic (talk modally and of characters), more intellectually discursive – that the real 'deviants' are those who 'disliked' the film. Given the controversial nature of the themes in the film, there is little reason to believe that such questionnaire responses are at all reliable. Without further, perhaps more sensitively situated, research, individuals in such circumstances are just as likely to give the response which corresponds to their 'workaday' view of themselves.[23] They may be motivated to respond in a particular way by a host of concerns, some of them repressive of 'true' responses, some mimicking imagined 'ideal' responses and so on. Even straight admissions that the film was enjoyed for the erotic idea of the sex-violence collision, may be vouchsafed for reasons not entirely appreciated by the respondent herself.[24] Indeed, this 'critical mass' neatly demonstrates that the film *Crash* can be identified with pornography/erotica, or with compounding an impoverished and prejudicial critique of it. Certainly the film version of *Crash*, by its very nature as a predominantly visual, rather than textual medium, tends to lose the problematising aspect. Two qualities arguably make the text more challenging, quite apart from the demand for greater intellectual engagement posed by textual as opposed to visual material. First, Ballard's prose anatomises the sexuality/violence/machinery problematic literally 'warts and all', and secondly, that he attempts, albeit in a somewhat hazy fashion, to explore what this might mean. At times one might wonder whether this is simply 'dressing up' an essentially prurient text. Rather, it seems an early prototype in Ballard's developing work, where, with some temerity, he deploys the anatomical, the physical, to critique the metaphysical.[25] It may be said that this can assist with a process of 'forensic' legal theory – with tracking every fragment of evidence bearing upon human nature. When law, with its brother religion, could simply demonise many practices and interests as the pursuits of an 'unnatural' and 'deviant' minority, the task of law seemed simple – to identify these few and continue to protect the many. Present caselaw reflects a new-found

---

23 Empirical findings are clearly fraught with difficulties even in the most rigorous study; how much more so when the human mind is the object of that study, and more so again when the mind is asked to report *on itself* – as David Hume is quick to point out.

24 Though the newly established convention 'herself' is used at this juncture perhaps advisedly, its widespread adoption in legal debate is, it might be argued, questionable. Emerging feminine cultures in the West, of boldly 'defiant' behaviour may be in part a reaction to former inhibitory factors and indeed, this entire field is the subject of sociological and socio-legal study in itself, an issue about which the researchers in the study seem blissfully unaware. In short, the recorded reactions of female and male respondents cannot be read as simple indicators in themselves.

25 For a discussion of the ethical implications of Ballard's more recent work, see Williams, M, 2002.

caution, yet remains powerless to advance a consequent rationale. Ballard, too, recognises that traditional notions of deviance present far too simple a picture – that we are all more or less implicated in such questions.[26] If the law once believed itself to be dealing with a social profile dominated by a somewhat mummified 'reasonable man', it might now question its model of human nature, in view of the vast access to forceful material.

In the absence of religion, this brave new world takes on more particular significance. Though society itself may fulfil the role of an authoritative and judgmental parent, current culture is hostile to such figuring, for understandable reasons. The 'paternalistic' community, or state, conflicts with the 'autonomous' individual. Indeed, both the authoritative and the nurturing aspects of parenting are absent – the benevolence of society lies in its willingness to tolerate the ongoing, unfolding human experiment. This is Ballard's point. Where is it taking us? Ballard's question – 'Can the writer leave out anything he prefers not to understand, including his own motives, prejudices and psychopathology?'[27] – is just as relevant to the jurist. Aware of the shortcomings and doubtful quasi-mystical origins of the reasonable man – the approved legal agent – the jurist may well adopt Ballard's assertion about the writer:

> His role is that of the scientist, whether on safari or in his laboratory, faced with an unknown terrain or subject. All he can do is to devise various hypotheses and test them against the facts.[28]

As Ballard points out, *Crash* is not simply situated in, but is also constituted by, a moral vacuum, a vacuum which resonates strongly with our own consumer culture. Indeed, addressing questions of what sort of creatures we are, so that society and law can consider what kind of constraints or debate should be put in place, demands a dispassionate objectivity, which law, as the creature of culture, seems no more equipped to produce than any other social institution.

With the movement from text to film, additional 'unknowns' arise in the impact of the medium upon the human psyche. The Williams Committee on Obscenity and Film Censorship[29] adopted a minimalist approach in its recommendations regarding legal constraints, bearing in mind the largely uncontrollable material viewed in 'private' clubs and venues on the one hand, and the underlying principle that law should be concerned with preventing exploitation of minors, or representations of physical harm in the production of film, on the other. Subsequent adaptations of the law aimed at extending some

---

26 'Throughout *Crash* I have used the car not only as a sexual image, but as a total metaphor for man's life in today's society. As such the novel has a political role quite apart from its sexual content, but I would still like to think that *Crash* is the first pornographic novel based on technology. In a sense, pornography is the most political form of fiction, dealing with how we use and exploit each other, in the most urgent and ruthless way' – Ballard, 1995, Introduction to *Crash*.

27 *Ibid.*

28 *Ibid.*

29 *Report of the Committee on Obscenity and Film Censorship*, Cmnd 7772 (1979) London: HMSO.

control over the Pandora's box of internet material, maintain this philosophy.[30] The emphasis is still upon the maximisation of freedoms alongside minimalist constraint, adopting a neutral, 'holding' position in the exponentially unfolding social experiment that is our cultural life. In considering the movement from text to film, JG Ballard himself appears to apprehend little alteration in the response of the reader; indeed, he has said of the film that he would be disturbed to think that an audience might set out deliberately to imitate, or recreate the film scenario 'in reality'.[31] Given that the location of the film and text of *Crash* is on the margins of popular culture, the risk of imitatory response may be minimised by dint of a less than 'mass' audience. In addition, the researchers in *The Crash Controversy* study would seem to believe that the film's 'art-house' location in the aesthetics of film render it somehow beyond the reach of ethical enquiry and indeed, an analogous rationale of permissible aesthetics of appetite seem to underlie the web market in pornographic imagery. Yet this dogged blindness to the philosophical implications of the film yields the deepest irony, as Ballard himself clearly appreciated in the very creation of *Crash*. The issue is not whether the film 'is' obscene, rather it is how the text and images, the 'collision' of ideas and values in the film provoke questions about ourselves which simple 'shoot 'em up' films, or sexually explicit websites, leave dormant.

Consider the following thought-experiment.[32] Suppose in observing spider monkeys in a compound, we 'discovered' that the 'collision' of sensory stimuli, for example the smell of the herb lovage at the edge of the compound, caused a uniform side-stimulus in a number (perhaps a large number) of individuals – say, a tingling in the left hand – but it had simply never been noted before. We would want to know why, what 'pathways', neuro-chemically, were responsible. Suppose also that we found a number of the creatures began to seek the sensation, as opposed to stumbling upon it. Now suppose that we also found that the tingling was accompanied, in a smaller sample of individuals, by a desire to relieve the tingling by pressing the affected hand hard on the face of a neighbouring spider monkey. Indeed, for some of those individuals, relief from the tingling could only be found by pressing hard on the face of another monkey. Pressing the hand on a cloth, a doll or some other similar object would not bring relief: the neuro-sensory synaptic circuit could not complete.[33]

---

30 See Akdeniz, 1997.

31 'People ask me how I would feel if young men, after seeing the movie, went and crashed their cars into other people, and of course, if this did happen, it would be a tragedy. But it hasn't happened anywhere in the world where it's been shown and it's highly unlikely to happen, because the sort of kids who go to see … non-stop, end-to-end violence are not going to be able to read a film like *Crash* …' – Ballard, quoted interview, at www.finelinefeatures.com/crash/cmp/ballard-interview.html.

32 The production of a practical ethics analogy at this point seemed appropriate, and the felt need to do so is illustrative of the intransigent, fixed location of different discourses. The choice of lovage is made to minimise reader response to a more commonplace herb – 'mint never has that effect on *me*' – so distracting from the model. The choice of spider monkeys is similarly less directly traceable to instantly anthropomorphic identification than, say, chimpanzees, though still sufficiently analogous.

33 For an introductory discussion, see J Bickle and P Mandik, 'The philosophy of neuroscience', in Edward N Zalta (ed), *The Stanford Encyclopaedia of Philosophy* (Winter 2002), at http://plato.stanford.edu/entries/neuroscience.

Now suppose that, added to this already bizarre series of circumstances, a behaviour pattern began to emerge amongst the non-participating members of the community. Spider monkeys normally engaged in tasks in other parts of the community began to drift towards the lovage-smelling spectacle, either to witness the visibly intoxicating inhalation-tingling sensation, or to observe the peripheral inhalation-tingling-relief-by-face-pressing scenario. At some point, 'outside' observers would have to log an alteration, not only in community activity, but also in evolving appetites for stimuli. At the very least, the change in community behaviour would have 'knock-on' implications for the investment in, or viability of, other potential activities. Even if only a small group formed the participant/audience population, this would be the case. There would be implications for the 'shaping' of the community and of individuals within it.

The reader may well feel their intelligence is somewhat insulted by this crude analogy between monkeys and ourselves, and in mitigation it must be pleaded that it is simply an attempt to move the debate beyond the improbable neutrality assumed by jurists and researchers alike. The belief that the Cartesian split in human nature is so effective as to entirely divide ourselves from the world of stimuli assaulting us from every side, is naïve in the extreme.[34] Not only does it disregard the interpersonal dynamics of evolving selves and concomitant links to community practices, it also disregards the first lessons of Aristotelian ethics – that our behaviours shape us, and that social organisation holds responsibility for that shaping.[35] This is not to say that any social or legal presumption should favour inhibitory or pre-emptive proscription. Indeed, the eccentric excesses now pouring from the internet, as well as the particular scenes depicted in *Crash*, pose a rather more complex question, poorly explored by popular debate, by committees or by caselaw. The creation and fostering of appetites, driven by market forces, provides fascinating potential insights into ourselves – holding a veritable hall of mirrors to our understanding of human nature; but as we discover such facts about ourselves, what do we do with the information? At present, we are rather strongly located within the passive compound audience and indeed the notion of scaling the fence may take the thought-experiment beyond viable realms of possibility; but we seem incapable of even planning an outbreak, preferring instead to groom ourselves whilst sitting back on the haunches of our ethical selves, willing only to see the mirror image best satisfying a regal vanity of all-encompassing power, over ourselves and our world.

The vocabulary of ethics seems quaint and singularly irrelevant to the world of *Crash*, where disability is simply another course in the widening and jaded erotic diet, where the character Vaughan:

---

34 For a brief history of Cartesian dualism, see Wozniak, Robert H, 'Mind and body: René Descartes to William James', at http://serendip.brynmawr.edu/Mind/Descartes.html.

35 An excellent critique of understandings of Aristotelian ethics, and especially of the relation between law and moral education as expounded in Aristotle's *Nicomachean Ethics*, can be found in Hunt, 2002.

... unfolded for me all his obsessions with the mysterious eroticism of wounds ... dreamed of ambassadorial limousines crashing into jack-knifing butane tankers, of taxis filled with celebrating children colliding head-on below the bright display windows of deserted supermarkets. He dreamed of alienated brothers and sisters, by chance meeting each other on collision courses on the access roads of petrochemical plants, their unconscious incest made explicit in this colliding metal, in the haemorrhages of their brain tissue flowering beneath the aluminised compression chambers and reaction vessels ...[36]

Just how far we have strayed from the allegedly 'known' conceptual territory of law and ethics becomes apparent when such prose from *Crash* is juxtaposed with a text concerned with moral valuations. To be sure, traditional moral philosophy, steeped in the lessons of classical thought, is directly relevant to us. The great classical philosophers dealt with the profound questions of human existence, which have not, despite appearances, altered in essence. In particular, they recognised that questions of individual freedom were intimately linked to those of moral, social and legal organisation; but making those insights work for us now is a challenge – indeed, there is a danger that moral philosophy, alongside its co-worker, law, may operate in a sealed unit of rationality far removed from the pressing subject matter of its discourse. Consider an essay entitled 'Shame and autonomy'[37] by Bernard Williams, the Chairman of the Committee on Censorship and Pornography. The very words examined in the essay – 'shame' and 'guilt' – seem quaint and singularly irrelevant to the world of *Crash*. Williams's critique of the minutiae of Homeric and Kantian notions of shame and guilt may seem otiose and obsolescent, a raindrop against a deluge; but Williams does point up concepts which, by their very deliberate impoverishment in *Crash*, help to clarify the points Ballard pursues. Asking himself 'what is involved in shame itself', Williams replies:

> The basic experience connected with shame (*aidos*) is that of being seen, inappropriately, by the wrong condition. It is straightforwardly connected with nakedness, particularly in sexual connections ... a further step is taken when the motive is fear of shame at what people will say about one's actions ... The reaction in Homer to someone who has done something that shame should have prevented is *nemesis*, ... defined as a reaction [such as indignation] ... depending on what particular violation of *aidos* it is a reaction to. As Redfield has put it, *aidos* and *nemesis* are a reflexive pair ... People can feel indignation or other forms of anger when honour is violated, in their own case or somebody else's. These are shared sentiments with similar objects, and they serve to bind people together in a community of feeling ...[38]

Now shame at nakedness, even shame at what people will say about one's actions, are both apparently irrelevant scruples in the world of *Crash*: the community works upon an entirely different logic. That is Ballard's point. We live

---

36   Ballard, 1995, pp 12–13.
37   Williams, B, 1994.
38   *Ibid*, pp 78–80.

in a surreal world where the obscene jostles with the mundane, where personal tragedy is another unit of consumption:

> I looked round at the crowd. A considerable number of children were present, many lifted on their parents' shoulders to give them a better view … None of the spectators showed any signs of alarm. They looked down at the scene with the calm and studied interest of intelligent buyers at a leading bloodstock sale …[39]

This deadening community is quite clearly a crucible for the more stylised and specialised proclivities or activities of particular groups, and within such groups – what Bernard Williams calls the community of feeling, in which shame would be a shared product – becomes a community of appetite. Shame and nemesis will be inverted – the root of indignation will lie in feeling shame. As Williams explains:

> Even if shame and its motivations always involve in some way or other an idea of a gaze of another, it is important that for many of its operations the imagined gaze of an imagined other will do … He might think that it was shameful to do it, not just to be seen doing it, and in that case an imagined watcher could be enough to trigger the reaction of shame.[40]

For the figures in *Crash*, the immediate and extended 'community' of watchers and imagined watchers endorse the aberrant behaviour. This should be a concern for the law, both in terms of understanding the growth of clearly 'deviant' communities – especially in the age of the internet – and in grasping the broader role of legal and other institutions in relation to the freedom and regulation of the legal subject.

Now this seems to be veering towards an hypothesis concerning the need for increased regulation of individuals 'adrift' in this moral void; but then one simply becomes enmeshed in the old polarised arguments – between freedom and censorship and so on. Ballard's approach strives to maintain a critical neutrality in relation to the uncertain journey of modern life. In so doing, he draws the debate away from conventional concerns, highlighting instead the experimental nature of the journey, the questions about ourselves left unanswered by the reciprocity of a doubtful shame culture. He is prepared to take risks with conventional assumptions about harm, recognising that we cannot understand the full implications – for good or bad – of our present emerging selves. It would be difficult for a legal theorist to find himself asking the question posed by this anthropologically orientated writer: 'Is this harnessing of our innate perversity conceivably of benefit to us? Is there some deviant logic unfolding more powerful that that provided by reason?'[41] For some, the question may offend in its apparent disregard for a world of normative value. Yet perhaps Ballard is after all a moralist crying: this is how we really are, all of us, more or less. The old myths have perpetrated as much harm as good, being merely cosmetic. Let us look full-square

---

39   Ballard, 1995, p 155.
40   Williams, B, 1994, p 82.
41   Quoted, as before, from JG Ballard's Introduction to *Crash*.

at the subject and without making condemnatory judgments, but with the cool eye of the scientist, have a keener sense of the factors weighing in the equation. Without truth, there can be no ethics.

In discussing shame, Bernard Williams concludes that:

> [*aidos*] [c]annot merely mean 'shame', but must cover something like guilt as well ... The idea of reparation is prominent in Homer, and the need for it, for gestures that compensate and heal, must surely be recognised in any society if the notion of holding oneself responsible is to have any content ... In the Greek world there was room, too, for forgiveness. It is often thought that forgiveness speaks more effectively to guilt than to shame: if the people who have been wronged forgive me, then perhaps the case is withdrawn from the internal judge ...[42]

Somehow in this new godless world of heartless externalities, it seems meet that the subject – for example the narrator in *Crash* – has as much compassion for his own disturbed and disturbing consciousness as for that of his fellow beings. The 'internal judge' is held in abeyance, whilst reparation, healing and forgiveness (to use Williams's terms) are liabilities flowing as justly toward the damaged subject as from him; his wounds are deeper than skin, his need endless, his vulnerability in the face of the machine acute. The legalistic relation of guilt and reparation loses clarity when all participants in the drama are not agents atop of the world, but linked orphans inching sideways on an existential precipice. Moreover, not guilt, but 'only shame' says Williams can help one:

> ... to understand one's relation to happenings or to rebuild the self that has done these things and the world in which that self has to live. Only shame can do that, because it embodies conceptions of what one is and of how one is related to others ...[43]

But this presupposes a sense of self and belonging ripe for such embodiment. Shame in the 'robust' context of *Crash* seems a somewhat superfluous and prudish emotion. It is after all through a surfeit of such scruples, a surface of respectability, that repressive and corrupt cultures are maintained. Yet Williams's analysis assists in understanding its potential relevance. Bereft of a conception of what one is and how one is related to others, one is deprived of the healing power of shame, or at least something akin to it. The difficulty lies in the realisation that the selfsame presumption of an ethical world ever-present, instantly accessed and deployed, underpins legal philosophy and doctrine just as surely as it forms the classical philosophy in the mouth of Williams. That such 'brakes' might be neutralised, in the pleasure dome that is our culture, leaves the law in an ethically discursive limbo. It would be unthinkable simply to invoke an 'anthropological' discourse in its place – to suggest that on our mother's or our father's side we are descended

---

42   Williams, B, 1994, pp 90–91.
43   Williams, B, 1994, p 94.

from the apes.[44] Yet we do need to consider how the gap, between the discourse of reasonableness and responsible free will and the course of unmediated appetites – whether lovage-, Hollywood-, or brave new web-scented – is taking us. In short, we are neuro-chemical selves as well as selves with an ethical capability. The sensory self interacts with the ethical self. Empirical corroboration that the sex-violence nexus produces 'positive' response tells us no more than a fleeting visitor to the zoo might divine from a notice declaring the lovage-smelling propensities of the monkeys: just another exotic fact on the way to the ice cream vendor. Remember that we are not secure in such a role of passing super-species. We understand little of how the reciprocity of values – the dynamic between individual and community – has faltered or failed. Williams's assertion that 'the internalised other … still has some independent identity … it is not just a screen for one's own ethical ideas, but is the locus of some genuine social expectations …',[45] is dependent upon an entrenched reciprocity between individual and community, whereas Ballard perceives his world and ours as systematically alienating, in the cathection of sensibility, where a:

> … coming autogeddon … conjunctions between elbow and chromium window sill, vulva and instrument binnacle, summed up the possibilities of a new logic created by these multiplying artefacts, the codes of a new marriage of sensation and possibility …[46] The destruction of this motor car and its occupants seemed, in turn to sanction the sexual penetration … both were conceptualised acts abstracted from all feeling, carrying any ideas or emotions with which we cared to freight them …[47]

How would Williams respond to the world of *Crash*? It is a world of as yet unmeasured possibilities for good and ill, stripped of the old cultures and old judgments. It is a world where individuals understand that autonomy is both blunted and sharpened by mortality, and their claim upon the fragments of selfhood frail, yet all the keener. For Williams, any such world of greater social heterogeneity must predicate not only the existence of a more discriminatory internalised other, but one which is the *locus* of 'genuine social expectations' – suggesting not just a responsible subject, but a responsible, reciprocal community. Williams suggests:

> If a charge of social heteronomy is to stick at a more interesting level, its claim will have to be that even this abstracted, improved neighbour lodged in one's inner life represents a compromise of genuine autonomy …[48]

It is not the primary work of the law to effect such compromise, but that of the social compact underpinning it. As with current culture, the agents of *Crash* are

---

44 Bishop Wilberforce was provoked by Darwin's theory of evolution to ask Julian Huxley '… whether it was on his mother's side, or his father's side that he was descended from the apes?'. Few people now share the Bishop's scepticism of evolutionary theory, though institutional human imagery is resistant to deriving implications from human location in the chain of primates, let alone in the chain of biological being. The Bishop's identity as primate remained, of course, purely ecclesiastical.

45 Williams, B, 1994, p 98.

46 Ballard, 1995, p 106.

47 Ballard, 1995, p 129.

48 Williams, B, 1994, p 99.

Secrets and Laws

drunk with possibility. That unbridled possibility leads both to new horizons and to chaos is clear, but who will determine which course prevails? *Crash* simply poses this question. Law, and legal argumentation, can make a useful contribution to the debate, as a source of development in the search for our own identifiers where, at its best, it forces refinement of the contest in ideas and values. The conundrum of whether we might all be described as cultivated citizen or popular savage is perhaps best informed by reflecting upon popular appetites, through the fragmented mirror to ourselves that is *Crash*. At present orchestrated primarily by the academic industry that is Film and Media Studies, the debate is easily reduced to a liberal presumption that freedom of expression must trump restrictions upon freedom.[49] Perhaps so; but freedoms must be understood to operate in a matrix of human relations in urgent need of more developed mechanisms for debate.

---

49 A recent letter from Professor Geoff Lealand in *The Independent* (2003) demonstrates the point: 'Television makes people happier, not more violent.' The letter takes issue with the suggestion that television 'makes people more violent'. Clearly, any suggested link, between television and a possible upsurge in violence, should not be expressed in such reductive and simplistic terms. Nevertheless, Lealand's conclusion – asserting that such links are 'not backed by the research evidence' – appears to bring a decisive empirical authority to the debate, yet it too appears to rely upon somewhat superficial and loosely delineated parameters, correlating, for example, to findings of 'happiness'.

PART III

LAW AND
PROSE NARRATIVE

LAW, MORALS, MARRIAGE AND COHABITATION – VIRTUOUS INDIVIDUALS AND VENAL LAWS – HARDY'S ETERNAL MESSAGE FOR ATTITUDES TO MARRIAGE AND COHABITATION

As debates concerning regulation of intimate partnerships and family life continue anon, Hardy's *Jude the Obscure* – published in 1896 – continues to be a relevant touchstone of pertinent issues. A central topic in current political and legal policy projections is that of marriage versus cohabitation – whether, and to what degree, unmarried partnerships should be supported, as well as regulated by law.

Current research on the subject of cohabitation is suffused with hypotheses of contrasting tenor. Whilst there is no doubt that cohabitation throughout Europe is on the increase (Kiernan, 2001), conclusions drawn from that pattern of increase are variable, and tend to focus upon perceived 'negative' readings, linking the breakdown of marriage to the breakdown of families, in turn heralding a collapse in the social fabric, increase in crime and so on – as Lewis (2001a, pp 159–84) summarises:

> For the most part, academic commentators have decided that what has happened to the family during the last quarter of the century is problematic ... the institution of marriage has long been viewed as the basic unit and bedrock of society ... The married couple has been viewed as the polis in miniature ...

The fact that this invokes, in Lewis's words, a model of marriage as 'a discipline and an order ... necessarily a matter of public interest and not just a private relationship'[1] may embrace an inevitable degree of *quid pro quo* in individual and civic relations. However it also imports a conception of a rights to responsibilities *locus* capable of bearing a repressive, rather than facilitative, tenor. Though units reflecting discipline and order may be constructive components within a larger unit of order, the relational position of the component individuals and partners to these orders may comprise radically different characteristics. In short, though persons may be helped by systems serving discipline and order, they may be hindered too. As Hardy understood well, the cultures underlying the model of marriage and/or cohabitation are crucial. Lewis notes, for example, that, on the one hand:

> A private contract model for personal relations may serve to widen the gap between the social reality of personal relationships and the legal assumptions ... (2001a, p 180)

---

1   Lewis, 2001a.

Whilst at the same time it may be said that:

> ... the legal and economic models of family behaviour that sustained traditional patters of dependency have largely disappeared, *but the erosion of normative prescription has outrun the social reality* ...[2]

Though our visions of partnership and family have been altered by material events, receptivity to trailing normative structures has altered and diminished more rapidly still. Though modern commentators such as Fukuyama (Lewis, 2001a) refurbish the anxieties attendant upon such developments,[3] there is a tendency for such critiques to underestimate the importance of broad underpinning ideologies in permitting perceptions of selfhood, whilst lacking breadth in imagining the possibilities for new ideologies and models of personal relations within the civic context.

Hardy understood only too well the power exerted in the play between ideological and normative structures. With a legal system which attempted to police intimate relations to a degree which resulted in patent absurdities, evasions and farce, such laws derived from an ecclesiastical ancestry that perpetuated a culture of moral censure (with its shadow still cast over today). The liminal service of discipline and order was achieved through structures of judgment and repression of real gravity in their results, especially in relation to women and children.

THE LAW OF MARRIAGE IN *JUDE THE OBSCURE*[4]

> It is so far from being natural for a man and woman in live in a state of marriage that we find all the motives which they have for remaining in that connection, and the restraints which civilised society imposes to prevent separation, are hardly sufficient to keep them together. (Samuel Johnson)

---

2   *Ibid*, emphasis added.

3   Lewis (2001a, p 161) indicates that Fukuyama continues the tradition carried by Talcott Parsons in the 1950s regarding the central focus upon the traditional family unit.

4   A substantial portion of this chapter first appeared as 'The Law of Marriage in *Jude the Obscure*' in (1996) 5(2) Nottingham Law Journal 168–86. As the first full-length academic article undertaken by the writer, the study of law in *Jude* presented itself as a clear choice for a 'law-through-literature' exposition. At that time, the 'negative' aspects of the textual message – that law created crushing and oppressive mechanisms forcing individuals inexorably towards deceit and ruin – effaced the more positive obverse, that law and attendant values might be recast to serve and support new ways of being. Overwhelmed by the complexity and variety of juristic, doctrinal questions presented by the text, the resultant account adopts a chronological, 'case by case' approach to the unfolding legal events – 'Marriage 1', 'Marriage 2', 'Divorce 1', 'Divorce 2', 'Remarriage 1', 'Remarriage 2'. Though coherent, a more experienced scholar might have choreographed an analysis tracking the doctrinal fits and starts, repressions and deceits, more clearly through the vehicles of character rather than case. For *Jude* is a clear indication that legal doctrine can all too easily come to serve those characters it least means to serve and, obscenely (as is the case with Sue and Jude) consume the virtuous drives of those it ought most clearly aim to preserve.

In conducting research into the legal-historical background to *Jude the Obscure*, primarily that of the law of marriage and divorce in the 19th century, the writer was struck not only by the wealth of contemporaneous legal material which could be brought to the text, but also by the potential of the text in supplementing the 'story' told by legal history. This process of exchange, between the legal, the literary and back again, comes to have significance not just to legal history, but to historicity. The blind spots of legal history, highlighted by the text, demonstrate both the incompleteness of legal record and the subsequent partiality of historical conclusions. Moving from the 'microscopy' of legal history, some degree of 'macroscopic' jurisprudential significance can be found in *Jude the Obscure* – the individual's collision with law, as depicted in fiction, can supplement our approach to material law, and our vision of law as 'a regime of adjusting relations and ordering human behaviour through the force of a socially organised group'.[5] Such an approach is in keeping with the aesthetic project of Thomas Hardy the novelist, for whom the universal resided – most typically – in the particular. It is perhaps salutary for that cohesive and impenetrable edifice, law, to be reminded by its historically and temperamentally unreliable cousin, literature, of the pure irrelevance, as well as the accidental, tragic or deformed significance that the law may hold for the lowly denizens it claims to serve. Through aesthetics – so relegated by the hierarchies of logical discourse – the abstractions of theory, the arsenals of empiricism, may be tested by the marshalling of all the senses in the depiction of lived human experience.

Jude the Obscure and legal history

Jude the Obscure presents a complex exposition of the formalities of marriage and divorce, providing an interesting record of the informed law person's filtered reception and knowledge of technical law, and the play between secular and canonical precepts, as well as a philosophical treatise upon the role of the law of marriage in the lives of ordinary people. Indeed, the philosophical and psychological ramifications of law, both secular and canonical, and the power of their associated moral codes, are major themes of the narrative. However, before embarking upon an examination of these issues, it may be pertinent to explore the legal background to the complex historiography of marriage that the narrative presents.

The formalisation and technical refinement of marriage in the civil law was a relatively recent development to a person looking back from the vantage point of the later 19th century. Lord Hardwicke's Act of 1753 marked the beginning of the bureaucratisation of marriage; the institution of records and legal requirements which spoke on the one hand of a movement away from the abstract aspirations of the divine in canon law marriage and, on the other, the annihilation of unreliable and corruptible proletarian 'self government' in the use of customary,

---

5   Walker, 1980.

'common law' marriage contracts.[6] The Act's requirement of the publication of banns[7] on purchase of a licence, the presence of at least two witnesses, and the recording of the marriage in a public register, signalled the ascendancy of secular over canon law, and the temporal court's desire to regularise its pragmatic dealings with property rights.[8] The 19th century later became a crucible within which the concept of the marriage contract was defined according to the evolving 'free radical', external element of cultural discourse and the internal purification of technical law, which selected and metabolised chosen elements of that discourse. The century saw an explosion of legislation in relation to marriage. There were Marriage Acts of 1822, 1823, 1824, 1825, 1830, 1835, 1836, 1840, 1847, 1857, 1860, 1886, 1898 and 1899. Many of these were concerned with legitimising marriages in places in which some minor detail might not have accorded with the stringent requirements of prior legislation. In addition, there were the Married Women's Property Acts of 1870 and 1882.

The appearance of a purely civil marriage ceremony through the Act of 1836, with its prosaic sounding officiator, the superintendent registrar, noted a further shift towards the laicisation of legal stewardship. Yet the law relating to the contents and termination of the marriage contract itself remained largely canonical, as secular law was content to tolerate the continued use of the long developed and sophisticated precepts of ecclesiastical law with its attendant moral *imprimatur*. The most significant secular incursion into the territory of ecclesiastical law was the passing of the Matrimonial Causes Act 1857, which established the Court for Divorce and Matrimonial Causes and abolished the divorce jurisdiction of the Church courts, so providing a more accessible machinery for the dissolution of marriage in place of the rare and expensive divorce by Act of Parliament, and canonical decrees of nullity (*divorce a vinculo*) and judicial separation (*divorce a mensa et thoro*). However, under the Act, adultery was the sole ground for dissolution and in the case of a wife petitioner an additional ingredient of cruelty or desertion had to be proved.

Jude the Obscure was published in 1896, and its modernity is located not only through the depiction of urban life, the use of trains as commonplace rather than novel events, and the radicalism of philosophical speculation, but also through the lack of novelty, amounting to disillusion, associated with the bureaucratic processes of marriage and divorce in the text. The story within the novel is complex. Apart from the central theme of Jude's quest for the unattainable university education, schematically it may be said to concern four individuals.

---

6   However, these common law pacts, including ceremonies based upon rituals, such as broom-jumping, did not completely die out: see Cornish, 1989.

7   Helmholz traces the pre-legislative status of banns according to canon law: from the 12th century:

    ... no public ceremony was required to make a marriage valid and indissoluble. Such a ceremony, preceded by publication of banns, was necessary to render a marriage fully licit. The parties sinned by marrying without publication of banns and blessing by a priest ... they rendered themselves liable to the spiritual penalties of penance ... but this failure did not affect the question of the validity of the marriage. (Helmholz, 1974)

8   For a clear summary of these events, see Baker, 1979.

First, Jude marries Arabella, to whom he is temperamentally unsuited, and from whom he soon parts. He falls in love with his cousin Sue Bridehead, who marries an older man, Phillotson, to whom she is unsuited. They part, and Sue and Jude cohabit, producing three children, as well as caring for Jude's putative son by Arabella. Both couples divorce. (Arabella has, prior to this, contracted a secret, bigamous marriage in Australia.) Sue and Jude attempt to marry, but their courage fails them. Jude's son tragically murders Sue's and Jude's children and then commits suicide. Distraught, Sue is convinced that she has been punished for flouting convention, and decides that she must atone by remarrying Phillotson. Jude, intoxicated by Arabella's artful provision of alcohol, remarries Arabella, but soon afterwards dies.

Marriage number 1: Jude and Arabella

Jude is tricked into marriage by Arabella's false claim that she is pregnant.[9] In the eyes of the law however, Arabella's falsehood is not capable of undermining the marriage contract. Under ecclesiastical law on the point (which becomes absorbed into secular law and in force until the Nullity of Marriage Act 1971) even a genuine pregnancy by some person other than the petitioner at the time of the marriage did not provide grounds for impeaching it. (For early canon law, simply embarking upon sexual relations suggested an irrevocable step towards commitment; carnal copulation effected physical union, the creation of one flesh by *commixtio sexuum*.)[10] The religious marriage ceremony was justified on spiritual grounds – the making of a solemn vow before God – whilst at the same time facilitating the incursion of institutional control in the lives of ordinary people. Thus the spiritual façade of the ceremony could be described as an arch counterfeit for the largely unacknowledged material purpose which it served – to mark and legitimise claims to the territory of the body – in particular, the female body. As the vessel which potentially would house the patrilineal product, the female body defined future property rights; this role as vessel was woman's only real, though attenuated, claim to power. Small wonder then that a knowing woman, Arabella, retaliates with her own effective form of colonisation – pre-empting the territorial claim through her own act of piracy – the fraudulent pregnancy. In practical terms, Jude's consent to the marriage had been induced by a fraud, and his plans and ambitions frustrated by it, yet the fraud was not of

---

9   Even before this event, Jude is becoming enmeshed. His 'walking out' with Arabella acquires the more permanent status of betrothal in the eyes of the community. In *Sullivan v Sullivan* (1818) 2 Hag Con 258, Sir William Scott stated:

   It is not imputed as a crime, if fair opportunities and facilities are allowed, for improving a favourable disposition that may appear in a respectable young man towards a female of the family, and for encouraging a prospect of what the law calls an advancement of a daughter in marriage …

10 Baker (1979, p 391): 'But, since there could be copulation without marriage, a mental element was also necessary. The early view, as stated by Gratian, was therefore that marriage was by agreement but became complete and indissoluble once the agreement was executed in a physical union.' The later canon law placed emphasis upon the agreement which constituted the marriage contract (see, also, Helmholz, 1974).

sufficient magnitude to negate the contract. (Ecclesiastical law, latterly secular law, distinguished between a mistake as to identity, which would avoid the marriage *ipso jure*, and mistakes as to quality which would not.)[11] Arabella knows as much: 'Every woman has a right to do such as that. The risk is hers', whilst Jude acknowledges the lifelong commitment which results: 'I quite deny it Bella. She might if no life-long penalty attached to it for the man ... but when effects stretch so far she should not go and do that which entraps a man if he is honest.' Nevertheless, Arabella's much later statement that she could not help feeling that she belonged to another more than to Jude 'since she had properly married him'[12] suggests that she apprehends the moral implications of Jude's artificially induced consent, even though the law lends no support to them; the text supplies us with sufficient detail to conclude that their marriage is otherwise a conventional and proper ceremony.

Marriage number 2: Sue and Phillotson

Sue and Phillotson also have a Church marriage; however, its orthodoxy is undermined by two factors which emotively amplify the moral offence that is being committed through the union. First, Sue and Jude (the man she really loves) undergo a bizarre mime 'rehearsal' of the marriage that is about to take place, and secondly, Jude performs the role of 'father' in giving Sue to her husband. In passing, the narrator mentions a more technically significant 'fault' in the formalities, since we are told that Sue undertakes 'a ten days' stay in the city prior to the ceremony, sufficiently representing a nominal residence of fifteen'. This formality was regulated by the Marriage Acts of 1822 and 1823, which required that the parties swear an affidavit in support of their claims as to names and residence, and even though the deceit might not have impeached the validity of the contract itself, if discovered it could have incurred a criminal charge of perjury.

Divorce number 1: Sue and Phillotson

Sue suffers from a feeling of physical aversion toward her elderly husband! That this is sexual is confirmed by Sue's act of jumping out of the window when Phillotson accidentally enters her bedroom. Sue asks Phillotson to allow her to leave him; it is understood that this will probably entail her going to live with Jude. Phillotson allows her to do so, and even shows concern about the practicalities of her departure, such as having enough to eat, enough money, etc. Subsequently, Phillotson is asked to leave his post as schoolmaster because of the social disapprobation he has incurred by 'condoning' Sue's adultery. Later, Phillotson petitions for divorce so that Sue and Jude may be free to marry.

---

11 *Moss v Moss* (1897) PD 263.
12 Hardy is being ironic, or at least reflecting Arabella's skewed workaday logic: the 'proper' marriage is bigamous.

Several issues of legal significance are raised by the narrated events. It seems likely that Sue's physical aversion has resulted from attempts to consummate the marriage: 'I have only been married a month or two ... and it is said that what a woman shrinks from – in the early days of her marriage – she shakes down to with comfortable indifference in half a dozen years'. That the marriage has been fully consummated is not entirely clear, however, from the 'evidence' in the book – whether her 'shrinking from' the intolerable has been a full or only partial retreat. Certainly, as Sue herself points out, '[n]o new interests in the shape of children have arisen'. If the marriage had not been consummated, Phillotson or Sue could have taken the alternative course of applying for annulment of the marriage. It is perhaps indicative of the incipiency of Freudian theory[13] that such cases were quite numerous in the 19th century and that law had developed a *ratio* for dealing with it. The incapacity of either party to consummate the marriage could originate, according to the law, from a disability arising from mental or moral causes, or from 'an invincible repugnance to the act of consummation with the particular man'[14] as seems to have been the case for Sue Bridehead. In the case of *G v G*,[15] the court pronounced a decree of nullity, 'although there was no structural defect in the woman'. It was stated that Mrs G '... was suffering from an excessive sensibility ... This condition was generally temporary and [the doctor, giving evidence] "had recommended soothing remedies such as morphia"'. In his musings upon the case, the Judge Ordinary echoes Sue's rueful expectations that she might become accustomed to that which she now shrinks from: 'Many difficulties of this peculiar nature, especially those which are associated with the moral feelings, pass away as time goes on ... it sometimes happens that a nervous condition has prevented consummation at first; but such a condition would be removed in the course of time.' A Dr Farre gave evidence that:

> ... her condition may be remedied, but in order that they should succeed it is necessary that she should lend herself to them. If she were to return to cohabitation, and were to refuse to take chloroform and the other remedies prescribed, I think there could be no consummation ... her condition is hysterical, and to a certain extent beyond her own control.

During the 19th century however, the law required cohabitation for three years – the *triennalis cohabitatio* – to ascertain whether the non-consummation was due to mere coyness, and to facilitate further attempts. (The chronology of Sue Bridehead's marriage suggests that a much shorter time had elapsed prior to Sue's departure; nevertheless the facts and language of the above case corroborate the depiction of Sue's mental and physical turmoil and the law's theoretical response.) The alternative mechanism of divorce thus remained the most practicable course of action. Yet this, too, was technically hazardous.

---

13 By this I mean the law's recognition of psychological justifications for non-consummation (see text to fn 10) may imply a growing awareness of the psyche as an entity.

14 *Rayden on Divorce* (1983) London: Butterworths, p 171.

15 (1871) LR 2 P & D 287 at p 291.

First, the removal of Phillotson from his teaching post because of the moral laxity he displayed in 'condoning' his wife's adultery is portrayed as a purely moral and social interdiction; however, the interdiction was also written into the law. 'Condonation', 'connivance' and 'collusion' were statutory bars to divorce, always providing that such nurturing behaviour was discoverable, either through direct evidence in court, or through the investigations of the Queen's Proctor. This intervention could occur at any time before the *decree nisi* was made absolute; the notoriety surrounding Phillotson's removal from office could certainly have given weight to such investigations. In *Goode v Goode and Hamson*,[16] the Judge Ordinary quotes the relevant statutory section:

> In case the Court ... shall find that the petitioner has, during the marriage, been accessory to or conniving at the adultery of the other party to the marriage, or has condoned the adultery complained of ... the Court shall dismiss the said petition.

Phillotson's behaviour is technically more correctly to be classified as 'connivance' rather than 'condonation', since condonation definitely took place where the husband, with knowledge of the wife's offence, should forgive her and should confirm his forgiveness by reinstating her as his wife; a 'blotting out of the offence imputed' (*Keats v Keats and Montezuma*).[17] 'Connivance' on the other hand, included:

> ... the case of a husband acquiescing in, by wilfully abstaining from taking any steps to prevent, that adulterous intercourse which, from what passes before his eyes, he cannot but believe or reasonably suspect is likely to occur ... (*Gipps v Gipps and Hume*)[18]

Phillotson himself undermines the normativity of the social interdiction with irony: 'They have requested me to send in my resignation on account of my scandalous conduct in giving my tortured wife her liberty or, as they call it, condoning her adultery.' Yet, as Jude himself indicates (in relation to the second technicality, below), obscurity has its advantage for, 'if we'd been patented nobilities we should have had infinite trouble, and days and weeks would have been spent in investigations'. As Baker points out: 'unless the prying nose of the Queen's proctor smelt collusion, the effect was virtually divorce by consent.'[19]

The second legal objection raised by the divorce petition in the case of *Phillotson v Phillotson and Fawley* is referred to by Sue herself. The ground for divorce – the only ground available under the Act of 1857 – was adultery, suggested by the fact of Sue's and Jude's cohabitation. Yet, as Sue confesses, when the decree is declared absolute: 'I have an uncomfortable feeling that my freedom has been obtained under false pretences ... if the truth about us had been known, the decree wouldn't have been pronounced.' The 'truth' to which Sue refers is the fact of her having lived with Jude, up to this point, in complete celibacy. This fact, if known would have been fatal to the decree; however the law, with a mixture of

---

16   (1861) 2 Sw & Tr at p 258.
17   (1859) 1 Sw & Tr at p 346.
18   (1864) II HLC – see Hall, 1966.
19   Baker, 1979, p 409.

perhaps pragmatism and cynicism, did not require proof of the direct fact of the adultery, but would have contented itself with 'strong surrounding circumstances'. Although 'the court must be satisfied that there was something more than opportunity before it will find that adultery has been committed; and evidence of an inclination or passion is needed in addition',[20] 'Proof of general cohabitation of the accused persons is sufficient and obviates the need to prove particular acts of adultery' (*Rutton v Rutton*).[21] Jude elaborates, 'We were not obliged to prove anything. That was their business', and a hint that a degree of complacency has become established in the availability of 'popular' secular divorce is suggested by Jude's remark that: 'however the decree may be brought about, a marriage is dissolved when it is dissolved. There is this advantage in being poor obscure people like us – that these things are done for us in a rough and ready fashion.'[22]

Divorce number 2: Jude and Arabella

After their brief and ill-started marriage, Arabella and Jude part and do not hear of one another for years. Arabella, having returned from Australia, confesses to Jude that whilst there she contracted a bigamous marriage with a man named Cartlett. She asks Jude to divorce her so that she may 'honestly and legally marry that man she has already married virtually'. Jude worries that this divorce might expose Arabella to criminal charges, but on enquiry, and since nobody knows of the bigamy 'over here', finds it will not be a difficult proceeding at all. Indeed, after he has petitioned and the decree is made absolute, he concludes: 'I was afraid her criminal second marriage would have been discovered and she punished; but nobody took any interest in her – nobody inquired, nobody suspected it.' The narrative has thus provided us with yet another covert impropriety in the legal arena, this time of criminal magnitude that, whilst not undermining the validity of the divorce itself, since Arabella has in fact committed adultery, points to a successful technical stand-off between the individual and their dealings with the mythical image of the law as a penetrative and inescapable forensic machine.

Remarriage: Sue and Phillotson

The central passion of the novel, the love between Sue and Jude, results in a tender, procreative, though impecunious and conscience-ridden, natural union.

---

20 *Rayden on Divorce* (1983) London: Butterworths, p 211.
21 (1796) 2 Hag Con 6n.
22 This suggests an interesting gloss to the commentary of academics on the subject: Baker recounts that: 'the abuses of the Victorian divorce court by society families became a scandal; formal evidence of adultery was often "provided" by the respondent and no defence was offered ...' Jude's remark might suggest that the higher profile accorded to these 'society families' was disadvantageous, and the abuses perhaps just as readily practised by the lower classes but with less detection, provided they could amass sufficient funds to apply for divorce in the first place.

Sue bears Jude three children, also caring for Jude's son by Arabella (known both as 'Little Jude' and 'Father Time'). Poverty, and anxiety about there being too many mouths to feed, leads little Jude to commit the tragic act of murdering Sue's children and then hanging himself ('Done because we are too menny'). Sue sees this as a divine judgment – 'Arabella's child killing mine was a judgment, the right slaying the wrong' – and resolves that she must correct her fault by remarrying Phillotson: 'I sacramentally joined myself to him for life. Nothing can alter it.' This marriage is, from a formal standpoint, the most technically unimpeachable. The narrative depicts a service which is a most correct and precise image of propriety:

> There they stood, five altogether: the parson, the clerk, the couple and Gillingham; and the holy ordinance was re-solemnized forthwith. In the nave of the edifice were two or three villagers, and when the clergyman came to the words 'Whom God hath joined', a woman's voice from amongst these was heard to mutter audibly: 'God hath jined indeed!' … When the books were signed the vicar congratulated the husband and wife on having performed a noble, and righteous, and mutually forgiving act. 'All's well that ends well', he said smiling. 'May you long be happy together, after thus having been "saved as by fire".'

The passage is steeped in heavy irony, since the preceding text gives ample evidence to disrupt the impression derived from pure formalities that 'all is well'. Sue is marrying Phillotson for 'self-abnegation'; she assures Jude that she does not love the older man. The mere sight of the marriage licence forces her to utter an involuntary cry of anguish; indeed, Jude feels that her state of mind borders upon insanity – 'bitter affliction came to us, and her intellect broke, and she veered round to darkness'. Phillotson too, enters the contract with the sensibility of a master bringing a recalcitrant creature to heel. He is supported in this view by his colleague Gillingham who urges: 'You must tighten the reins by degrees only. Don't be too strenuous at first. She'll come to any terms in time.' This one, and perhaps only, technically unimpeded contract is thus revealed as a travesty.[23]

Remarriage: Arabella and Jude

Broken hearted at the loss of Sue, Jude falls an easy victim to his weakness for alcohol. Arabella reappears, and feeling that Jude may yet prove to be useful as a spouse, determines to ensnare him. Carefully setting a trap, which will render him intoxicated for a period of several days, Arabella coaxes and coerces Jude, whilst still drunk, to participate as principal in a marriage service, 'though I knew you were seeing double all the time, from the way you fumbled with my finger'. Later, his sobriety returned, Jude expresses the view that both he and Sue have 'remarried out of our senses. I was gin-drunk; you were creed drunk'. Nevertheless, the narrative concludes, inexorably, that both these marriages subsist to the bitter end, with Sue herself finally to submit to consummation with

---

23 An (arguably singular) example of dissonance between the perverse personal motivations to marriage and doctrinal justifications of it, which in turn throws some doubt upon reading marriage statistics as evidence of doctrinal success.

the detested Phillotson and Jude to die neglected and despised by the callous Arabella.

The depiction of these two marriages as contractual travesties, which perpetuate a moral crime, is deliberately crafted to be a culminating and lasting memorial to the role of law in serving the logic of unreason in a world where chaos prevails. Thus it is necessary, structurally speaking, to insist that, within the interstices of 'realist' representation, the marriages would in all likelihood prevail in the world as both permanent and valid. Nevertheless, some legal commentary may give a perspective upon this authorial position, for although Jude recognises the moral injustice that the contracts create, he does not for a moment consider any legal redress, considering it only in the light of a 'mistake' that might, with Sue's agreement, justify 'running away'.

As indicated, the remarriage of Jude and Arabella is contracted whilst Jude is intoxicated. In law, the validity of the contract may be clearly impugned. If a person is induced to go though a ceremony of marriage by threats or duress, or in a state of intoxication, without any real consent to the marriage, it is invalid. Common law precedent for this principle is well established; in *Sullivan v Sullivan*[24] it was stated by Sir William Scott that:

> I will not lay it down that in no possible case can a marriage be set aside on the ground of having been effected by a conspiracy. Suppose three or four persons were to combine to effect such a purpose by intoxicating another, and marrying him in that perverted state of mind, this Court would not hesitate to annul a marriage with a clear proof of such a case with such an effect. Not many other cases occur to me in which the co-operation of other persons to produce a marriage can be so considered, if the party was not in a state of disability, natural or artificial, which created a want of reason or volition amounting to an incapacity to consent.

The judge is thus locating intoxication as the *locus classicus* within a range of nullifying factors. Yet Jude never considers seeking a remedy.

Similarly, Sue's mental instability at the time of her remarriage to Phillotson is capable of undermining her ability to consent; it is born of grief bordering upon insanity. Jude describes the contract as a 'fanatic prostitution' and Sue persuades herself that the marriage will somehow atone for the death of her children; they were 'sin-begotten. They were sacrifices to teach me how to live! – their death was the first stage of my purification. That's why they have not died in vain!' That her motive in marrying is self-immolatory is illustrated by her rending her wedding night gown, tearing the linen into strips and laying the pieces in the fire, crying, 'It signifies what I don't feel!', and the Widow Edlin's comment that 'She's forcing herself to it, poor dear little thing, and you've no notion what she's suffering!'. Such behaviour could well be brought as evidence of such instability as to undermine the ability to form a valid consent to the contract, so founding a suit of nullity. (However, the rationale of the novel accords with the failure to pursue this avenue – the petitioner would classically be a husband who wishes to rid himself of an encumbrance – Phillotson has every reason to sustain the bond, however

---

24 (1818) 2 Hag Con 258.

bizarre its underlying features.) Nevertheless, a court of the time would have quite blithely tolerated the recounting of such events as evidence of insanity. In the case of *Durham v Durham*,[25] the Earl of Durham petitioned for a declaration of nullity of his marriage with the Countess of Durham, by reason that at the time of the celebration of the ceremony she was of unsound mind and incapable of contracting marriage. Sir J Hannen stated that the contract of marriage:

> … is expanded in the promises of the marriage ceremony by words having reference to the natural relations which spring from that engagement, such as protection on the part of the man, and submission on the part of the woman … a mere comprehension of the words of the promises exchanged is not sufficient. The mind of one of the parties may be capable of understanding the language used, but may yet be affected by such delusions, or other symptoms of insanity.

The Countess of Durham's history had in some respects been similar to that of Sue Bridehead:

> The evidence satisfies me that the respondent's affections had been fixed upon a gentleman whom she knew before the petitioner … Lord Durham naturally complains that when his proposal had been accepted, Miss Milner (as she was then) did not return his kiss, and that neither then, nor at any other time, did any word of endearment pass her lips.

Further, that the day before the engagement, her dress:

> … in some way or other, took fire, and she sustained a burn on her chest. The respondent made little of it, changed her dress and rejoined the company without complaining of pain … evidence of her insensibility to pain which, it said, was not without a bearing on her mental condition …

Despite the court's knowledge of the Countess's tortured loyalties regarding her first love, evidence of her mental instability included the suggestion that:

> The respondent's coldness and reticence to Lord Durham after their engagement is so unnatural in the circumstances that it is evidence of a deranged intellect. Lord Durham states that she avoided walking near him, shrinking from him, and walking on the grass border of the path at Lambton in order to keep away from him.

In the case of *Hunter v Edney*,[26] a husband petitioned for nullity of marriage stating that:

> On the morning of the marriage she received him very coldly, and was continually rubbing her hands, and at first refused to be dressed for church, and after the wedding to change her dress to go away. All day long, and on the journey to London, she was quite quiet, and when [they] arrived at their apartments she refused to have supper … She lay down on the bed in her clothes, and for three hours refused to undress, and in the morning asked her husband to cut her throat. The marriage was not consummated. In the morning a medical man was called in, who pronounced her to be insane …

---

25   (1885) PD 80. The ensuing two to three paragraphs provide a snapshot of the detailed study in Chapter 8 of this book.
26   (1885) PD 92.

These cases are of course worthy of attention as 'literary' and cultural, as well as legal, texts. The condensation of lives, comments and behaviour into the legal format reveals a still, a hazy daguerreotype of the legal subject, dimly glimpsed through the *camera obscura* of the law. The detachment of legal language contributes to the distancing, the atrophy of the subjects' identity and humanity; the Countess of Durham's emotional bond with another man becomes 'the respondent's affections'. That these emotions are in some sense illegitimate in the eyes of the court is conveyed though the notion of evidence, not merely incidental, but 'satisfying' – comprehensive and replete. These affections are depicted not as natural and fluid, but hysterical, adulatory, 'fixed'. The Countess of Durham's voice is unheard, though we hear the muted and injured tones of Lord Durham, with whom the judge sympathises; his complaint is after all 'natural', the weight of evidence cumulative and conclusive 'neither then, nor at any other time'. Even heroic self-restraint in not complaining of pain is capable of being transmuted by legal alchemy into potential evidence of insanity. Clearly, the most blatant medical and legal metamorphosis is affected through the depiction of 'coldness and reticence' as 'evidence of a deranged intellect'.[27] Similarly, one can only speculate as to the social coercions which must have brought the respondent in *Hunter v Edney* to such a state of resistance and anxiety. It would appear that the petitioner did not attempt to evince any sense of the reasons for her behaviour, which was clearly indicative of massive conflict paralleled today only by the unwilling female victims of arranged marriages. The description of Sue's behaviour accords chillingly with the images culled from the cases. In law the assumption was inevitably that the undemonstrative, anxious and reticent female subject must necessarily be insane; in *Jude* we see the influences, the potency of religious and cultural coercion, which contributed to such behaviour. The conclusion evinced in the reader is that the culture itself is insane, the besieged female merely a vehicle for the insanity. It is clear that Sue Bridehead could as easily have been dealt with, had the purposes of plot called for her disposal. The text's criticism of cultural insanity is arguably even more potent where feminine suffering is primarily self-destructive and, thus, does not incur husbandly unease. Sue's 'consent' to the

---

27 This is an issue that is deserving of more comprehensive research. Certainly writers of medical tracts in the Victorian period were (predictably) ready to make poorly corroborated diagnoses of women's mental illness. Henry Maudsley, in *The Physiology of Mind* (1876) wrote: 'The weaker the conscious factors in mental function, the more power have the unconscious factors, as we plainly see by the examples of women and of children, of persons labouring under sickness and of those who are dying ...' Roger Smith (1981) notes: 'the network of correspondences between woman, nature, passivity, emotion and irresponsibility.' Victorian medical texts of authority reveal a bizarre mixture of apparently 'objective' scientific analysis, eroticism and outright misogyny. In the *Journal of Psychological Medicine and Mental Pathology* (1851, Part 4) an article, entitled 'Woman in her psychological relations', refers to woman as organism: 'of all animals, woman has the most acute faculties; and when we consider how much these may be exalted by the influences of the reproductive organs, there is not much ground for surprise at the grotesque forms which cunning assumes in the hysterical female.' The article goes on to explain how woman's behaviour is affected by '... ovarian irritation, burst[ing] us, false, malicious, devoid of affection, thievish in a thousand petty ways, bold – may be erotic, self-willed and quarrelsome ... what seems to be vice, but is really moral insanity. Dr Laycock, we are happy to learn, has been able to treat cases of this kind with perfect success, by a course of galvanism directed through the ovaria, and by suitable medication and moral and hygienic treatment ...'.

marriage contract, clearly questionable on legal and ethical grounds, thus remains on record as perfectly valid.

The legal and literary historian will, I hope, have taken some pleasure in the contextualisation and juxtaposition of contemporary legal issues and case law. However, apart from making us technically more informed readers of the novel, what can this retrieval exercise teach us about the law? One of the most tantalising questions is, to what extent was Hardy's use of technically significant legal issues deliberate? Certainly there are instances that demonstrate a conscious utilisation of the law. Taking each event independently, we may ruminate upon their effect.

Arabella's 'fraud' concerning her pregnancy is properly understood within the text as not justiciable; however its potential for wreaking ruin clearly locates it as a moral crime, which the law could not or would not address. Sue's 'casual' attitude to the residency requirements before her marriage to Phillotson may serve several purposes: to illustrate the casual attitude sustained by individual citizens towards particularly 'bureaucratic' formalities; to illustrate, in particular, the likelihood that an emancipated, educated citizen such as Sue would see such requirements clearly and without embellishment as mere formalities, to be adhered to with only a modicum of concern; or to suggest an unconscious psychological 'resistance' in Sue to the prospect of marriage with Phillotson, contributing contextually to her growing sense of unease and ambivalence. Sue's failure to justify the accusation of adultery at the time of Phillotson's divorce petition serves a narrative purpose, confirming her extreme fastidiousness and moral anguish. The branding of her as an adulteress reveals the law as an inexact science, with a brutalising tendency to assume the worst; an inversion of the principle that the accused is innocent until proven guilty. Phillotson's act of 'collusion' (though not pursued to its legal conclusion in the text) is shown to be a humane and conscientious act; contemporaneous law's utilisation of such an empathic stance as a 'bar' to divorce at a time when adultery was the only ground, highlights the law's blindness to the extenuating motive driving the apparent contradiction of 'collusion'. Arabella's divorce from Jude, tainted as it is by the knowledge that her relationship has not been merely adulterous, but bigamous, demonstrates her essential pragmatism, and locates her entry to the 'new world' culture (Australia) where the tough material conditions, demographic mobility and resultant lack of sentiment, foster an attitude of casual acquiescence to such crimes. Law's institutional elevation of bigamy to the grave status of crime with its implication of moral turpitude is of little consequence to commoners, except as a potential complication that must be evaded by stealth.

Jude's intoxication during his remarriage to Arabella would clearly have negated his consent and nullified the contract; nevertheless he lives out his remaining life in apathetic acceptance of the daily misery that the formal pact has thrust upon him. This supports the textual treatment of Jude's overall decline and his psychic descent into passive fatalism. Conjecturally, so many unrecorded 'real' lives must have suffered the same fate.

Sue's marriage to Phillotson is detailed as perfectly correct in form, whilst the reader is left in no doubt that it is a travesty. Jude's comment that she was 'out of her senses' and 'creed drunk' suggests a state of mind capable of negating her contractual consent.[28] That this is not developed as a legal issue may simply be in order to serve greater narrative concerns, for example the chilling and permanent effectiveness of this use of marriage by Sue as an instrument of self destruction. In addition, it underscores the contingent and incidental relationship that the law has to its proclaimed pursuit of justice. The potential negativing factor of Sue's mental condition remains unseen by the gaze of law and, as the contemporaneous caselaw demonstrates, law's involvement in such cases was instrumental in promoting abuses of power through conjecture and bigotry. Such judgments must have held undocumented and tragic consequences for their victims, delivering formal justice to the extent of recognising the absence of a valid consent, whilst condoning the substantive injustice – the branding of women, subject to impossible cultural constraints, as insane. In addition, Sue's repugnance to the act of consummation with Phillotson is contextually justified by their being ill-matched in terms of age and disposition, and by her extreme sense of delicacy: even with Jude, a 'twin soul', her sensibilities create some obstacle to simple enjoyment of her sexuality. However, Victorian values were creative of the dilemma; 'womanhood' was the 'empty signifier' filled with the social valuation placed upon piety, purity and submission. Women frequently came to the marriage bed not as participants, even less as equal contracting parties, but as victims. Jude himself succumbs at times to the rhetorical force of this cultural gloss: 'I seduced you … you were a distinct type – a refined creature, intended by Nature to be left intact.' Having received these values from infancy, and often being kept in ignorance, or given representations of sexuality as the bestial manifestation of man's basest instincts, it is little wonder that Victorian caselaw is studded (am I guilty of a Freudian slip?) with the issue of non-consummation. Yet what the caselaw, as cited, reveals is a zealous readiness to impute insanity where the bride's nervousness resulted in slightly eccentric or ambivalent behaviour, or she (quite understandably) refused to undress. The patriarchal call for the administration of chloroform to remedy such resistance, and allow penetration to take place presumably whilst the bride was insensible, was symptomatic of the sickness of the culture, fully supported by the law.[29] This instance of the court tolerating the suggestion that one of the contracting parties should be rendered unconscious in order to facilitate the fulfilment of a contractual term, is surely one of the most unprincipled events in the history of the law of contract. Materially it

---

28 In *Allcard v Skinner* (1887) 36 Ch D, the Court of Appeal returned to the petitioner money that she had donated to a sisterhood while a novice, on the ground that the gift had been voidable by reason of undue influence, which interfered with the donor's ability to exercise free will. Lindley LJ stated that the equitable doctrine of undue influence had been developed '… by the necessity of grappling with insidious forms of spiritual tyranny … of all influences religious influence is the most dangerous and most powerful …'. Jude's assessment of Sue's condition as 'creed drunk', neatly summarises her seduction by fanatic dogmatism. It is one thing to uphold that a gift of money has been so obtained, quite another to suggest that the 'sacramental' pact of marriage, culturally and institutionally entrenched, might come to have the brooding power of an 'insidious form' of spiritual tyranny.

29 The Judge Ordinary from *G v G* did not at any time question or doubt the recommendations of the medical men; however he did assert that forcible penetration could not be countenanced: 'Is he by mere brute force to oblige his wife to submit to connection? Every one must reject such an idea.' (But, see text to fn 26.)

is an accurate reflection, a chilling exposure of the subliminal rationale of the contract. The promises in the marriage ceremony, the exchange of rings, the mutual worship of bodies, suggest reciprocity. Militating against these soothing palliatives are the sinister overtones of the word 'submission'. Conjugal rights were both a culturally supported 'rite' and a right. Lord Hale, in *The History of the Pleas of the Crown*, laid down in the 18th century that:

> ... the husband cannot be guilty of a rape committed by himself upon his lawful wife, for by their mutual matrimonial consent and contract the wife hath given up herself in this kind unto her husband, which she cannot retract.

Until 1884 in Britain, a wife could be jailed for refusing conjugal rights and, until 1891, husbands were allowed to imprison their wives in the matrimonial home to obtain their rights.[30] Thus the administration of chloroform would have been a humane method of facilitating specific performance of the contract, which otherwise could lawfully have been concluded brutally. Both symbolically and materially, the chloroform would have conjured the effacement of feminine autonomy, of identity, which had already been officially effected through matrimonial rites: the chemical inducement of an expedient and tantalisingly malleable degree of 'submission' as prescribed both by the medical and legal fraternities. The male bastion of medical science was quick to recommend the use of this virtually untried nostrum – how 'modern' to be able to neutralise incongruous feminine resistance through the beautiful symmetry of science. As we have seen, in *G v G*, Mrs G objected, with unseemly selfishness, to the administration of chemical correctives as potentially injurious to her health; the court did not respond to this tentative note of insurrection.[31]

Little wonder that Sue Bridehead is consumed by guilt for her inconvenient resistance. Consummation was, after all, a term of the contract, and by the end of *Jude*, when Sue's sanity is in question, she is all the more able to digest these values and see her prior inability to consummate the marriage with Phillotson as a grave breach of contract. The only remedy is to renew the contract, and this time strictly adhere to the terms ('I have nearly brought my body into complete subjection').[32]

---

30 Pateman, 1988, p 123.
31 In the course of his judgment, the Judge Ordinary concluded:

> The absence of a physical structural defect cannot be sufficient to render a marriage valid if it be shown that connection is practically impossible, or even if it be shewn that it is only practicable after a remedy has been applied which the husband cannot enforce, and which the wife, whether wilfully or acting under the influence of hysteria, is determined not to submit to.

The choice of words – 'wilfully' and 'hysteria' – is in itself telling: at no time does the Judge Ordinary acknowledge that Mrs G might be justified in resisting treatment which she thought dangerous to her health and life.

32 Looking towards a fictive totalitarian future, Margaret Atwood (1987) charts the cultural normalisation of the wholesale 'consumption' of women, and their inability to resist this devolution when their identity as object effaces any viable claim to subjecthood. It is interesting to consider the extent to which this image is not merely a nightmare vision of a totalitarian future, but can be retrieved from the normative texts of the literary and legal canons.

The broader insights derived from this analysis of the law in *Jude* thus take on a jurisprudential significance. Historically, the attempt to loosen the mordant stranglehold of canon law, and provide access to 'divorce for all' through secular machinery was attenuated by the moral and doctrinal spectre of attributing 'fault', which haunted Sue personally, and distorted legal usage. Since the ground for divorce was limited to the narrow scope of adultery (presumably it was feared that a wider variety of grounds would have 'opened the floodgates' to a tide of divorce petitions, so contributing to the moral disintegration of society), petitioners seeking a divorce were forced to be economical, or just plain misleading, with the facts. Note, again, Baker's comment that: '[t]he abuses of the Victorian divorce court by society families became a scandal; formal evidence of adultery was often "provided" by the respondent ...'[33] The 'bars' to divorce, collusion, condonation and so on, were no doubt considered by their legal advocates to be an effective form of resistance to such 'abuse'. Yet Hardy's depiction of Phillotson's charitable release of Sue evinces a view of 'collusion', in contrast to its harsh moral overtones, as creating a potential abuse of the individual by the law. Driven by the purest moral imperatives, yet forced to untie the contract by attributing blame, petitioners such as Phillotson would have been roundly castigated for pleading the fault since their prior behaviour fell short of Victorian expectations of spousal wrath and instead indicated sympathy with the errant partner bordering upon a 'sinful' tolerance.[34] *Jude* itself was to suffer an ignominious fate at the hands of public and critical opinion: the novel's 'collusion' in condoning cohabitation outside of marriage was vilified as immoral. This acted as a successful 'bar' to Hardy's continued petitioning of the public – *Jude* was his last novel. Modern law generally, and the marriage contract in particular, still suffer from the 'mortmain' of moral values, so at variance with social practice as to produce doctrinal schizophrenia. (In the novel itself, the replacement of the canonical contract with a purely bureaucratic machinery, housed in the registry office, was portrayed as having failed to meet the need for some recognition of the profoundly spiritual element of the pact, and thus Sue's and Jude's attempts to marry one another failed.)

Social histories and juristic surveys provide us with statistics on the development and use of the law; fiction can remind us not only of the incidence and outcome of this use, but also of the many instances when it remains lost to recorded law, unused, or fails the purported aims of its usage. Locating 'real', technical legal events within an emotive and aesthetic framework is a form of 'law in action' that pure theory, however elegant, cannot explore. The vision of law as facilitator, cultivated particularly through the eyes of positivists, is interrogated by the event. In *Jude*, the law is a disembodied entity with a rationale which impinges accidentally upon the life of the individual, if at all. Contingent upon so many factors, the intervention of fate, ignorance, desire, malice or guile, the law is as likely to forge injustice as it is to do justice. In this 'real' world, Hart's penumbra of uncertainty, the hard case, derives from the point of origin; it is an effect, not a

---

33 Baker, 1979, p 409.
34 Whether divorce can be designed on a completely 'no fault' basis is still a contentious issue for some.

cause, of the law. The aesthetics of fiction reveal that the mechanism of law, distant and remote, is considered rarely by the citizen as a viable medium for resolving either theoretical or practical conundrums; and when, through a precipitous, imperfect filtration process the citizen 'receives' the law, its mutated form is already ripe for personal exploitation, morbid devolution or wholesale reconstitution. Since the law is used to police the values of the citizen as well as serve their needs, the citizen may be forced to avoid its facilities when their own moral code departs from the law's dictat. Caught between its proclaimed adherence to a synthetic ethical code and an intrinsic denial of passion, the law of marriage – the law – subsists in an uneasy limbo between order and chaos, the general and the particular, and forms of human flourishing are as likely to be hampered as fostered by its use.[35]

CONCLUSION

Putting aside the intriguing technical legal-historical and social commentary upon marriage and divorce provided in *Jude*, the crucial surviving message of the book for modern thought derives from the depiction of the characters of Jude and his partner Sue. Though current society has been confronted with countless challenges to orthodoxy, this message survives as somewhat radical and novel. It is simply this: that cohabitees may choose cohabitation over marriage as a conscientious strategy – they may be 'virtuous cohabitants'. Jude and (especially) Sue are wholly aware of the fact that the spiritual and sentimental bases of marriage are easily colonised by a base and heartless state machinery, paving the way for invidious, deceitful journeys through marriage as well as divorce.

Current academic and political debate upon trends in marriage and cohabitation remains remarkably shy of such a possibility. Though discussions envisage possible new models of partnership, the focus upon public- and private-law repercussions becomes absorbed by doctrinal prognostication. Valuable and politically aware, such discussions may nevertheless lose sight of the meaningful identification process that must accompany effective change. In discussing the future possibilities for 'cohabitation contracts and the democratisation of personal relations', Kingdom (2000) provides a striking critique of current and potential reformulations of the notion of contract underlying domestic partnership, highlighting the possibility of a 'relational' contract model which can adapt to individual and changing needs and inequalities (Kingdom, 2000, p 20). The resultant potential diminution in the influence of rigidly commercial, mercantile models for private contract would be welcome – Hardy's text recognises the reduction in human values and dignity attendant upon such models. Most dramatically, Kingdom's enumeration of the elements forming an 'immorality

---

35 The characters in *Jude the Obscure* attempt to mediate this collision between the law and the individual through the range of discourses available to them, the tempered and *extempore*: the resultant rhetorical excursus upon the law, in particular the law of marriage, may be reserved for separate treatment.

doctrine' (Kingdom, 2000, p 7)[36] derived from classical contract law, ties directly to the assumptions Hardy so forcefully disrupts. Any uniformity imposed by such law presupposes citizens ruled by base motives and instincts. Yet, though Kingdom's analysis corresponds to Hardy's in this regard, paving the way to greater equality and autonomy between partners, it does not extend to empowerment prefiguring a visionary, proud emancipation. By implication, Hardy's figures, dignified and heroic in their quest for an ethical union, suggest just this, symbolising a new 'morality doctrine' – to counter the current 'immorality doctrine' – of honesty, family and civic responsibility, if only permitted to be so. Radical for its time, the model might herald something akin to the Scandinavian poise of social liberation coupled with private and civic duty. In particular, modern scholarship tends to overlook the central influence of 'lost' religious values that, coupled with the failure on the part of civic structures to offer a spiritually meaningful secular replacement, lends further fragmentation to already piecemeal notions of civic partnership.[37]

---

36 Kingdom's summary of the components of the immorality doctrine identifies eight components: the presumption that contracting cohabitants are sexually involved; the presumption that this sexual involvement is the object of the consideration for which is the basis of all the other clauses in the contract; the presumption that the said sexual involvement takes the form of heterosexual intercourse; the presumption that this heterosexual intercourse takes place between men and women who are not married to each other; the definition of this heterosexual intercourse as an act of prostitution; the designation of prostitution as illicit sexual intercourse, where 'illicit' typically means 'not authorised by law or custom'; the inclusion of illicit sexual intercourse in the category of immoral actions; and the inclusion of immoral actions in the category of illegal actions.

37 For example, Kingdom's critique, exemplary in its analysis of contractual histories and repercussions, barely mentions this crucial role of religious ideology as a vehicle not only of political, but also spiritual, power.

CHAPTER 8

EXPERT EVIDENCE, INSANITY, NULLITY – MEDICO-LEGAL STORIES OF FEMALE INSANITY: THREE NULLITY SUITS

INTRODUCTION

The article produced in this chapter 'grew' from the preceding study of the law in *Jude the Obscure*. In sifting through the late 19th century cases relating to marriage law, the three cases that follow in this chapter served not only to illustrate a broad context of discourses concerning women, marriage and subjection in relation to *Jude*, but also presented themselves as richly deserving of separate attention in their own right.[1] Rich in the terrific untold drama playing out in each case, they seemed forlorn in having tales of such personal tragedy embedded within the formalities of evidence and doctrine, demanding to be resurrected and permitted a different hearing for their plight. Such is the context to these Victorian cases – recorded as mere examples of the doctrine of nullity of marriage – but actually revealing, despite rhetorics of sincerity and sympathy, disturbing prejudices in judicial and medical mores. Here are real tragedies in the lives scrutinised, with secret 'inner' lives whose silencing by the prevailing culture only served to enhance the tragic turn. Blinking in the light of day, these figures insisted upon a new telling of their stories, a new reading of their cases. In so doing, the cases provide a snapshot in the history of evidence and medical pathologies, denoting the cultural drives, still relevant today, in the detection of illness.[2] Current events and scholarship maintain several topical links of direct relevance to these cases. First, psychiatry continues to operate within a regime of unfolding new pathologies, though sometimes with a broad sensibility of the tension between those aspects of illness which may be 'scientifically' or 'biologically' corroborated, and alterations in social and medical cultures that 'feed' certain evaluations over others. Secondly, this phenomenon presents particular difficulties for the law, since psychiatric evaluations impinge upon so many principles of central importance to the law – of capacity, competence, responsibility and so on. Thirdly,

---

1   At an early stage in the experience of producing scholarship, this event served to demonstrate the extent to which research and scholarship had, and has, a 'life of its own' such that three cases of apparently peripheral relevance to an initial study insist upon a swerve of attention. Such experience is heady. The cases were exciting as well as poignant – down the years they had received virtually no academic attention, emerging from the Victorian reports as a rich, yet forlorn and neglected, 'archival' phenomenon.

2   As an example of modern medical evidence cases in the wider domain, see 'Experts in the dock', *The Guardian*, 4 February 2004, for an account of the review of expert evidence prompted by recent doubtful identifications of 'cot death' cases. For doubt concerning the ready diagnosis of psychiatric conditions in general, see www.mentalhealth law.co.uk/ukanpd.htm; for concerns regarding the ambit of the Mental Health Bill – and the impact on civil liberties debates – see discussions at www.liberty-human-rights.org.uk. This chapter first appeared in (1998) 1(1) Feminist Legal Studies.

these factors continue to raise particular difficulties when psychiatric questions and legal questions impinge upon issues of gender. Finally, all these factors are players in a crucial current debate linking law, scholarship and the professions generally, that is, the status and reliability of expert evidence. In Britain, the debate has been rekindled by high profile miscarriages of justice where the fault was revealed to lie with representations made by experts and later discredited.[3] Such cases exemplify the difficulties raised by the implicit credibility accorded to persons of elevated status, as well as the notion of scientifically verifiable 'fact'; but the difficulties extend further – to our understanding of the role played by subtle cultural change, and also that played by the 'slippage' between cultural production and cultural product, where doctor and patient, witness and subject, become such products, their interactions so much the outcome of invisible processes of reception.

A recent article by Metzl (2003) provides an example. Discussing the 'psychodynamics of psychotropic advertising', Metzl explores alterations in medical cultures through the latter half of the 20th century (specifically alterations in attitudes towards women and illness) taken up and elaborated in the advertising of psychotropic drugs. Placed alongside the nullity cases, the article amplifies an already discernible vision – of cases epitomising not only the shortcomings of their own time, nor simply part of an ongoing history of medical and gender cultures, but a place in a tapestry of ideological and political, as well as medical and legal, cultures. Metzl's review of links between specific representations of women, illness and marital status chimes eerily. Where in the nullity cases a 'drooping head' and awkward 'picking of fingers' could prefigure a finding of insanity, Metzl recounts that, in the pharmaceutical advertisements of the early 1960s:

> [t]he married woman was not only the victim of mental illness, she was the cause of it as well ... even the least astute professional surely would have noticed that the unmedicated woman to the left of the doctor appears to demonstrate the conventions of psychoneurotic distress. Her brow for example, is markedly furrowed, her gaze nervous and indirect, and her hand clutches her heart as if she is in throes of painful emotion ... (Metzl, 2003, p 85)

Meanwhile, the image of the expert medical witness is redolent too, not just of a classical stance of authority, but of the pre-emptive position of judgment:

> From his position behind the desk the physician is clearly allowed to gaze at the patient with what [an] art historian calls the 'socially legitimated, historically specific socially and psychically produced look, the non-innocent look of culture ...' (Metzl, 2003, pp 86–87)[4]

---

3   See fn 2.
4   Metzl's description is consistent with many feminist critiques – he continues:
      The woman patient, in the less powerful position of object, is therefore defined in opposition to the doctor's medically legitimated gaze ... with the meticulously constructed image the woman quite purposefully holds up her left hand ... that wedding ring features prominently on these hands [and] shores up a woman's place in a cosmology ... The wedding ring in the Deprol advertisement however is quite problematically meant to have exactly the opposite narrative effect: rather than being a symbol of closure and resolution, it is a locus of ambiguity ... [it] ironically implies that the married woman is the source of a mental illness ... unable to fulfil her socially determined role ... (ibid).

The trajectory from consultation to politics is thus swift and complete. Metzl's analysis goes on to discuss the link between female emancipation and the social hostility all too ready to identify independence and unconventional behaviour as symptomatic of illness, whether in married or unmarried women. This again echoes the Victorian cases, where there were instances of notable spirited independence prior to marriage, apparently 'broken' upon marriage. The persistence of the steady psychiatric gaze described by Metzl underscores the aggressively cyclical dominance of this *locus* of 'witnessing' experts, and the concomitant effective silencing of the observed subject. To some extent then, not only must the cycles of medical cultures be brought into question, but some discursive purchase gained to recover the silenced subject. Professional discussions explore the difficulties encountered by psychiatry in engaging with subjects in its treatment of victims of trauma (see, for example, Larrabee *et al*, 2003, p 354):

> Where the meaning of one's life is disrupted, what words can be found? ... the feeling of a chaos of seemingly unutterable experiences collapsing into that 'wordless nothing' ...

Though recognising the need to promote a more effective 'intersubjective' dialogue, consciously striving to break the bonds of prior constructions,[5] such scholarship, falls short of engaging with the problem of the 'illegitimate' claim. In other words, though perhaps ready to modify its sensitivity to the subject in order to facilitate the subjective discourse, such analysis must still work within its conceptions of what 'counts' as trauma and symptoms of trauma – in the first place a socially and medically constructed phenomenon. For the women at the centre of the 'nullity' cases, 'silence' was necessitated by the absence of social and linguistic structures capable of 'hearing' their stories – ironically, then, 'silence' was sanity writ large.

In an article entitled 'Faulty judgment, expert opinion and decision-making capacity',[6] Silberfeld and Checkland (1999, pp 377–78) explore modern assessments of decision-making capacity, concluding that:

> ... assessors' uses of diagnostic information is frequently not up to the task of bridging the inferential gap in a justifiable way [and that] the requisite expertise to be developed in the long term [should be] a distinct multidisciplinary endeavour ... Statutes or the courts often take the judgement of an expert witness, without any wide agreement regarding who possesses the relevant expertise.

Such sensitivity to the task is to be welcomed, though agreeing an appropriate interdisciplinary *locus* for expertise in relation to the widely differing contexts

---

5   As elaborated by Larrabee *et al* (2003, p 355), by Bakhtin's theory of dialogic interaction and utterance, with the realisation that 'the speaker is already taking cognizance in some way of the actual listener and thus is framing language according to certain expectations about or held by *that* listener'.

6   It would seem that whilst the title is meant to refer to the diagnosis of faulty judgment in the medical and legal subject, it bears an ironic reference to the *imposition* of faulty judgment *upon* the subject.

calling for expert opinion in the courtroom could exacerbate difficulties and create justifiable fears of substantive inconsistency. The realisation that 'the issues of who are experts and how they should be selected and have their evidence assessed are … pressing matters'[7] only touches upon the enormity of the questions facing us.

THE THREE NULLITY CASES

'Who breaks a butterfly upon a wheel?'[8]

The members of the medical profession have long and anxiously endeavoured to frame a definition of insanity, which is an attempt in a few words to exhibit the essential character of this disorder; so that it may be recognised when it exists; – these efforts have been hitherto fruitless, nor is there any rational expectation that this desideratum will be speedily accomplished. The Lawyer has taken a different view of the subject: he has been little solicitous to become acquainted with the physiological distinctions of disordered intellect, or the causes producing such state: – these he has confided to the medical evidence to explain …

John Haslam MD, *Medical Jurisprudence as it Relates to Insanity*
According to the Law of England (1817)[9]

As explained, this chapter explores three Victorian actions for nullity of marriage. The three cases share a common theme in that all were cases of husbands pleading nullity on the ground that their wives were insane at the time of marriage, thus vitiating the ability to give a valid consent to the contract. To the judges of the day, the basis of the inquiry seemed clear – that the court ensure that the evidential burden of proving insanity was discharged before a decree of nullity could be declared. Yet, to modern eyes, the cases present tantalising cues to cultural currents and influences, which at the very least cast doubt over the apparent simplicity of the question the court asks of itself and its witnesses.

The professions of medicine and law have known intimate and troubled relationships with the concept of insanity. Theories of insanity – particularly female insanity – raise issues of narrative and authorship, which are central to the feminist critique of history, the production of ideology, and of notions of 'truth'. It is hoped that these three cases contribute a small, perhaps singular, fragment to the debate.

The first section of this chapter will recount the cases in some detail. Subsequently, undercurrents and themes – meta-narratives – are explored, finally linking to modern feminist evaluations of medical doctrine. The cases are as replete with examples of great and petty unconscious tyrannies, as with the glimpses of individual tragedy they yield.

---

7   See Allan Levy QC, (2004) *The Guardian*, 20 January, 'Value of experts and their evidence must be questioned if justice is to be done'.

8   Alexander Pope, *Epistle to the Earl of Oxford and Earl Mortimer* (1721), reproduced in *The Oxford Dictionary of Quotations* (3rd edn) (1990) Oxford: OUP.

9   London: Hunter, pp 62–63.

In the history of the law of marriage, the nullity suit has experienced a chequered career. As with most legal doctrines, fluctuations, both in the use of actions and grounds pleaded, derive from changes in social and cultural mores – changes which may be reflected in relaxations of law, or legislative prohibitions. So, for the legal historian, a sudden rise or fall in the use of particular actions may itself produce a 'master narrative'.[10] Stone[11] narrates several such correlations in the career of the nullity suit: for example, he explains that, 'by the early nineteenth century there was an increase in the number of nullity cases brought on technicalities (for prior legislation had created several petty technical grounds for annulment) "which created a scandal by giving the appearance of being the equivalent of divorces. As a result of this evidence, in 1823, Parliament passed an act amending the 1753 Marriage Act so as to block this avenue to easy divorce"'.[12] Here, the master narrative appears to be the 'linear' relationship between legislative 'prohibitions' and the increase in actions. A 'meta-narrative', only hinted by Stone, is the fact that this increase reflected a societal appetite for accessible divorce – the 'prohibition' thus becoming reconstituted as a permission.

Stone's survey takes us to the mid-19th century. This chapter is concerned with three of the cases that were reported in the later 1800s. The second half of the 18th century is generally most notable for the relative liberalisation of the law of divorce through the Matrimonial Causes Act of 1857. Again, this period reflects a distinctive pattern in the grounds pleaded in nullity suits – of cases reported in the probate and divorce reports in the period 1865–90, three cases cite irregularities in formality requirements, two concern marriages within the prohibited degrees, and one cites duress vitiating consent. In the same period, 14 cases cite impotence as a nullifying factor – seven cases of male impotence, seven female. In the midst of these cases, there quite abruptly appear the three cases pleading insanity in the wife as the nullifying factor. At first glance, the three arrest attention as a poignant oddity in the fabric of later-Victorian private law; on reflection, they may appear intimately connected to the more numerous counterparts pleading impotence.

Within the three cases there is also a pattern of master- and meta-narratives, which to some extent reflects this link in the interplay of social norms operating at the time; social norms which were repressive of women and lead to a tragic outcome for the three female respondents – three butterflies, broken upon a wheel.

Case number 1: *Hunter v Edney* otherwise *Hunter*[13]

In this case, the parties were of modest social standing. The petitioner was an organ builder, the respondent the daughter of an innkeeper. Nothing untoward

---

10 This term is used to denote a narrative model which hypothesises the (apparently dominant) external factors that direct a particular outcome.

11 Stone, 1990.

12 Stone, 1990, p 152.

13 (1881) X PD 93.

was apparent in the behaviour of the respondent prior to the marriage, except perhaps that there may have been untold significance in the fact that she attempted to postpone the marriage. By the morning of the marriage, however, the respondent was showing signs of distress:

> She received him very coldly, and was continually rubbing her hands, and at first refused to be dressed for church, and after the wedding to change her dress to go away. All day long, and on the journey to London, she was quite quiet, and when they arrived at their apartments she refused to have supper, and said that she did not want to get married, and that she was false. She lay down on the bed in her clothes, and for three hours refused to undress, and in the morning asked her husband to cut her throat. The marriage was not consummated. In the morning a medical man was called in, who pronounced her to be insane ...[14]

Since the depositions recorded the respondent's strange behaviour as dating at least from the morning of the marriage, the judge, Sir J Hannen, concluded that the respondent had not been the mistress of her mind at the time of the marriage contract but instead '... took an entirely morbid and diseased view of it'.[15] The case for nullity was therefore established. The respondent's condition was referable to 'evidence of her manner', which established '... that excitement had been set up by the idea of her approaching marriage'.[16] Earlier in his judgment, Sir J Hannen commented, 'whether it was the effect of insanity or not, it is certain she exhibited the greatest repugnance to entering upon the condition of a married woman'[17] and that, since her mother had testified that the respondent '... has always been a well conducted and virtuous young woman', it was 'obvious that the respondent must have been labouring under a morbid delusion and imagining things that never existed; – that she had committed some crime, that she was so wicked that she was unfit to be married to an honest man'.[18]

In addition, the evidence of Dr Savage, who visited the respondent after her marriage, carried much weight. Dr Savage, the senior physician of the Bethlehem Hospital, reported that:

> In my opinion the patient is suffering from melancholia, owing in the first instance to hereditary insanity excited by the idea of marriage. I should think she was of unsound mind at the time of the marriage, as her actions point to a complete change of character and disposition. She shewed an unreasonable aversion to the lover of her own choice; she thought herself unfaithful, which is not true, fit to go to prison, and unworthy to live ... The patient may probably recover, but be liable to a relapse; and if she have children may probably have recurrences of melancholia and transmit the insane tendency.[19]

---

14 *Ibid*, at p 93.
15 *Ibid*, at p 96.
16 *Ibid*.
17 *Ibid*, at p 94.
18 *Ibid*, at p 95.
19 *Ibid*, at p 94.

Case number 2: *Cannon v Smalley, otherwise Cannon*[20]

This is perhaps the most poignant case. Again, the husband petitioned for annulment of marriage by reason of insanity of the respondent. The respondent had performed her usual duties, including giving singing lessons until the day of the marriage, and:

> ... nothing unremarkable had been noticed except that she was at times dull and reticent. She was very quiet on the day of the wedding, and in the afternoon the petitioner and respondent left for Wigan, and on the way she said she was not worthy of him ... on 4th or 5th of January he could not get her to take interest in any thing. On the 6th he called in Dr Jeffries [who] arrived at the conclusion that her mind was affected.[21]

Again, Dr Savage makes an appearance, also finding that 'her mind was affected'. The respondent attempted suicide, and was removed to the Bethlehem Hospital. Dr Savage stated that during his interview with the respondent, 'the patient had her head bent down and was picking her fingers', that her replies to his questions were made '... in a very low tone by words to the effect that she could not help it, or could not understand. He came to the conclusion that she was suffering from melancholia ... In Bethlehem she had marked delusions – such as that the petitioner was not her husband, and that she was not married'.[22] He was of the opinion that 'to a certain extent the respondent understood what she was doing when she was contracting the marriage, but that to the full extent she did not understand the marriage relations'.[23] He concluded by saying that, in cases of melancholia, the transition, from sanity to insanity could be very rapid: '[a] patient might appear to be mentally competent one day and be plainly of unsound mind the day after ...'[24]

Case number 3: *Durham v Durham*[25]

In this case, the Right Honourable the Earl of Durham sought a declaration of nullity of his marriage with Ethel Elizabeth Louisa, the Countess of Durham. The affidavits identified Ethel Elizabeth by the surname of Milner, her maiden name (a usual practice no doubt, meant to assert at the outset the validity of the claim, which nevertheless might be read as a symbolic attempt to pre-empt the issue). On the evidence, the court could not affirm the assertion that Miss Milner was insane at the time of contracting the marriage, although it was driven to conclude that she had become insane shortly afterwards. This rejection of the petitioner's

---

20 (1885) X PD 96.
21 *Ibid*.
22 *Ibid*, at p 97.
23 *Ibid*, at p 98.
24 *Ibid*.
25 (1885) X PD 80.

case should not too readily be construed as a demonstration of law's impartial dispensation on the matter. Although it may be said that formal justice prevailed (the imputation of insanity was insupportable on the evidence pertaining to the time that the marriage was contracted), substantive justice did not, since the respondent still emerged with the brand of insanity as far as the post-nuptial period was concerned. It will be seen that the evidence relating to this period was similarly impugnable.

At the outset, the petitioner wished to show that expert medical opinion to the effect that the respondent was insane some months after the marriage could be made referable to a period prior to and including the time of the marriage. The marriage had taken place in October 1882. A Dr Matthew Duncan first saw Lady Durham in April 1883. Dr Duncan was consulted for 'certain functional derangements'.[26] To his questions, Lady Durham gave no answers, or only 'I don't know', and he concluded that at that time '... she only exhibited imbecility'.[27] Subsequent visits, during which Lady Durham continued to answer only 'Yes' and 'No', or 'I don't know', led him to conclude that she had '... more decided marks of insanity – more marked insanity – not mere imbecility'.[28] A Dr Playfair saw Lady Durham in June 1883. He came to the conclusion '... that her symptoms were not those of hysteria, but of unsound mind, but he added that he could not give an opinion as to its duration'.[29] Dr Blandford saw her two days later, on 2 July 1883. The case records his account that:

> ... she stood the whole time he saw her, that he could get no answers to his questions except 'I do not know'; that she may have said 'Yes' and 'No', but that practically he got no answer to his questions, and that he came to the conclusion that she was of unsound mind.[30]

At this point the judge surmised: 'I assume that there was something in the manner of the respondent which justified these gentlemen in coming to the conclusion that she was imbecile or insane at the times they have respectively spoken to [sic].'[31] He continued: 'I now proceed to examine the evidence to see whether her condition was the same previous to her marriage.'[32] He considered the imputation of imbecility in the respondent. He suggested that the letters of Lady Durham implied that she was:

> ... a person of low intellectual powers, but she was capable of receiving the ordinary education of young ladies of her class ... She acquired some accomplishments, and took part in private theatricals ... she was everywhere received and treated as an ordinary person, at any rate until her engagement ... Her grandfather, the Archbishop of Armagh, states that he regarded her as the most sensible of his granddaughters, a statement quite consistent with her intellectual powers being

---

26   *Ibid*, at p 83.
27   *Ibid*.
28   *Ibid*.
29   *Ibid*.
30   *Ibid*.
31   *Ibid*, at p 84.
32   *Ibid*.

feebler than those of her sisters, but entirely excluding the idea of her being imbecile.[33]

The judge went on to confirm his view, based upon numerous witness accounts, that Lady Durham was more shy than imbecile. He added that the engagement (to Lord Durham) was itself the strongest possible testimony in her favour as evidencing her sanity and intelligence at the time, although he suspected that Lord Durham '... was no doubt in the first instance attracted by her beauty',[34] and the judge added a further gloss to his observations with a quotation from Milton's *The Doctrine and Discipline of Divorce* as 'no doubt applicable to this case': 'Who knows not that the bashful muteness of a virgin may ofttimes hide all the unliveliness and natural sloth which is really unfit for conversation.'[35]

The judge went on to consider the evidence proffered to support the claim of unsoundness of mind in the respondent from the time of her engagement. In August 1882, the respondent's dress caught fire, causing injury to her chest.

> [She] made little of it, changed her dress and rejoined the company without complaining of pain ... evidence of her insensibility to pain which, it was said was not without a bearing on her mental condition. No evidence, however, has been given to shew that insensibility to pain is an accompaniment to insanity.[36]

The judge thus remained sceptical on this point, and found no evidence of insanity before, or at the time of, the marriage; therefore the plea of nullity was rejected. However, in considering all of the evidence placed before him, the judge noted the demonstrable change in Lady Durham's behaviour after the marriage. There are indications that Lord Durham was from the first a somewhat boorish husband: 'Lord Durham did not, on the third night after the marriage, shew that tenderness and consideration with the condition of his bride demanded.'[37] Many acquaintances who saw the respondent subsequently noted a change in her manner – that she was 'cross and irritable' – and Lord Durham darkly volunteered that whilst in Cannes, she '... there walked out by herself and did not return until after sunset'.[38] The judge added: 'this wandering has been repeated many times since.'[39] The respondent's sister testified 'that she was excessively cold to her'.[40]

The culmination of lay and professional witness statements to this effect led the judge to conclude that, after the marriage, Lady Durham had succumbed to insanity: 'It manifested itself in a perversion of the affections, she became cold, distant and unkind to those whom she had formerly loved'.[41] This finding of insanity did not avail the petitioner as far as the nullity suit was concerned.

---

33   *Ibid*.
34   *Ibid*, at p 85.
35   *Ibid*.
36   *Ibid*, at p 86.
37   *Ibid*, at p 90.
38   *Ibid*, at p 91.
39   *Ibid*.
40   *Ibid*.
41   *Ibid*, at p 92.

However, one wonders what repercussions may have ensued for the respondent from having been declared insane in a court of law, especially bearing in mind the high profile that such a case must have held within 'society' circles.[42]

EVIDENCE: A RE-EXAMINATION

In the case of *Durham v Durham*, Sir J Hannen, the presiding judge, should be given some credit for resisting the attempt to make the evidence put forward to establish insanity (or imbecility, which could equally have provided a nullifying factor) referable to a time before the dates upon which the doctors first interviewed the respondent. Nevertheless, it is disturbing to mark the willingness with which the court accepted expert testimony relating to those dates. No question was asked to clarify what might be meant by the term 'certain functional derangements'. Most tellingly, the evidence of Drs Duncan and Blandford, making a direct correlation between the respondent's muted answers and a conclusive insanity, was not questioned. For both doctors, their diagnosis seemed to rest upon an insult to their professional solicitousness, that insult being the unwillingness of the respondent to give more comprehensive answers to their questions. We are given no indication of the substance or ambit of those questions, but there is no suggestion that the responses were logically inappropriate, as might be the case, for example, when in testing for derangement a doctor asks a patient, 'Do you believe that you are a cat'?, and the patient answers 'yes' or 'I don't know'. Rather, the offence was one of quantitative inadequacy of response, which in itself might have offended against the practitioner's pride in his professional capability to 'get to the heart of the matter'. Dr Playfair's more cautious response, that he could give no opinion as to the duration of the insanity, was nonetheless derogated by the virtually admitted inadequacy inhering in his diagnoses: the respondent's symptoms 'were not those of hysteria'. Stating the parameters of what the symptoms *do not* constitute, however, should arguably be followed by a clear diagnostic indication of what they are, rather than resorting to the semantically ambiguous '*unsound mind*'[43] (a refuge which may well have been common to many members of the profession). It is almost as if Dr Playfair wished to disguise the inadequacy of such an indefinite diagnosis by prefixing it with a definite diagnosis *in specie*, even though this happens to be in the negative. Dr Blandford's diagnosis of unsound mind, based upon the quantitatively inadequate responses of the respondent, would also appear to claim evidential support for his conclusion by his attaching significance to the fact that the respondent, perhaps 'unnaturally' for a woman, *stood* throughout the interview. The scurrility of so readily associating unresponsiveness with imbecility seems

---

42 In the 1916 edition of *The Complete Peerage* (London: St Catherine's Press) the entry for Earl Durham is concerned almost solely with recording the failed nullity suit. *Burke's Peerage* (London: Burke's Peerage, 1959) is more informative: the Earl became a Chancellor of Durham University, Mayor of Durham in 1899, and was appointed Lord High Steward to King George V. Earl Durham and Ethel Elizabeth Louisa did not divorce or remarry; the Earl died in 1928, Ethel Elizabeth in 1931.

43 Emphasis added – not present in case report.

almost more distasteful than the association of insanity. It would seem that the judge harboured some latent scepticism in this regard. Remarkably however, given his legal and ethical mandate, judge stilled his disquiet concerning the inadequacy of the evidential correlation between the respondent's reserve and the finding of insanity, by departing altogether from the realm of presented evidence, into that of his own unsubstantiated assumption:

> I assume that there was something in the manner of the respondent which justified these gentlemen in coming to the conclusion that she was imbecile or insane ...[44]

Thus, to the *inadequacy* of expert testimony is superadded a replenishing *something* that is quite speciously made to reside in an unattested *manner*, yet the conclusion of insanity made by the judge in his closing statement makes direct reference to this expert testimony.

The judge's statement that the description of the respondent as 'the most sensible' is 'quite consistent with her intellectual powers being feebler than those of her sisters' could itself be regarded as either perverse or sensible, depending upon point of view, though he qualified the observation with the conclusion that the description excluded imbecility.[45] To the mind of the judge, the strongest attestation of the respondent's sanity and intelligence prior to the marriage was not however the evidence of family, friends and general social competence in the respondent, but the engagement itself. The respondent's ability to arrest the attention of a man (and especially a man of standing) thus acts as a formal validation of both sanity and intelligence, Milton's caveat notwithstanding.

The attempt to cite the episode of the burn, and the respondent's ensuing 'insensitivity to pain', as evidence of instability was rejected for lack of expert corroboration. Indeed, in the given context (a quick change of clothes and rejoining the social circle) it would seem that the respondent was exhibiting a stalwart strength of character, rather than the reverse.

Aside from the medical testimony gleaned from the doctor-patient interviews (or interrogatories), the judge's finding of insanity in the respondent referred to lay accounts of her changed manner, that she was *cross and irritable*, that she *walked out by herself*, that she became *cold and distant*. We will have cause to return to these patterns of behaviour later.

In *Hunter v Edney*, we again meet a respondent whose behaviour is, at the very least, not that of a loving bride. For the moment we will not speculate as to the range of reasons for this behaviour. Her quietness, suicidal wish, and resistance to consummate the marriage were swiftly construed as evidencing insanity – less than 24 hours after her marriage she had been pronounced insane. In support of

---

44 (1885) X PD 84.

45 The judge's refutation of imbecility in the respondent has an ironic flavour to modern eyes – it is based upon the evidence that the respondent had coped with an education suited to her sex and class, including the fact that she had taken part in amateur theatricals. Today this level of stimulus is thought appropriate in homes for the mentally handicapped and those suffering from mild senile dementia. Indeed, in the narrative of feminine amusements amongst the better classes in the novel *Jane Eyre* such accomplishments were lampooned as absurdities.

this finding, the opinion of Dr Savage is quoted at length. He gave an exact diagnosis – that of melancholia, and amplified the legitimating force of this diagnosis by presenting the court with an even more astonishing instance of his arcane virtuosity: that this was not merely a transient melancholia, but one springing from *hereditary insanity*. The court did appear not to attempt to make any enquiry as to the meaning and symptomatology of either melancholia or hereditary insanity. The doctor's conclusion that she might be liable to a relapse, and to transmit the insane tendency to her children, was not doubted. According to the evidence available in the case report, neither Dr Savage, in using the term 'hereditary', nor the court, in receiving it, seem perturbed by the complete lack of corroborative familial history in support of such a claim. (Perhaps unsurprisingly, Dr Savage was a keen exponent of psychiatric Darwinism and warned in his writings that 'the transmission of insanity leads gradually to the abasement and ultimate extinction of our race'.)[46]

In *Cannon v Smalley*, we again meet a bride who suddenly became dull and listless, ultimately developing suicidal tendencies. Within days she had apparently transformed from a competent singing teacher to an appropriate candidate for incarceration at the Bethlehem Hospital. No doubt this swift change of status to inhabitant of an asylum sealed the respondent's fate incontrovertibly; the resultant account of the medical history would have been merely a dutiful formality. Again the diagnosis is a definitive melancholia; again the patient is subdued, unresponsive: before the eminent doctor she significantly 'keeps her head bent down' and 'picks her fingers'. Her desire to deny her marital status is treated as a literal statement and thus elevated to the status of 'delusion'.[47] The rapidity of her decline is also presented as perfectly explicable in clinical terms: 'A patient might appear to be mentally competent one day and be plainly of unsound mind *the day after*.'[48]

We must perhaps accept that the readiness of the court to submit to, and even fortify, medical opinion upon the issue of insanity in these cases springs from a widespread cultural deference to professional medical authority and expertise, amounting almost to reverence, coupled with an innate acquiescence in the ready conclusion that women were psychologically frail. As Porter notes, 'the somewhat less disturbed woman living in society – the nervous case, the hysteric, the so-called "neurasthenic" – came under a distinctively penalising psychiatric gaze'.[49] This tolerance of diagnostic fashions, whims and ambiguities, would seem to have been particularly indulgent, if our trio of cases is any indication, in the arena of civil law. Generally in the realm of criminal law, the medical profession were under greater pressure to justify and corroborate their diagnoses with a more refined, precise and developed reference to clinical history, pathology and nomenclature. Of course this aetiological process was amply facilitated by the

---

46 Quoted in Showalter (1987, p 110), from Savage and Goodall, *Insanity and Allied Neuroses* (1907) London: Cassell.
47 Thus, with ironic symmetry, the denial of marital status is used as evidence of insanity in a nullity suit – itself a denial of marital status.
48 Emphasis added.
49 Porter, 1987, p 118.

very overt symptomatology of the accused – that his or her condition had been outwardly expressed through an act of violence; conversely the pressure to demonstrate clinical precision was greater because such diagnoses must have been sufficiently weighty to militate against the drive of public policy to impose criminal responsibility. Wariness of medical opinion could be given formal and logical credence; so, for example, a judge could direct a jury in a criminal case: 'You are not to be deprived of the exercise of your common sense because a gentleman comes from London and tells you scientific sense.'[50]

The acceptance of medical opinion in our three nullity cases possibly extended in some degree into the criminal arena where the accused was a woman. Here, then, it may be said that judicial deference to the medical man's greater understanding of the mysteries of the organism[51] 'woman' worked in her favour. So, Smith remarks of infanticide cases that:

> Lay and medical discourse coincided to render women – especially in activities connected with reproduction – lacking in responsibility ... But the willingness to excuse women is remarkable, especially as infanticide was thought to be widespread throughout the century ... The cumulative effect was a legally exculpatory attitude towards infanticidal women.[52]

The key issue connecting both civil and criminal adjudication of female insanity is perhaps this presumption of lack of responsibility as a foundational characteristic – how simple to step from such infantilism to complete unreason in the civil and criminal cases. Yet in the criminal cases, such indulgence was often patently justifiable on purely clinical grounds: unlike other types of violent derangement, the aberrant behaviour was directly referable to a chronologically and physiologically precise event in itself of some violence and trauma – childbirth. Indeed, knowledge of the association of childbirth with at least temporary insanity was so widespread that the courts did not always feel the need to adduce precise medical diagnoses, of 'puerperal insanity' or 'lactational insanity' for example, but were prepared to rely upon 'common sense'. In the trial of Eliza Dart, Lord Justice Brett directed that:

> It was a mistake to suppose that, in order to satisfy a jury of insanity, scientific evidence must be adduced. If the evidence of facts were such as to indicate an unsound state of mind that was quite sufficient.[53]

Smith pertinently concludes that:

> ... the medical language of individual internal disorder emptied the violent act of external social meaning. The insanity verdict classified child-killing as a problem to

---

50 Quoted in Smith, 1981, p 142.
51 *Ibid*, at p 142: 'Medical men identified women as natural objects and therefore described them with all the objective standing associated with science.' This is taken to its extreme in an article in the 1851 edition of the *Journal of Psychological Medicine and Mental Pathology* (Part 4, pp 18–50) entitled 'Woman in her psychological relations', which records a Dr Laycock's observation that: 'of all animals, woman has the most acute faculties ... there is not much ground for surprise at the grotesque forms which cunning assumes in the hysterical female ...' (at p 32).
52 Smith, 1981, p 144.
53 Smith, 1981, p 149.

be solved by custodial therapy ... this was humanitarian (in Victorian terms), but it also detracted from examining women's position in relation to power and wealth.[54]

One may even suggest that compared to the respondents in the nullity suits, physically resisting the institution of marriage, the 'temporary insanity' of maternity was less offensive. In the latter cases, the women had succumbed to their procreative role, albeit imperfectly – they had offended against the infant individual, even against an aspect of 'natural' law, but the greater 'natural' law of masculine order had not been transgressed. The crime could be understood as a singular act, not a threat to social order. Goodrich comments of woman:

> The law states her place as ancillary or secondary, the woman waits, she remains, she gestates or otherwise registers an external imperative ... the worst of all feminine crimes, a kind of madness, is that of the woman who takes off or leaves the home ...[55]

The reader may care to remember the degree of disquiet engendered by Lady Durham's *walking out alone*. Further, rejection of physical intimacy may itself be regarded as a profound abandonment of place, an assertion of autonomy.

These comments are of course suggestive of many contextual themes, but in particular can be made referable to the three nullity cases in two ways. First, and most obviously, we may see that the preservation of the status quo in terms of masculine polar values towards women was as well served in the civil suit, in deferring to medical opinion, as in the criminal. Secondly, and this is a less direct but nonetheless related inference, the ability of medical discourse to influence and contain social responses to individual behaviour was not merely the product of its relative supremacy in the hierarchy of existing discourses. It dominated and suppressed alternative discourses both in broad hermeneutic terms (for example the positing, as Smith indicates, of socially based explanations), but also in narrow doctrinal terms (the insistence upon organic, rather than affective or reactive, pathologies). In mitigation, it must be said that such alternative discourses, although available, occupied only penumbral cultural spheres, from marginal feminist writings to the most trivial locale of fiction.[56] In addition, the development of precise pathological nomenclature in the sphere of criminal law was indirectly 'encouraged' by the high profile of issues of public policy and the need to oppose moral, protective and retributive drives with developed discourses of equal sophistication. In the private sphere, the adjudication of the individual state of mind had no such pressures attendant upon it, thus the medical production of 'organic' pathology, however vague, weakly grounded, or transient in origin, could go unchallenged. I have said that alternative discourses, alternative explanations for individual 'aberrant' behaviour, were only available in marginal spheres. This is true in so far as they were overtly made. However, if

---

54 Smith, 1981, p 149.

55 Goodrich, 1995, p 135.

56 There are many examples however. Showalter (1987) quotes extensively from Florence Nightingale's *Cassandra*, and adds the gloss (at p 65): 'Middle class Victorian women were Cassandras rendered so crazy and powerless by their society that they could rail and rave but never act.'

we examine our three nullity cases again, looking both at the material evidence already supplied in this chapter and some additional commentary until now withheld, we may retrieve at least some vestige of those alternatives.

Meta-narrative I: enforced modesty

In the case of *Hunter v Edney*, we may remember the bride who was exhibiting her unwillingness to enter upon the marriage contract quite overtly even on the day. In this, as in all the cases, the narrative provides a vision of tragedy enhanced by the linguistic frame and productive of almost beautiful Victorian poetics. One might even arrange it as such:

> All day long
> and on the journey to London
> she was quite quiet
> and when they arrived at their apartments
> she refused to have supper
> said she did not want to get married
> and that she was false.[57]

The respondent's claim that she was 'false', that she had 'committed some crime', that she was 'so wicked that she was unfit to be married to an honest man', and that she was 'unfaithful', suggests two possible interpretations. The first is that she was hiding a previous liaison, perhaps even one which had been consummated. However, this scenario squares poorly with the evidence available in the case. The comments can be aligned more pertinently with the fact of her unwillingness to undress and consummate the marriage, and of judicial comments upon this resistance that she 'shewed an unreasonable aversion to the lover of her choice', that she 'exhibited the greatest repugnance to entering upon the condition of a married woman', that she 'took a morbid and diseased view' of marriage.

Bearing in mind the fact that young women were kept in a condition of ignorance, often total, with regard to sexuality, and were taught that their bodies were objects of shame to be hidden from view, this resistance to consummation is perfectly explicable. In the criminal case of *R v Flattery* (1877),[58] a girl submitted to intercourse believing that the act was a surgical operation; in *R v Case* (1850),[59] a medical practitioner similarly represented to a fourteen-year-old girl that he was 'treating' her medically, whilst in *R v Williams* (1923),[60] the accused, a singing master, had intercourse with a pupil under the pretence that it was a method of training her voice. Even more pertinent to the three nullity cases is evidence gleaned from the contemporary suits pleading female impotence. In *G v G*

---

57 *Supra*, at fn 13, poetic 'form' added.
58 (1877) 2 QBD 410.
59 (1850) 4 Cox 220.
60 (1923) 1 KB 340.

(1871),[61] where female impotence was claimed, it was admitted that there was 'no structural defect',[62] but that attempts at intercourse produced 'hysteria'.[63] The respondent refused to submit to the use of chloroform (as recommended by the doctors) in order to facilitate intercourse. In *P v L* (1873) (reported in *S v A* (1878)),[64] the petitioner said:

> At the time of my marriage I was thirty, and the respondent eighteen. I attempted to consummate the marriage, but there was an obstruction. She screamed and became hysterical, and afterwards complained of pain and suffering. In appearance she seemed to be a child not a woman. I made other attempts, but she resisted me, and on one occasion hit me in the face. She also threatened to drown herself.[65]

A Dr Hicks examined the respondent, who said that 'when she married she had no idea that there would be sexual intercourse – that she had no sexual desire … she said it was like the beasts of the field'.[66] In *L v L* (1882),[67] the respondent refused to accompany her husband home after the wedding ceremony, but a week afterwards they slept together at her father's house for three or four nights:

> … when she objected altogether to any attempt to consummate the marriage, and on one occasion threatened to leave the house … she was examined by a medical man, who gave evidence that she was suffering from vaginismus,[68] that there was a spasmodic affection of the parts … but that a cure might be effected with no great risk to life.[69]

Thus it is likely that the respondent was only acquainted with the physical requirements of consummation shortly before the marriage.[70] The culture thus presented her with an irreconcilable statement of her identity and role. The social coercion to move from a condition of modesty and secrecy to one of nakedness and total intimacy with a person of the opposite sex may explain not only her physical resistance, but also her sense of guilt. Society had taught her that her existence would be best justified and expressed by entering upon marital union, that it would afford her not only security, but status. The man who was willing to 'rescue' her, to elevate her to this sublime condition, must be a good man, an *honest* man. That she harboured fears, reservations and a sense of repugnance made her *false*, a *criminal*, *wicked* and *unfaithful*, both to him and to social norms. The bifurcation could be rendered more extreme and inexpressible by the

---

61　(1871) II PD 287.
62　*Ibid*, at p 288.
63　'Her condition is hysterical, and to a certain extent beyond her own control' – *ibid*, p 289.
64　(1878) III PD 72.
65　*Ibid*, at p 73, fn 2.
66　*Ibid*, at p 74.
67　(1882) VII PD 16.
68　Vaginismus is a spasmodic contraction of the vagina caused by anxiety. This condition may have accounted for some of the cases of 'impotence'. Surgical intervention, as was sometimes recommended, would be inappropriate and probably harmful.
69　*L v L* (1882) PD Vol VII 16.
70　Again, in fiction this theme is reproduced. For example, it is strongly suggested in *Jude the Obscure* by Thomas Hardy, that Sue Bridehead is ignorant of the physical nature of consummation, despite her unusually advanced education. Jude inwardly cries to Sue, 'You don't know what marriage means!' – Hardy, 1985a, p 225.

sublimating effects of available discourse: the judge glosses the issue of consummation through veiled language, her repugnance was to entering upon the *condition* of a married woman, the question before the court was not whether she was aware that she was going through the ceremony of marriage, but whether she was capable of understanding the *nature* of the contract she was entering into. In addition, the court could not take cognisance of the correlation between the immanence, the violence of the words 'repugnant', 'false', 'criminal' and 'wicked' as pertaining to the violence inhering in a physical consummation that may have been represented hitherto as an act, at best, unclean, but to be endured, and, at worst, bestial. Indeed, the dissonance between her avowed virtue and self-denunciation was itself taken to be evidence of her insanity.

Meta-narrative II: autonomy denied?

As already noted, the respondent in the second case, *Cannon v Smalley*, was transmuted within a few days from a person of competence, a singing teacher (the daughter of a professional musician), to inmate of the Bethlehem Hospital. Modern interpretation might take greater note of the trajectory of her mental condition from being dull and reticent to the expressions of denial, classified as 'delusions', when she said that the petitioner 'was not her husband'. Dr Savage felt that her apparent melancholia did not preclude her from sustaining a 'co-existent' mental capacity sufficient to contract marriage. He felt that, to a certain extent, the respondent understood what she was doing when she was contracting the marriage, 'but that to the full extent she did not understand *the marriage relations*' (emphasis added). Again, the veiled language, the semiotic code, 'patri-speak' for the unintelligible feminine rejection of masculine rights.

Meta-narrative III: prohibited love

In *Durham v Durham*, the presiding judge regretfully felt compelled to refer to an issue 'which may cause pain'.[71] The issue in question was that Lady Durham's affections 'had been fixed upon a gentleman whom she knew before the petitioner'.[72] The gentleman had communicated his wish to marry the respondent, but her brother, Mr Edward Milner disapproved of this connection on account of that gentleman's 'want of means'.[73] Over time it seems that the respondent was persuaded that such a marriage would be unwise, and was quoted by her sister as having later stated that 'a marriage with a poor man did not answer'.[74] Mrs Gerard, the sister, seems to have done much to encourage the match with Lord Durham. At one stage she reassured him, with a Shakespearean

---

71 *Durham v Durham* (1885) X PD 80, p 88.
72 *Ibid.*
73 *Ibid.*
74 *Ibid.*

flourish, 'that her sister's coldness to him arose from her love'.[75] Both Mrs Gerard and the respondent's other sister, Miss Emily Milner, were among those who gave eloquent testimony of the change they noted in their sister after the marriage, of her coldness and hostility towards them, testimony which, along with the expert medical evidence, compounded the judge's conclusion that after the marriage Lady Durham was mad. ('I find it impossible to doubt the concurrent testimony of so many witnesses, and it is to be observed that from this change was in its nature *such as commonly arises from insanity*'.)[76] It does not take a brilliant forensic mind to deduce that the hostility of the respondent towards her sisters was perfectly explicable, an arguably healthy expression of her anger towards those who had pressurised and coerced her into an ill-starred union. Thus the evidence, which Lord Durham tried (unsuccessfully) to adduce, of an existing mental instability prior to the marriage is explicable on other grounds. After the proposal of marriage, Lord Durham remonstrated with his betrothed for her silence and reticence, and she replied, 'Oh there is something dreadful and awful I ought to tell you',[77] but she could not or would not elaborate upon this statement. Lord Durham averred that the respondent's coldness and reticence towards him was so unnatural as to be 'evidence of a deranged intellect'.[78] It seems likely, as the judge himself seemed to realise, that the behaviour and veiled comments of the respondent were linked to the issue of which she dared not speak – her love for another man; but this issue comprised the unsayable, the inadmissible, promising only loss of face and general ignominy. So, when visiting doctors ask in a perhaps rather peremptory fashion, why you seem so ungrateful, so undemonstrative, so unhappy, it is better to be monosyllabic, to answer 'yes', 'no', or 'I don't know' than to betray yourself with comprehensive explanations (assuming you have acquired a sufficiently objective mastery of the events and facts yourself to be able to supply such answers). In addition, another issue is unsayable, too monstrous to give voice to: that the intimacy required by the marriage relationship is a matter of repugnance when you are in love with someone else, or not in love with your husband. Perhaps an empathic and shrewd medical practitioner could have inspired the patient with sufficient confidence to enable her to indicate the source of her troubles; but one can imagine that the formal interrogation, with the patient *standing* awkwardly throughout, may not have been conducive to such confidences.

The headnote to *Durham v Durham* tells us that it was admitted that, by the time of the hearing of the case, the respondent was 'hopelessly insane'. Perhaps this had become 'true'. Perhaps also it is easy to be persuaded, having become isolated by the opinion not only of medical experts, but of family, friends and society, with no legitimate discourse available with which to voice your version of events, that you are indeed insane. Perhaps even the 'discourse' of insanity, giving at least partial relief from the pressures of a socially approved and repressive lie,

---

75   *Ibid*, p 89.
76   *Ibid*, p 92, emphasis added.
77   *Ibid*, p 87.
78   *Ibid*, p 89.

offers the most logical resolution of the dilemma, and provides the most cogent expression of an insoluble turmoil.

Medical theories of 'organic' insanity – the master narrative

The single and overwhelming theme throughout the three cases – the master narrative – is the presentation of evidence to support the notion of an 'organic' insanity particular to women. The dominance of this theory suppresses the alternative explanations present in the text of the cases – the 'meta-narratives' – to effective extinction. At the time, the theory was part of a normative process which would continue until the chance incursion of war, and was directly referable to its theoretical and social context.

First, we should recognise the diagnostic difficulties with which the medical profession had to contend. Retrospective analyses of the development of theoretical and practical approaches to the issue of insanity recognise the difficulty encountered by the burgeoning discipline of psychiatry in its attempts to define insanity. Whilst noting that 'definitions of insanity and discussion of how the condition is to be recognised abound in early 19th century "psychiatric" literature', Scull[79] recognises that 'while the definitions are full of medical terms and phrases, and are frequently long and cumbersome, they make no progress at all towards the actual identification of cases'. Even later treatises quoted by Scull reveal inadequate and imprecise criteria: the insane person is 'one whose intellect has been perverted'.[80] In addition, the identification of 'specific' pathologies was charged with uncertainty, despite the implication derived from specific diagnostic nomenclature; of 'monomania', 'hysteria', 'melancholia', and of an irrefutable and arcane professional expertise. Added to this development of a legitimating 'scientific' approach to madness, the 19th century marked a professional (and civic) pride in its growing awareness of, and response to, insanity, by the development of asylums as therapeutic and humane institutions, which in itself, as Scull points out, provided an incentive for the adoption of a wide criterion for madness. The culmination of this process, of definitional ambiguity at source and the investment in institutional treatment (which in turn enhanced the scope and status of the profession), was that 'the profession began to create new realms of madness'.[81] Apart from the intrinsic caution that must ensue from retrospective awareness of this 'liberal' interpretation of madness, it should be remembered that many of the case histories to which they referred did display, for whatever reason, overtly disturbed, violent or socially disruptive forms of behaviour.

We should note too, that retrospectively we can identify the 'seduction factor' of prevalent ideas and discourses that blind practitioners to the subjectivity of

---

79 Scull, 1979, p 234.
80 Thomas Mayo, *Medical Testimony and Evidence in Cases of Lunacy* (1854) London: JW Parker & Son, quoted in Scull, 1979, p 234.
81 Scull, 1979, p 239.

their assumptions. In charting the history of the psychopathic disorder, Prins[82] notes that the conception of 'constitutional psychopathy' in the 1880s, with its link to notions of heredity, was followed by the early 20th century concentration upon neurological factors, in turn followed by psychoanalytic interpretations, and the subsequent development of 'socially based' explanations of behaviour in the later 20th century. Certainly, the theoretical explanations of deviant behaviour in the 19th century seemed inextricably linked to the identification of inherent 'constitutional' causes of illness rather than to affective or reactive ones. The net result of this tendency was a determination to 'contain' the deleterious effects upon society, which might be created by these inherently 'faulty' individuals, rather than to discover extraneous social causes that might produce an affective disorder. To have done so would have been to indict a society that took pride in its controlled and formulaic structures, at a stroke removing the foundation of medical expertise insofar as it claimed to be able to divine and define the disordered individual.

The emphasis upon constitutional, rather than extraneous, causes of 'aberrant' behaviour is strongly revealed by the medical testimony in the cases. As we have seen from the exegesis by Prins, this merely typified medical theory of the period. Within the particular context of medical predilections given as evidence in a court of law, however, this emphasis is not only provided with an enhanced legitimacy because of the formal legal context; it is also supported by the format of that context, since the normal ethical reliance of the law upon an adversarial inquiry of evidence is absent. First, all three of the respondents in the cases did not actively refute the allegations, and appeared only in a position of lateral removal. So, in *Durham v Durham*, we are simply told in the headnote that the respondent appeared by her brother, Edward Milner,[83] and denied the insanity. In *Hunter v Edney*, we are intriguingly told that an answer denying insanity was filed on the respondent's behalf, but she had instructed her counsel that she did not wish to oppose the petition. Although we are told in the headnote that she, with her mother, was examined as a witness, their evidence was dilute, incomplete and finally used to corroborate the imputation; for example, the mother's testimony of her daughter's virtue is used to demonstrate that the respondent's comment to the effect that she was 'wicked' was proof of delusion and madness. In *Cannon v Smalley*, the respondent appeared 'by her father as guardian' and denied the allegation. Although in all the cases, a statement of denial formed part of the headnote, the subsequent recorded material evidence and discussion gives little or no opportunity to substantiate these denials, if indeed any substantiation was offered.

Secondly, although medical evidence was used as the very foundation of the imputation of insanity, no professional opinion was offered or called to challenge this evidence. Was this due to passivity on the part of the respondents and their

---

82 Prins, 1995, pp 307–15.
83 Readers may apprehend that Edward Milner may not have been the sympathetic champion of his sister's cause implied by his fraternal status. In addition, the issue of property is latent in the cases, not least that of who should bear the continuing burden of maintaining the respondent.

representatives? Certainly, in the case of *Hunter v Edney*, since the respondent did not wish to oppose the petition, there may have been reason to allow the formal judgment to proceed unimpeded upon the basis of unifactoral presentation, although even here it was strange, bearing in mind the probable social ignominy attached to a legal pronouncement of insanity. Certainly, the lack of challenging opinion is not questioned by the court, suggesting that no visible offence to legal ethics was committed by this absence; the existing structural composition of nullity hearings was indulgent of unifactoral, rather than adversarial presentation. This had not universally been the case in legal examination of insanity. John Haslam, writing in 1809,[84] commented that '[m]edical men have been subjected to much ridicule in our courts of law for the great variety, and sometimes total dissimilarity, of opinions entertained by them' in defining insanity. Perhaps by the 1880s, the appropriation of the notion of scientific objectivity in the analysis of pathologies had acquired such force, especially through a developed nomenclature, that authoritative diagnoses were irrefutable, at any rate in the penumbral area of civil suits of nullity. This may be especially true bearing in mind the eminence of the medical experts who appeared; and, of particular relevance to these cases, was the virtually universal acceptance of, and cultural acquiescence in, a polarised analysis of the feminine psyche which, as Smith[85] notes, created 'a network of correspondences between woman, nature, passivity, emotion and irresponsibility … in a socially contingent contrast to man, culture, activity, intellect, and responsibility'. However, having noted these correspondences, and admitting that they were almost certainly 'unconscious' polarisations (in the Derridean sense) rather than consciously malignant, we must remember that the social and professional indulgence toward such theoretical constructs (which, after all, 'merely restated the terms of women's existing position' (Smith, p 143) should be viewed less critically than *legal* indulgence when the very credibility and authority of the law is founded upon its impartiality and forensic expertise. It is admitted that the cultural partiality of evidence becomes visible in retrospect, yet it is still salutary to observe how weakly the judicial and procedural buttress stood up to the currents of medical opinion.

Legal ethics have thus been 'found wanting' in this regard, and so too must medical ethics. As early as 1817, John Haslam[86] had written in his treatise, *Medical Jurisprudence as it Relates to Insanity*, of the 'important duty which the medical practitioner has to perform, when he delivers his testimony before a court of justice'; and that the testimony should be:

> … clearly defined, conscientiously felt, and thoroughly understood, – his opinion ought to be conveyed in a perspicacious manner; he should be solemnly impressed that he speaks upon oath, the most sacred pledge before God, between man and man – and that the life of a human being depends on the clearness and truth of his deposition.

---

84 Haslam, J, *Observations on Madness and Melancholy*, 2nd edn (1809) London: Callow, quoted in Scull, 1979, p 236.

85 Smith, 1981, p 143.

86 *Op cit*, fn 9, pp 3–4.

At this stage in his treatise, Haslam is referring to the inquisition of insanity for the purpose of deciding criminal responsibility, hence his reference to the 'life' of a human being.[87] Yet his disquisition upon the giving of medical evidence in civil suits is equally conscientious. Later, he comments that:

> ... our knowledge of the intellectual faculties, and of their operations is very limited, and that for the progress of the philosophy of Mind has borne no proportion to the rapid advances which have been made by Anatomy, Physiology and Pathology.[88]

With a precocious foresight of later apprehensions in philosophical and linguistic theory, he warns that:

> All that we can know of the mind of an individual is from the communication of his ideas in terms or signs which are conventional between us, in order to be intelligible, or from his actions.[89]

It would seem that this attempt to imbue the profession with an ethical code, a heightened awareness of the grave responsibility pertaining to the potential effects of its pronouncements in a court of law, was not universally followed.

CONCLUSION

It may seem somewhat uncharitable to charge the professional lawyers and doctors with ethical mismanagement of these three cases, given the cogent indications of mental instability exhibited by the women – two showed suicidal tendencies – and the power of beliefs held about women at the time. We can only note that the power resided in the professionals' hands, and that ethical codes were inherent to the framing of their respective practices. For the lawyer and judge, the rules of evidence and of forensic investigation could have operated as a brake on the one hand, and a stimulus on the other, in recognising indications of a repressed narrative; but this would have entailed aiming a broadside at the doctrinal certainties of the marriage contract, requiring, as it did, 'submission on the part of the woman, protection on the part of the man'. For the medical practitioner, then as now, the absence of controls upon their pronouncements in private practice vested them with a pervasive power. The failure to temper their hazarded diagnostic decrees with a consciousness of the gravity of the effect of such decrees, particularly when they were based upon little more than unexplored conjecture, served with the garnish of nomenclature, was arguably a failure of medical ethics. In his treatise on medical jurisprudence of 1817, John Haslam urges[90] his professional readers to remember that:

---

87 Arguably, in a broader sense, the 'life' of a human being was also at issue in the civil cases.
88 *Op cit*, fn 9, p 78.
89 *Op cit*, fn 9, p 78.
90 *Op cit*, fn 9, p 48.

The medical evidence, in order to impress and satisfy the tribunal before which his testimony is given, should not merely pronounce the party to be insane, but ought to adduce sufficient reasons as the foundation of his opinion. For this purpose it behoves him to have investigated accurately the collateral circumstances. It should be enquired if he had experienced an attack at any former period of his life? If insanity had prevailed in his family? If any of those circumstances which are generally acknowledged to be causes of this disease had occurred? ... It should likewise be ascertained, if previous depression of mind had prevailed resulting from grief, anxiety or disappointment ...

Perhaps here we have evidence that the recognition of experiential, reactive or socially based pathology originated not in the 20th century, but in the early 19th century, only to be submerged by the rigid and seductive power of 'organic' theories. Nevertheless, the passage can be read simply as an ethical caution which, had it been practised by the eminent medical practitioners of the 1880s, might have tempered their diagnostic conclusions. It would appear that the dramatic identification of hereditary disease in *Hunter v Edney* was without foundation, and the assumption of insanity in *Durham v Durham* (based upon a 'perversion of the affections') was tenuous. The aversion to physical contact in all three cases remained unexplored, though darkly acknowledged by the veiled discourse. In addition, an ominous subtext seems to run through the cases – that the rejection of masculine sexual rights was itself indicative of madness. Could the homosocial community of patriarchs really have taken feminine sexual inhibition, ingrained by their own tenets, as so universal a rejection of the masculine as to militate against reason? Certainly Lord Durham somewhat pettishly claimed that his wife's coldness and reticence was so unnatural as to be 'evidence of a deranged intellect', whilst Miss Edney suffered from an *unreasonable* aversion. In fact, this line of reasoning could have presented theoretical difficulties for the doctors, since it was believed that one of the symptoms of insanity in women was the abandonment of sexual reserve. John Millar, the medical superintendent at Bethnal House Asylum in London, observed that nymphomaniac symptoms were 'constantly present' when young women were insane, and Showalter concludes that 'uncontrolled sexuality seemed the major, almost defining symptom of insanity in women'.[91]

---

91 Showalter (1987) includes the quotation from Millar on p 74. Authoritative Victorian medical texts reveal a bizarre mixture of apparently 'objective' scientific analysis, eroticism and outright misogyny. The article entitled 'Woman in her psychological relations' (*supra*, fn 51) refers to woman as organism:

> ... of all animals, woman has the most acute faculties; and when we consider how much these may be exalted by the influences of the reproductive organs, there is not much ground for surprise at the grotesque forms which cunning assumes in the hysterical female.

The article goes on to explain how woman's behaviour is affected by 'ovarian irritation, burst[ing] forth beyond all control', leading her to be irreligious, selfish, slanderous, false, malicious, devoid of affection, thievish in a thousand petty ways, bold – may be erotic, self-willed and quarrelsome ... what seems to be vice, but is really moral insanity. Dr Laycock, we are happy to learn, has been able to treat cases of this kind with perfect success, by a course of galvanism directed through the ovaria, and by suitable medication and moral and hygienic treatment' (p 34).

With the comparison of the three cases to hand, it would seem that women were as much in danger of being classified as insane for exhibiting an overly controlled sexuality. The offence common to both behaviour patterns, of 'uncontrolled' and 'controlled' sexuality, is inherent in the notion of 'control' itself, since it would seem an anathema to patriarchal rule that the parameters of sexual control could reside in the hands of antinomian woman. At the heart of the cases it can be seen that the question of sexuality and sexual autonomy is intimately bound to the notion of the marriage contract itself; as Sir J Hannen stated, the question to be determined by the court was not whether the woman was aware that she was going through the ceremony of marriage, but whether she was capable of understanding the 'nature' of the contract she was entering into. This could be read as a conventional inquiry into the viability of capacity *simpliciter*, as in orthodox inquiries into contractual capacity; but it would seem that the reference to an inability to understand the 'nature' of the contract was not so much referable to an analytic dissection of the components of the contact, as an implosion of the unspoken requirement to willingly respond and consummate; an implosion which was well served and expressed through the annexation of the professional discourse on insanity.

Thus, not only did medical and legal discourse fail to address the factor common to all three cases of the strangely immediate appearance of 'aberrant' behaviour upon marriage, and what that might indicate in terms of trauma to the personal and sexual autonomy of the individual, but their practices actively obscured the issue in a fabric of semantic play. The 'impenetrable' notion of an 'organic' insanity was sustained in equilibrium with the juristic and evidential indulgence of the impenetrable, 'organic' nature of the marriage contract. Showalter historicises the movement from 19th century adherence to 'organic' theory in psychiatric medicine, to the 20th century recognition of reactive disorder. The recognition was rather forced upon medical practitioners, who were confronted by the thousands of men returning from the front in the First World War with variable forms of shell shock. Showalter states:[92]

> The experience of male hysteria inevitably had a number of effects on psychiatric practice. It forced a reconsideration of all the positions that Darwinian psychiatry had taken on the causation of mental illness, on male and female roles, and on therapeutic responsibility. The overwhelming allegiance of English psychiatry to organic explanations of mental disorders was breached and subverted by the experience of war, as it became clear that shell shock had an emotional, not a physical origin.

For Showalter, there is a direct correlation between the trauma of repression and loss of autonomy for women in the domestic setting, and that for men in the war zone, and that in both cases the causative factors could be cumulative. The three nullity cases add to this picture by suggesting that the moment of marriage, like the moment of bombardment, could be a catalyst for the expression of that trauma through simply rebellious, or patently disturbed responses. For men at war, the

---

92   Showalter, 1987, p 189.

reaction to powerlessness in the war zone was invoked by a trauma both violent and public. For the woman in the bridal chamber the trauma, or prospective trauma, may have seemed, or been, just as violent although admittedly not so public.

Feminist objections to the marriage contract recognise the dangerous fluidity resulting from the association of the notion of marriage with that of contract. The word contract imports a sense, not just of legality, gravity and formality, but of agreement and impartiality. Schouler stated, in *A Treatise on the Law of the Domestic Relations*, that:

> ... we are to consider marriage, not as a contract in the ordinary acceptance of the term; but as a contract sui generis ... as an agreement to enter into a solemn relation which imposes its own terms.[93]

The statement was intended to be instrumental in defining the *locus* of divergence between the classical contact and the marriage contact, but neatly indicates the source of the problem. For the marriage contract is not simply discernible through its self-referential, self-defining terms, it is also submersible, placed beyond or below the reach of forensic legal scrutiny by its inward nature, and this elision is entrenched and legitimised in the 19th century cases through the judicial use of formal discourse which clothes itself as exegesis. The male spouse, the judge, counsel and doctors all have a (largely unspoken) understanding of the offence against masculine power and law itself. The male 'representatives' of the respondents are passive counterparts, 'eunuchs' at the court of adjudication of the feminine transgression of order. Feminist critiques of the marriage contract recognise that central to it is the surrender by one party of bodily autonomy and integrity. To critique the issue of unilateral surrender as a contractual term would have made the inherent inequalities of the contract a justifiable issue in itself, which would have been a source of no little discomfort and indeed an act of anarchy; for the law nurtured and sustained the inequality. In the absence of a legitimate and legitimating discourse, the women could only vent their anger through the primitive discourse of denial, recrimination and self-recrimination, itself so perilously close to the chaotic cries of the incompetent. Yet, if their legal and medical interlocutors had adhered to ethical formulae – to listen, to analyse, but not to judge – justice could have been realised in the particular case, and medical progress would have been served. The failure, in John Haslam's words, 'to investigate accurately the collateral circumstances' was instrumental to the perpetuation of the flimsy myths of organic pathology, obstructing recognition of the infinitely variable (in terms of origin and response) *reactive* condition; but to have listened to the feminine subject, to have allowed her access to the integrity of a valid experience and response to masculine norms, would have endangered not only the 'laws' of medicine, but the law itself.

Effectively unrepresented in the cases, the feminine subjects were mere ciphers for the literal effacement of integrity and autonomy already practised upon women by the law, an effacement conveniently facilitated by the discourse of

---

93   Quoted in Pateman, 1988, p 189.

medicine. For both law and medicine, the 'singularity' of this voice and experience, had articulation been possible, could have undermined the somewhat *louche* and comfortable recourse to 'pathology' and its passive reception by the law. Kessler[94] reminds us that law, like every other cultural institution, is a place where we tell one another stories about our relationships with ourselves, one another and authority. Dalton adds that:

> ... when we tell one another stories, we use languages and themes that different pieces of the culture make available to us, and that limit the stories we can tell. Since our stories influence how we imagine, as well as how we describe our relationships, our stories also limit who we can be.[95]

The 'stories' told by medicine and by law in these three cases outlawed not only the story of the feminine subject. They allowed the doctor and the lawyer to recline together in a 'story' of their own brotherly alliance, a story of power, of paternalism, of fraternal sympathy. Their abandonment of ethics was subliminal and partial, and did not detract from their belief that, as players in the story, they served justice and truth.

---

94 Quoted in Dalton, 1985, p 997.
95 *Ibid*.

CHAPTER 9

RAPE OR SEDUCTION? FACTS AND FICTIONS – LAW, LITERATURE AND THE 'IDEAL' VICTIM – 'IS ALEC A RAPIST?'– A REPLY TO PROFESSOR JOHN SUTHERLAND

INTRODUCTION

> The space between the myth and the truth contributes to a further myth – that if a man a woman knows, as one High Court judge put it to me, goes a bit too far when she does not want it, that may be misbehaviour but it is not a serious crime. As a result of that myth, the sympathy in a rape trial between parties who know each other will be with the defendant ...

> V Baird MP, House of Commons Debates, 24 April 2002

As this quotation suggests, the current law of rape grapples with predispositions concerning the prior familiarity of parties,[1] itself a key component in the unfolding tale which ensues. However, this chapter includes other, unusual features. First, it documents a true research story, wherein a 'reply' was provoked by the clear 'skewing' of materials and arguments presented by a leading academic – a skewing that exemplified the very stereotypes and prejudices that academics are expected to resist and expose. In his essay 'Is Alec a rapist?', Professor John Sutherland suggests that readings of the rape/seduction scene in *Tess of the d'Urbervilles*[2] have been shaped by literary-political fashions, culminating, for Sutherland, in a modern interpretation which 'favours' rape and unfairly demonises the character of Alec d'Urberville: 'She who was seduced in 1892 is she who is raped in the permissive 1960s.' The simple 'polarisation' of the notions of 'rape' and 'seduction' that this statement entails is dramatically undermined by Victorian caselaw, in which both 'rape' and 'seduction' could attract legal notice. This chapter takes issue with Sutherland's account, demonstrating a selective use of the evidence and predisposition that is sadly still mirrored in modern court cases involving charges of rape.

---

1   Dispositions most recently reflected in the debates surrounding the case of *R v A* [2001] UKHL 25.

2   *Tess of the d'Urbervilles* by Thomas Hardy was published in 1891. John Sutherland's essay 'Is Alec a rapist?' appeared in his collection *Is Heathcliff a Murderer? Puzzles in 19th Century Fiction* in 1996.

The process of reply[3] undertaken here also induced scholarly excavation work on the definition and history of the word 'rape' in relation to that of 'seduction', revealing an intriguing pattern of usage and case law. These patterns – the perpetuation of stereotypes and the transmission of such stereotypes through subliminal etymologies – continue to be present in courtroom practice. For Larcombe (2002, p 134), who reviewed recent empirical and theoretical work on rape trials, the typecasting in 'the real' of the courtroom is reflected in the validation of certain types of victimhood – the rape complainant should be an 'unequivocal victim'[4] – a monolithic character. In addition, the etymological currency of the courtroom supports this validation process; Bavelas and Coates (2001, pp 37–38) chart the semiotic patina overlying the use of key words at trial, especially where sexual offences are in issue. They explain that:

> Our main interest was in how the judgments tended to characterise these offences, especially in whether the language cast them as sexual or as violent acts ... the most frequent description was in erotic or affectionate language ... there were also a small but noteworthy number of sexual-violent oxymorons, such as 'She stopped struggling and ... acquiesced ... although the intercourse was still without her consent.' ... The analysis revealed a strong tendency for these judgments to characterise sexual assaults as sex rather than as assault. We propose that this use of a sexual vocabulary ... minimizes and even hides the intrinsic violence of an assault ... The language used does not just euphemize; it actively misleads and misdirects ...

Both phenomena – the monolithic and the semiotic – pervade the discussion produced by the influential Sutherland. In situating his discussion of rape and

---

3   Author's note: this chapter first appeared as 'Is Alec a rapist? – a reply to Professor Sutherland' in (1999) 7(3) Feminist Legal Studies. It also forms part of a chapter in Melanie Williams, *Empty Justice: One Hundred Years of Law, Literature and Philosophy* (2002), London: Cavendish Publishing. It is included in the current book as a separate chapter in itself since it complements the identity of the essay collection dedicated to revealing 'stories' behind law and policy. The rape/seduction scene in *Tess*, though depicted in veiled language, seems to leave little doubt as to the identity of perpetrator and victim. But by chance, on a long train journey through Wales, I read the collection of essays referred to, designed for popular consumption, by Professor John Sutherland, subtitled 'Puzzles in 19th century fiction'. One essay glossed *Tess*, with specific focus upon the issue of rape. It became clear that what I considered to be virtually incontestable aspects of the text (as to *both* 'legal events' – rape and homicide – but chiefly with regard to the rape/seduction scene) could be metamorphosed, by adroit, persuasive rhetoric, into something quite different. The essay did not simply amount to a different point of view. Having studied the text of *Tess* in detail for the previous work, I was sure that I detected odd trails and adroit elisions in the essay that created a very different impression of the person and text of *Tess* from that evident in the original. Particularly striking was the degree to which the transformation of fact and opinion could produce a credible version of events radically different from that which I believed to be true. In short, Sutherland had arranged a cogent, but, I believed, wholly erroneous and misleading 'case for the defence': I felt bound to investigate a response, not least because the transformation resembles those which take place 'in the real'.

4   Larcombe (2002, p 134):

> This valourised victim speaks of woman as a sex and reproduces the generalized construct of the 'natural', biological woman vulnerable to, and physically weaker than, her male counterpart ... Being a liberal construct, she appreciates the *risk* of rape and takes all sensible and logical precautions to avoid creating the opportunity for such an attack. She modifies her behaviour to exhibit caution ... she fears being out of control ...

seduction within a popular paperback entertainment collection that reflects upon great (legal) mysteries in literature – such as 'Was Alec a rapist?' – he appears to undertake a disinterested, 'outsider's' quest in search of a workaday 'truth', perhaps more forgivable than the tired replications prevalent in the courtroom. Yet laying claim to an underlying, historicised and culturally aware scholarly 'truth' carries its own debt to integrity, a debt sustained in the real and fictional lives whose 'truth' is on trial.

Tess of the d'Urbervilles, by Thomas Hardy, is a classic English novel of the late Victorian period, a tragedy of perennially urgent themes. Briefly, it is the story of a young girl, Tess Durbeyfield, ignorant and innocent of sexual matters, who experiences a sexual encounter with Alec d'Urberville, a local member of the *nouveau riche*. She gives birth to an illegitimate child, who subsequently dies. Later she falls in love, and marries Angel Clare, a pleasant young man. On their wedding night, he confesses a youthful peccadillo. She in turn feels permitted to disclose her past, but her husband's idealisation of her purity means that he cannot accept these facts. He insists that they part. The young woman spends some time in hardship and poverty, but feels unable to appeal to her estranged husband. Destitute, convinced that her husband is lost to her, and careless of her fate, she allows the seducer to establish her as his mistress, partly in order to secure aid for her impoverished family. Meanwhile her husband has relented. He returns to see his wife. Desperate to regain the love of her husband and in an attempt to negate the past, she kills her seducer. Husband and wife are reunited. After a brief period as fugitives, the young woman is captured, tried and hanged for the murder.

In keeping with Victorian literary/cultural constraints, the sexual scene is indicated only circumstantially. Nevertheless, textual indications most strongly indicate rape. This study will explore, as in 'real' life and law, the premise that demonstrating the categories and agencies driving an event 'beyond reasonable doubt' involves an elaborate assembly of disparate elements. 'Doubt' is as much the product of cultural norms as of empirical finding, whilst what is 'reasonable' remains very much in the eye of the beholder.

Tess is a book so powerful in its depiction of a person of honesty, integrity and powerlessness overwhelmed by factors beyond her control and drawn towards a terrible end, of her condemnation by law *at* that end – with no formal mitigation drawn from preceding events – that a person with no direct connections with the study of law must be troubled by it. Two issues of legal note arise in the text – a possible rape, and a murder. A story involving a probable rape, murder and an execution, but little *law*, might seem at the very least a conscious omission on the part of the author. When that omission is coupled with the strongest intimations that the *spectre* of the law promotes indifference or injustice, a moral imperative commands that the subtext to the omissions and spectres of law be explored.

The absence of a murder trial in *Tess* serves as a reminder that the law's response to such facts would have been swift and draconian. Yet the narrative pleads that the law thereby enacts a substantial injustice. How would modern law respond to the case of *R v Tess of the d'Urbervilles*? A comparison of the narrat of law and of literature reveals the latter to be a prescient source of practical jurisprudence as *Tess* explores the notions of social, psychological and physical/legal death. Our understanding of words such as 'provocation' and 'self-defence' is rooted in history, a history that reflects social and juristic prejudice and paralysis. This obliquity is further demonstrated in the enigmatic portrayal of the role of sexuality – of 'courtship', seduction and rape. The histories of the law of provocation, of seduction, rape and associated caselaw reveal the intimacy of links between individual and institutional conquest, a savage private sphere from woodland to drawing room.

Thus *Tess of the d'Urbervilles* is a text that stimulates jurisprudential enquiry of some breadth. The initial impetus to writing this essay was to 'assay' the clearly sophisticated rationale underlying the message of *Tess*: that a person of goodness and virtue would have been viewed by the law as tarnished and malevolent. Apart from the desire to clarify the anomaly, and the clear indication in the text that the class and gender of this malefactor seemed relevant to her fate, the study was begun with no particular preconception of how the fictional account would compare or link with that of law, or of the doctrinal issues that might become implicated. Attentive reading of the text reveals that the rape *itself* was not (as one might expect) portrayed as deeply traumatic and life-changing, despite the textual indication of a non-consensual and invasive encounter. Initially therefore, the study focused upon those events or beliefs in the book that led the 'realistic' – that is, driven by feasible responses and decisions – character of Tess to bloodshed, and how the law would view such responses: these concerns motivate the second part of this chapter, linking to current as well as contemporaneous case law.

At the time of writing, however, an article on *Tess* was published by a leading academic in English literature – Professor John Sutherland – asserting that Tess was both a willing participant to the sexual encounter, as well as a malevolent character. This surprising assertion demanded a re-examination of the denominations of 'rape' and 'seduction' and of the provenance of this 'modern' interpretation which, in its overt reading *against* the spirit of the text, reveals a persistently 'skewed' viewpoint, wonderfully mirrored in past and, to some extent, present legal culture.[5] Finally, the chapter reflects upon the significance of this exploration of 'the particular' in the more general purview of jurisprudence.

As a late Victorian writer, Hardy laboured under conflicting tensions[6] – wishing to depict the moral frailties and weaknesses of individuals, great and small, his writing was received with some ambivalence by a bourgeois Victorian society guarding its claim to moral propriety. A self-educated natural sceptic,

---

5   As is reflected in concerns about low reporting and conviction rates and adversarial exploitation of already established vulnerabilities in the victim – a global problem; see, for example, Murphy, 2001.

6   Hardy's writing cuts across many conceptual boundaries; critical responses appear in several fields. Texts are numerous; foundational scholarship can be located in, for example, Raymond Williams (1987), Widdowson (1989), Hawkins (1989) and Millgate (1982).

Hardy explored conflicts in the philosophical and theological domains which mirrored, and to some extent presaged, *fin de siècle* and early 20th century anxieties concerning the nature of being; this too posed a threat to more traditional sections of society. Hardy's extensive diaries and notebooks, which often formed the basis of fictional developments, referred to contemporary philosophical debates, current affairs and newspaper accounts of individual tragedies and incidents. Of rural background, Hardy understood, practically and intellectually, the hardship and privations of peasant life and the pretences of the bourgeoisie. Thus, Hardy was alive to the likely repercussions of his writings: textual ambiguities, as exemplified in this sexual encounter, at least in part reflected the social constraints imposed upon him as author *and* upon the experiences to which his characters could lay claim.[7]

POLAR VERSUS RELATIONAL, 'SEDUCTION' VERSUS 'RAPE' – THE CULTURAL OPPOSITION IN REPRESENTATION

The courtroom is not the only location in which a trial may take place. In 'Is Alec a rapist?'(Sutherland, 1996) Professor John Sutherland conducts an enquiry into the nature of the sexual encounter that occurs in *Tess of the d'Urbervilles*. As occurs in many trials, both within and outside the courtroom, the evidence in the fictional account is open to some conjecture and, in common with the zealous courtroom advocate, Professor Sutherland is selective in the interpretation and use of evidence. Thus, in reading his account one may begin with an enthusiasm to discover the new insights that literary criticism can provide for the legal issue and potential analogues with 'real' possible rape cases. Yet the encounter ends with the realisation that the juristic analogue in this particular encounter between law and literature is more sinister: it is in the partiality of the account itself, a partiality which mirrors some of the devices used in legal advocacy.

Sutherland's piece begins with an interesting survey of 19th and 20th century literary accounts of the novel, accounts which vary in their view of the sexual encounter. Sutherland uses this historiographical background to refute the suggestion that Tess was raped: 'She who was seduced in 1892 is she who is raped in the permissive 1960s' (p 203). With this laconic phrase, Sutherland suggests that initial, critical readings of the text of *Tess* that view the scene as one of 'seduction' are, by the 'permissive' 1960s, displaced by critical readings which 'cry rape'. However, as will be seen, independent reference to the legal history of rape and

---

7   Rooney (1998, p 475), in her wide-ranging critique, asserts that:
    ... the meaning of the contested interaction from Tess's point of view is radically unavailable, and so we too face the problem of reading the silent, seductive Tess as a text, confined by the limits that mark every reading of the scene of sexual violence.
    The evidential difficulties in such events are indeed problematic but, as will be seen, although Tess herself may – culturally – be disabled from anatomising her experience, the textual indications concerning the nature of the 'contested interaction' take us beyond the silent, and apart from the seductive.

seduction in both English and American caselaw reveals a more complex background.

Sutherland's analysis is focused upon the textual evidence of the sexual encounter and is similar to the analysis that would take place in a legal context; certain facts, circumstantial evidence, points of view and verbal statements made by the parties to the encounter are selected as material to the case. The case is of some additional interest to lawyers because it involved the suggestion, as in some 'real life' sexual offence cases, that the act took place whilst the victim was asleep. A review of Sutherland's account, in conjunction with the text of the novel, provides an opportunity to test his reading of the evidence.

TESS VERSUS SUTHERLAND

Just prior to the sexual encounter, Tess is obliged to accept a ride on horseback from Alec. Exhausted, she falls asleep momentarily and Alec places his arm around her waist. Tess responds with 'a little push' which almost unbalances Alex. Sutherland's gloss reads:

> A little push ... stresses that even when her body is dormant, Tess's purity is vigilant and well capable of defending itself. This is important, since she will be sleeping when the seduction/rape occurs. (Sutherland, 1996, p 206)

Already Sutherland is establishing the foundation of his view that Tess is more participant than victim. In making this connection between the early and later 'sleep' response however, he does not acknowledge a material fact provided by the text: the 'little push' ensues from a 'moment' of oblivion, whereas just prior to the later time when intercourse takes place, Tess, we are told, 'was sleeping soundly' (Hardy, 1985b, p 119). In addition, one may question whether the physical dormancy of sleep, momentary or otherwise, can be opposed by an autonomously active 'vigilant purity' that is 'well capable of defending itself'. Sutherland clothes an abstract virtue with independent and kinetic power.

Reviewing the textual account of the ride on horseback prior to the sexual act, Sutherland concludes: 'Tess repulses his love-making as they ride, without ever distinctly denying that she loves him. He is much encouraged by her lack of frigidity' (Sutherland, 1996, p 207). Yet the text tells us otherwise:

> Tess, why do you always dislike my kissing you?
> I suppose – because I don't love you.
> ... What am I, to be repulsed by a mere chit like you?
> Put me down, I beg you. I don't mind where it is, only let me get down sir
> please! (Hardy, 1985b, pp 114–15)

Alec informs Tess that he has made gifts to her impoverished family, a statement which may be intended to increase Tess's sense of indebtedness to her rescuer. Yet even then when asked, 'Tessy – don't you love me ever so little now?', she regretfully admits, 'I'm grateful ... but I fear I do not' (Hardy, 1985b, p 117). Thus, in direct contradiction of Sutherland, Tess twice denies any love of Alec, and the text merely indicates that Tess is willing to voice her past anger *as opposed to* remaining frigid, not simply that she 'lacks frigidity'. Instead the text indicates her clear discomfiture – she is told that they are hopelessly lost in the foggy forest, miles away from the village, and she feels so compromised by his gift to her impoverished family that we are told 'she wept outright'(Hardy, 1985b, p 117). In addition, the clear imbalance in status and power between Tess and Alec adds to her entrapment. There are verbal instances of her will being overborne ('on one condition', 'whatever you may yourself feel about it') and Alec's remark, 'That is devilish unkind!', invokes the humble response, 'I beg your pardon, sir', whilst his 'What am I, to be repulsed so by a mere chit like you … I won't stand it!' is a clear assertion of social superiority. Tess's demeanour is awkwardly resistant, she 'writhes uneasily on her seat' (Hardy, 1985b, pp 115–16) and asks to be released, behaviour not easily characterised as 'lacking frigidity'.

Alec leaves Tess to rest deep in the forest and returns to find her sleeping soundly. The narrator does not describe the sexual encounter, but discourses upon its significance concluding that: 'An immeasurable social chasm was to divide our heroine's personality thereafter' (Hardy, 1985b, p 119). Sutherland glosses this narrative as the 'lofty moralising' of a narrator who 'prates about olden times' (Sutherland, 1996, p 208). Certainly, the narrative does not conclusively classify the sexual act, but the textual suggestion that Tess's guardian angel, like Tess, is asleep, that 'the coarse' (Alec) 'appropriates' the finer (Tess), and the reference to the 'possibility of retribution' and of 'the same measure' being 'dealt' 'even more ruthlessly' by Tess's mailed ancestors towards peasants of ancient times (Hardy, 1985b, p 119), all involve active verbs associated with *the will being overborne*, rather than with consensual intercourse. Sutherland clutches at the fact that Alec is not *as* 'ruthless' as those ancient ravishers as somehow lending support to this case and reiterates his analogue regarding sleep:

> The point is made earlier in the chapter that even when asleep, Tess is able to fend off unwanted sexual advances. Why does she not protect her imperilled virtue with one of those timely 'impulses of reprisal'? (Sutherland, 1996, p 208)

To support his case still further, Sutherland refers to Tess later upbraiding Alec:

> She does not accuse him of rape, but of having duped her: 'I didn't understand your meaning until it was too late'. Nor, when upbraiding her mother for not warning her against men, does Tess claim that she has been raped … (Sutherland, 1996, p 208)

'I didn't understand your meaning' is indeed an indication that, once awake, consent is either falsely induced, or never given. If Tess was indeed 'duped' – misled as to the nature of the encounter (consent induced by fraud) – this would rightly invalidate the consent. The most likely explanation of this 'misunderstanding' is sexual ignorance. Tess may not have understood the act of intercourse, a possibility not explored by Sutherland, although this was a common and now well-documented phenomenon, resulting from the infantilising ignorance forced upon women. There are several 'classic' cases: *R v Williams*,[8] in which a conviction for rape was upheld where a singing master had

---

8   [1923] 1 KB 340.

engaged in sexual intercourse with a girl pupil by pretending that it was a method of training her voice; in *R v Case*,[9] a medical practitioner represented to a girl that he was 'treating' her medically; in *R v Flattery*,[10] a girl submitted to intercourse believing that the act was a surgical operation. Tess herself supports this contention, and later later rebukes her mother:

> How could I be expected to know? I was a child when I left this house four months ago. Why didn't you tell me there was danger in men-folk? Why didn't you warn me? Ladies know what to fend hands against, because they read novels that tell them of these tricks ... (Hardy, 1985b, p 131)

Yet Sutherland dismisses this extensive plea (which indicates real anatomical ignorance – 'Ladies know what to fend hands against') with the gloss, 'Nor, when upbraiding her mother for not warning her against men, does Tess claim that she has been raped' (Sutherland, 1996, p 208) – for Sutherland, failure to use the *word* 'rape' is conclusive.[11] Yet had the plot so centred upon the crime of rape, clear rape in Tess's mind and published abroad by her as such, insuperable demands would have been made upon the plot. The whole novel centres upon her unwitting victimhood and that she is 'a pure woman'[12] despite society branding her otherwise. It is an indictment of Victorian double standards, which by the 1890s a few enlightened members of society could begin to critique. A novel centred upon a more overt rape would have been utterly dominated by crude imperatives. In addition, then, as now, rape was one of the most difficult crimes to prove, since it generally occurs without witness other than the parties themselves, and fear, ignorance, unconsciousness (or a combination of these) can mask the non-voluntary stance of the victim.

It would seem that Hardy appreciated this. Of Tess's view of Alec, the narrator much later tells us that:

> She had never wholly cared for him, she did not at all care for him now. She had dreaded him, winced before him, succumbed to adroit advantages he took of her helplessness; then, temporarily blinded by his ardent manners, had been stirred to confused surrender awhile: had suddenly despised and disliked him, and had run away. (Hardy, 1985b, p 130)

Sutherland uses this selfsame passage to suggest that Tess is sexually aroused, a 'willing, if misguided, participant of her own undoing' (Sutherland, 1996, p 209) – in particular, that the word 'stirred' suggests 'erection',[13] 'physical reciprocation' which is a response to Alec's 'stimulating foreplay', and the existence of Tess's 'aroused feelings' (Sutherland, 1996, p 209). Yet objectively, rather than feminine potency and 'willing participation', the passage evokes Tess's impotence and active dislike; she experienced 'dread', 'helplessness', she 'winced' and

---

9   (1850) 4 Cox 220.
10 (1877) 2 QBD 410.
11 As may be seen, the word 'rape' is frequently avoided by 19th century culture; from writers of fiction to witness statements, euphemisms are preferred to the precise noun.
12 *Tess of the d'Urbervilles* is subtitled 'A Pure Woman'.
13 Sutherland appears to imply here female 'erection'.

'succumbed' (Hardy, 1985b, p 130). 'Stirred' Tess may have been, but it was to 'confused surrender', not the equality implied by Sutherland's 'physical reciprocation'.

Given the context, of Alec's deliberate exploitation of his social superiority, his worldliness and his adroit use of his gifts to Tess's family in order to increase her sense of obligation to him, it seems that Tess is 'stirred' to 'confused surrender' of some part of her *emotional* self *after* the sexual act. Whilst honestly maintaining her stance that she does not love Alec, she nevertheless 'succumbs' to the relentless pressure of his alternate threats, attentions, scorn and favours, in that she feels 'grateful', yet 'hampered', by his gifts to her family; her 'confused surrender' simply an unwilling diminution of her formerly obdurate stance. Not only is Sutherland's *interpretation* of evidence a departure from the indications in the text, his analysis relies upon a glaring omission of evidence – albeit circumstantial. Observing her later with the product of the encounter – an illegitimate child – Tess's peasant companions agree:

> A little more than persuading had to do wi' the coming o't, I reckon. There were they that heard a sobbing one night last year in The Chase; and it mid ha' gone hard wi' a certain party if folks had come along. (Hardy, 1985b, p 140)

This is a clear textual suggestion that although Tess may have borne her fate without recourse to law, there was a local impression, corroborated by unidentified witnesses, that Tess was the victim of non-consensual intercourse, which is rape.

As already indicated, had Tess 'cried rape', the complex tale of emotional and social dislocation that is *Tess of the d'Urbervilles* would have been denied. Instead, the text explores the subtleties of victim experience – strongly mirrored by modern accounts; the exploitation of unequal gender and power relations; the fatalism of the peasant class; the scepticism and readiness of wider society to judge and condemn in error; and the isolation and sense of guilt experienced by the victim. All of these issues, still of contemporary relevance, are clearly signalled by the plot.

The legal implications of the scene in *Tess of the d'Urbervilles* have been explored with great scholarship by Davis (1997), who examines not only some of the caselaw of the period, but who also provides a fascinating study of the probable influence of contemporary newspaper articles, noted by Hardy, upon earlier textual versions of the plot. Davis concludes that the scene *does* appear to depict rape. Like Sutherland, however, Davis feels bound to assert that the ambiguity at the heart of the text allows Hardy to use the novel form 'to argue for a definition of female purity that includes Tess's sexual nature and her sexual responses to men' (Davis, 1997, p 228). Such an approach implies a reading of the text that appears sympathetically 'feminist'– asserting that a woman can be both 'pure' and sexually responsive. This leads Davis to conclude that:

> Alec's brutal mastery of Tess through rape makes possible his subsequent mastery of her through seduction. Hardy wants the equation to read a particular way: Tess is seduced because she was raped. (Davis, 1997, p 230)

Leaving aside the fact that Davis, like Sutherland, is assuming that the word 'seduction' can be juxtaposed with that of 'rape' unambiguously – questionable bearing in mind the overt variation in 'workaday' use of the word, as well as at the more subtle deconstructive level – he appears to be implying that, having been 'mastered' non-consensually through rape, Tess becomes more receptive to a less involuntary, perhaps more sexually responsive, liaison with Alec. Yet again, the text of *Tess* militates against this reading. Even after the rape scene, d'Urberville continues to be Tess's employer and the benefactor of her destitute family; a destitution which Tess blames, in part, upon herself. Tess attempts to retain some shred of dignity in the aftermath by wearing only the clothes which she can pay for herself and working in the fields. Despite Alec's protestation that she need not work and can 'clothe herself with the best', Tess replies 'I *should* be your creature to go on doing that, and I won't' (Hardy, 1985b, p 125). She allows Alec to kiss her on the cheek, but is 'indifferent' to this and repeats her assertion that she cannot love Alec, despite her apprehension that future events[14] might justify her being less than truthful on the point.

To many readers, the idea of rape as a *prelude* to seduction (given the view of the word as intimating sexual responsiveness) is, at the very least, anomalous. More consistent with the particular and overall themes of the novel is a reading that acknowledges that the nature of Tess's relationship with Alec d'Urberville, in the 'few weeks' (Hardy, 1985b, p 123) subsequent to the assault in 'The Chase', is one of abject victimhood. The separation of 'rape' from 'seduction' in Davis's thesis springs in part from his otherwise compelling analysis of Hardy's *Literary Notes*, coupled with a belief that the existence of similar Victorian rape cases could have given justice to Tess:

> Such laws and case rulings suggest that the courts would have interpreted Tess's situation as a case of rape. Why, then does Hardy keep Tess away from an apparently sympathetic judicial system? (Davis, 1997, p 227)

Davis concludes that:

> Hardy, I believe, wanted Tess's sexuality and the matter of her purity to be considered in the minds of his readers rather than argued (with perhaps predictable results) in a fictional court of law. (Davis, 1997, p 228)

Yet the case of Tess is miserably typical of the type of case that might well then, as now, have failed. For although the 'successful' caselaw is similar in *some* facts – as we shall see – Tess's account would be undermined, first, by having allowed herself to be led – without witness – into a wood and, secondly, by her lowly status as against that of her suave attacker. Tess's tale is thus largely *untold* by precedent, like many hundreds of cases not reported or not pursued.

---

14   Probably pregnancy: 'If I did love you I may have the best o' causes for letting you know it. But I don't' (Hardy, 1985b, p 126).

SEDUCTION AND RAPE: BLURRED CONCEPTIONS

Davis's evidence that Hardy himself referred only to the 'seduction' of Tess is not inconsistent with this: the word 'rape' was virtually unsayable in the Victorian mouth whilst 'seduction', 'ruination' and so forth, were words used broadly, with little reference to the presence or absence of consent. As a creature of the patriarchal *logos*, the word served a multitude of material and ideological purposes.

Of contextual relevance is the subtle interplay of values and assumptions revealed by the laws of the period – laws which appear to have been explored at times more completely by American than by English academic commentary. Sutherland's case, in part, springs from the verbal and conceptual anomaly that was played out in Victorian law, in the ambiguous relationship between the words 'seduction' and 'rape'. For some Victorian commentators – as for Sutherland – 'seduction' more readily implies mutuality, complicity. In present assumptions of sexual liberation and equality, 'seduction' is no longer a crime,[15] yet we may still find ourselves speaking of a 'victim' of seduction. At the time of *Tess*, seduction could be subject to legal notice. In English law, the terms of this legal response were rooted in the history of women as property. In *Jason v Norton*,[16] where Norton entered the plaintiff's house and made an assault upon his daughter thereby 'getting a bastard child upon her', the case was in the power of the plaintiff father 'for the loss of her service' – *per quod servicium amsit*. In the 20th century American case of *Wendt v Lentz*,[17] an action for seduction, the defendant had sexual relations with the plaintiff's 'previously chaste' 15-year-old daughter. According to the case, this resulted in the girl becoming 'wild and unmanageable' and she was subsequently committed to a home as being 'incorrigible'. The defendant was held not responsible for the plaintiff's loss of his daughter's services, since it was concluded that the girl's 'abnormal' behaviour could not be wholly attributable to the defendant. The case gave rise to the response by Edgerton (1929–30)[18] that:

> The defendant's unauthorised interference with the plaintiff's interests was not negligent, but intentional; and it is commonly recognised, both by the law and by public opinion, that the risk even of exceedingly unlikely consequences of an unauthorised and intentional interference should fall on the perpetrator rather than the sufferer. If A tramples the valuable plants in B's garden, it is no defense that he reasonably mistook them for weeds.

Thus, in the bizarre displacement activity that often typifies law, the 'victim' of seduction is clearly identified as the *father* whose *property* has been interfered with. Even where that female chattel later exhibits such wrongful conduct as to make her analogous to a weed, that weed is still as much actionable property as

---

15 Note however the recent resurrection of the notion of criminalising 'seduction' in England and Wales in the context of schoolteachers and their 16 to 17 year old charges – 'Teachers criticise "seduction law" plan' (1998) *The Times*, 4 October.

16 (1653) cited in Baker and Milsom, 1986, p 353.

17 (1928) 249 NY 253, 164 NE 42.

18 HW Edgerton, 'Seduction – loss of services' (1929–30) Illinois L Rev 24, at pp 233–34.

the carefully tended valuable plant. Edgerton's conclusion appears to occupy moral territory:

> ... without being Victorian one may regret on social grounds a decision which encourages or gratuitously refuses to discourage the seduction of fifteen year old girls. (Edgerton, p 236)

However, the concern is 'social' in that the predominant masculine order is keen to preserve property rights. In *R v Mycock*,[19] an action for abduction, Willes J uses a similar analogy when he says that:

> The prisoner had no more right to deprive the father of the girl of his property, as it were, in her, and his possession of her, than he would have a right to go into his shop and carry away one of his telescopes or optical instruments.[20]

The language and forms of these cases reveal that women were very far from being the autonomous beings that Sutherland's use of the word 'seduction' assumes; in some the masculine 'duel' over ruined property occludes evidence bearing a close resemblance to the facts of rape. This is because the focus of the action was upon the preservation of *physical* integrity; whether the girl consented or understood was irrelevant to the men of law. Not only might seduction be classified as a trespass against property – a tort – in 1921, 37 American jurisdictions maintained statutes defining seduction as a crime, which was defined, subject to various limitations and exceptions, as:

> The act of a male person in having intercourse with a woman of chaste character under promise of marriage, or by the use of enticement or persuasion ... in jurisdictions wherein the statute is not confined to seduction under promise of marriage, but expressly covers seduction, it is interesting to note that the statute has been construed to be broad enough to cover practically every case of intercourse with consent. The word 'seduce' (in such statutes) is used in its ordinary legal meaning and implied the use of arts, persuasions, or wiles to overcome the resistance of the female who is not disposed of her volition, to step aside from the path of virtue ... Any seductive arts or promises, where the female involuntarily and reluctantly yields thereto, are sufficient ...[21]

No doubt there were men who suffered unjustly from measures that so readily assumed the overweening power of the male. Nevertheless the passage is interesting in that it conflates the term 'intercourse with consent' with 'involuntary' yielding. The dominant references to acts designed to 'overcome the resistance' of the female who is 'not disposed of her volition' seem closer to definitions of rape, recognising that the will can be overborne in ways other than violence and that 'reluctant yielding' to whatever pressure, is not consent. Certainly in the realm of more overtly commercial 'contracts' such duress could operate as a vitiating factor. Yet in the realm of contract too, woman may be effaced by her identity with property; in the English case of *Moss v Moss*,[22]

---

19   (1871) Cox CC 28.
20   *Ibid* at 30.
21   HW Humble, 'Seduction as a crime' (1921) 21 Columbia Law Review 145–54.
22   (1897) PD 263.

consideration was given to whether a marriage contract could be annulled on the basis that the wife was pregnant by another man at the time of marriage. In the language of contract utilised by the court, the issue was 'whether the mistake about the condition of the bride, or indeed any bride found not to be intact, was a mistake as to her identity, or merely a mistake as to the *quality* of the bride *thing*' (Williams, 1999, p 189). Thus, underpinning the actions for seduction lay the very complex network of social values that made feminine autonomy – the autonomy of desire, as much as that of repulsion – unsayable. The diverse circumstances encompassed by the words 'seduction' and 'rape' contained a penumbral overlap, made less transparent by the identity created in law between the concepts of 'woman' and 'property', and by the resultant need to crush recalcitrant autonomy. The case of Tess is a *locus classicus* of the penumbra; a reminder that for all the vagaries of the rape-seduction scenario women were, by reason of their weaker bargaining position, poor status and education (not to mention a likely physical disadvantage), more vulnerable to exploitation. Strict legal analysis of such facts, of the manipulation of sexual ignorance, of superior status used to negate any attempt to exercise free will or the right to consent, would, to most modern jurists, fulfil the definition of rape. The novel is *not* about a girl who is aroused, but cannot say so. This would have been easy to depict with weak protestations and coy refusals. Nor is it a tale of brutal rape. It reflects the much more common and subtle concatenation of circumstances that allowed young men to exploit their greater worldliness and ease with opportunism and who were then largely indulged by the world for doing so. Later, Alec admits this:

> What a blind young thing you were as to possibilities! I say in all earnestness that it is a shame for parents to bring up their girls in such dangerous ignorance of the gins and nets that the wicked may set for them, whether their motive be a good one, or the result of simple indifference. (Hardy, 1985b, p 394)

Reviewing the evidence so far, we can make the following summary of the sexual encounter. Prior to the act, Tess is compromised by her relation to Alec, her employer's son; he has cajoled her, threatened her, made her feel indebted on behalf of her family and finally, deliberately or otherwise, disorientated her. Tess is left in the wood in an exhausted state. She falls into a sound sleep. Alex returns and embarks upon intercourse. At some point during this event Tess wakes up. She does not fully understand what is happening until it is too late. She does not know what to 'fend hands' against. Nevertheless, according to witness testimony, she is 'sobbing' at some stage in the encounter. By her own later account she was 'a child' who did not know of the 'danger in men-folk' and even Alec describes her as having lived in a state of 'dangerous ignorance'. This suggests that, even if Tess was no longer asleep, penetration was initiated without her full understanding or consent and then, as now, this should have been classified as rape. It may be that penetration began whilst Tess was sleeping soundly and that, given her anatomical ignorance, she was, upon waking, confused enough for completion of the act to occur ('succumbed to adroit advantages he took of her helplessness'). Like many rape victims, Tess felt foolish and guilty for having allowed herself to fall into such a trap and was unsure as to whether she had any claim to moral integrity. When she later met a religious slogan-writer inscribing 'THY, DAMNATION, SLUMBERETH, NOT', she asked, 'suppose your sin was not of your own seeking?' (Hardy, 1985b, p 128), thus quite independently classifying the act as *unsought*. Once the deed was done, Tess lapsed into a state of fatalistic apathy. This was a credible response: aware of the contribution made by her own ignorance, a girl in her lowly position would also have had difficulty sustaining a complaint against a gentleman, albeit a gentleman who has proved himself calculating and amoral. Forensic science, such as that which more recently identified President Clinton, could not have aided Tess, and the social hierarchy, coupled with the fatalism of the peasant class, both of which were clearly evidenced in the book, would have confirmed her view that she was powerless in the matter. For a short time Tess remained in the neighbourhood. During that time she could not bear to think of her former self; she feels 'sorrow', is 'listless', 'indifferent' and is still prone to tears. Alec was, by then, cold and mocking, although Tess allowed him to kiss her cheek – 'If you wish … see how you've mastered me' (Hardy, 1985b, p 126) – she answers 'indifferently'. It is *after* this stage in the text that we meet the passage to which Sutherland alludes, thus 'stirred to confused surrender awhile' could well refer to Tess's submission after the event.

SLEEP, SEX AND THE LAW

As has been noted, Victorian caselaw gives clear indications that women could be tricked into allowing intercourse as a result of their sexual ignorance. In addition, the caselaw, which most closely mirrors the case of Tess, has long established that rape can occur whilst the victim is asleep. In *R v Young*,[23] the prisoner 'proceeded to have connexion' with the victim, she 'then being asleep'. It was held that the prisoner was guilty of the crime of rape. In *R v Mayers*,[24] Sarah Mayers testified that she 'fell asleep; the first thing after that which I remember was finding the prisoner in bed with me, he was agate of me when I awoke; … I cannot say that he did it altogether; his person was to mine …'. Taylor, for the accused, argued that 'There was no evidence of force or intent to use force, or that she resisted the prisoner, and therefore the prisoner could not be found guilty of the attempt'. However, Lush J concluded: 'Yes, but if she was asleep, she is incapable of consent, and therefore it would be a rape' (or attempted rape).

Mrs Mayers, being the married sister-in-law of the accused, was likely to have been sufficiently cognisant of sexual matters to understand the nature of full penetration and that the complete act may not have taken place. Nevertheless, the case is authority for the proposition that a sleeping victim is incapable of consent. Where intercourse commences during sleep, but continues without objection upon awaking, the absence of consent is more difficult to assert. So, in the sad case of *R v Page*,[25] on the trial of an indictment for rape:

---

23 (1878) 14 Cox CC 114.
24 (1872) Cox C Vol XII (1871–74) 311. Again, note the euphemistic terms.
25 (1846) Cox CLC 133.

... it appeared that the prisoner had commenced having connexion with the prosecutrix, his own daughter, a girl about thirteen years of age, while she was asleep, but that she awoke before it was at an end and made no resistance, until she saw that a third person was present watching her.

It was held that in such circumstances (and with an established sexual history between father and daughter) '[t]he jury would not be justified in finding the prisoner guilty of rape'. In this case, a child's passivity was sufficient to undermine the charge, demonstrating, at the very least, some cultural and legal ambivalence. Nevertheless, the cases do not cast doubt on the contention that penetration can be initiated whilst the victim is asleep. In 1987 Hom noted that:

> Some readers may consider it beyond the realm of credibility to believe that a man could engage in sexual intercourse with a woman before she awakens. Although rare, such occurrences have been reported in other cases. (Hom, 1987, p 1246)

In the case of *State v Moorman* itself a college student, 'in the hazy period between sleep and wakefulness ... dreamed of having sexual intercourse. The dream however, became a nightmarish reality when the woman awoke to find a man, a slight acquaintance, *flagrante delicto*' (Hom, 1987, p 1246).

A notable aspect of the prosecutions for rape recorded in 19th century criminal cases is that, apart from the few dramatic cases already cited of men procuring intercourse by various forms of fraud or during sleep, many sickeningly mundane prosecutions seem to have involved young or handicapped children. So, in *R v Nicholls*,[26] the prisoner '... was indicted for an assault to commit a rape on a girl under eight years of age ... There were also marks on the child's linen which made it doubtful whether the graver offence had not been completed'. In *R v Barratt*,[27] Robert Barratt was tried for the rape of Mary Redman, an idiot girl aged fourteen who was blind, dumb and severely handicapped. *R v Woodhurst*,[28] was an indictment for carnal knowledge and assault of the ten-year-old daughter of the accused. The direction to the jury reviewed the issue of consent, but concluded that: 'if the child submitted under the influence of terror, or because she felt herself in the power of the man, her father, there was no real consent.'

If consent could have been an issue in crimes against such young children, it is little wonder that rape claims by ordinary women seem to have been singularly rare. This paradoxical reference to consent may be resolved by viewing it as involving an unspoken *presumption* of consent, as opposed to the modern ideal of establishing whether consent was real or, from diverse pressures, apparent. It would appear that the case of *Woodhurst* adverted to the negation of consent through terror because it involved a ten-year-old child; such 'psychological' pressure has come to be recognised, only latterly, as a viable negating factor for adult women.

---

26 (1847) Cox CLC 182.
27 (1873) Cox CLC 498.
28 (1870) Cox CLC 443.

CONCLUSION

In criminal trials for rape, there is a clear motive for construing the evidence either to strengthen or undermine the case against the accused. It is the *raison d'être* of prosecution and defence counsel, and the very purpose of the theatre of law, to test the credibility of conflicting accounts. In the text of *Tess of the d'Urbervilles* there exists an additional source of evidence to which the real-life courtroom cannot advert – the philosophically enlightened and reliably clairvoyant eye of the omniscient narrator. Those events which are obscured, because they are unsayable in the Victorian text, are made more transparent by judgments offered by the omniscient narrator. The voice of the narrator vindicates Tess as an innocent who is consumed, first for her beauty and again for daring to hope that the absence of agency in her own sexual fate will preserve her from further harm. The plot confirms this view: Alec is a cad who admits full blame and Tess's husband Angel Clare rejects her because of the mechanical fact of her lost maidenhood notwithstanding the blameless context of that loss.

Tess is painfully honest, loyal and trusting, the bearer of a sin 'not of her own seeking' (Hardy, 1985b, p 128). This being the case, any questions not wholly answered by the text should be examined with at least a suspension of judgment, if not a degree of partiality for the victim, clearly signalled by the text. Why then does Sutherland choose to present the case so roundly in the role of an avid defence counsel for Alec? Perhaps, primarily, he feels challenged to construct the least automatic analysis in the pursuit of critical refinement. The process is fuelled by evidence of a change of emphasis in successive critical views – the 'seduction' of the 1890s becomes 'rape' in the 1960s. Yet this fails to take account not only of the clear message signalled by the text, but of the socio-legal context of that message. Whilst contemporary Victorian commentators might, predictably, have railed against a novel that sympathetically portrays the sexually injured Tess, the novel was ahead of its time in critiquing the double standards of a culture too ready to judge by superficial lights. The transcendent importance of preserving virginity as the emblem of unsullied property meant that women were divided into two basic groups determined not by the modern emphasis upon whether intercourse was consensual or not, but by whether anatomical invasion had occurred. The fact of such damage raised a presumption in the minds of 'respectable' souls – a kind of *res ipsa loquitur* that only the clearest mortal resistance could gainsay. This evaluation still obtains today. As Helena Kennedy explains:

> The persistent cross-examination ploy of defence counsel is to deny that fear might paralyse the victim and to insist that a woman guarding her virtue would fight like a lioness. We are still haunted by powerful cultural images of what good women do in the face of ravishment. In a long literary tradition which begins with Livy and Ovid, Lucretia fights off her attacker and refuses to yield to his threats. The deed done, she takes her own life. (Kennedy, 1993, p 123)

Such leonine vigilance is clearly expected, by Sutherland, in the sleeping Tess.[29] Whilst Tess's peasant companions clearly understood that the protections vouchsafed to bourgeois females did not extend to them, writers of critical essays languished in the deluded certainties of middle-class prejudice. It was believed that girls who found themselves in compromising situations at the very least contributed to, if not actively sought, their fate. Sutherland relies on the views of the Victorian critic Mrs Oliphant,[30] a literary critic who, as Sutherland must know, represented extreme sanctimony – the Mary Whitehouse of the 1800s. Lyndall Gordon calls Mrs Oliphant 'the foremost opponent of emancipation'.[31] Not only did she oppose Hardy's work, in *Blackwoods Magazine* Mrs Oliphant dismissed *Jane Eyre* by Charlotte Bronte as a production of 'grossness', 'such grossness as could only be perpetrated by a woman' (Oliphant, 1855).

Tess was little more than a child at the time of the encounter. The text describes her bastard offspring as 'a child's child' (Hardy, 1985b, p 144); but this was at a time when childhood, in fact and in law, was fleeting and sexual maturation all too easily implied a guilty mind. Tess's sensual appeal and her downfall lie partly in that very combination of childish womanliness: 'Here was I thinking you a new-sprung child of nature; there were you, the belated seedling of an effete aristocracy', rails her husband (Hardy, 1985b, p 302). Yet the evidence dispersed throughout the book suggests that Tess was the victim of her own sexual ignorance and innocence, that the encounter was unwanted, but that in Victorian terms, surely 'The Woman Pays'.[32] This is a conclusion made available to any fair reader of the text, Victorian or otherwise. Sutherland's view, that '[s]he who was seduced in 1892 is she who is raped in the permissive 1960s' (Sutherland, 1996, p 203), betrays a similarly strange inversion. Surely to 'modern' eyes a 'censorious' age would have recognised as 'rape' that which in a more 'permissive' age is dismissed as mere 'seduction'? On the other hand, if a 'permissive' age is that which 'permits' a hitherto unsayable, yet justifiable, plea of rape to surface, it is surely a permissiveness to be welcomed.

Like the judge for whom a woman victim's 'No' may really mean 'Yes', Sutherland's inversion and ultimate melding of the terms 'seduction' and 'rape' is an expression of a dominant phallogocentrism. Yet, as Carol Smart explains:

---

29 On the classical Greek background to rape and seduction, see Harris (1990), a scholarly examination of the claim that 'seduction' was a more serious offence than 'rape' in classical Athens: 'Euphiletus' explanation … is that while the rapist incurs the hatred of his victim, the seducer corrupts the very soul of the woman …' (Harris, 1990, p 370).

30 Sutherland (1996, p 202) quotes Mrs Oliphant's assertion that:
    … we do not object to the defiant blazon of a Pure Woman, notwithstanding the early stain. But a Pure Woman is not betrayed into fine living and fine clothes as the mistress of her seducer by any stress of poverty or misery; and Tess was a skilled labourer, for whom it is very rare that nothing can be found to do. Here the elaborate and indignant plea for Vice, that is really Virtue, breaks down altogether …
    Sutherland adds that: 'Morris and Oliphant take it for granted that Tess was "seduced" – that is, led astray, not violated or forced into sexual intercourse against her will.'

31 L Gordon, *Charlotte Bronte* (1994) London: Chatto & Windus, p 162.

32 *Tess of the d'Urbervilles* – 'Phase the Fifth – The Woman Pays' – title to the fifth section of the book.

The concept of phallogocentrism is, however, not without its limitations. Basically the identification of a system of knowledge and logic based on binary meanings does not help us to go beyond this form of conceptualisation ... the law cannot accommodate the supposed ambiguity of a submission to sexual assault ... Hence, in law's domain the more that non-consent can be made to look like submission, the more it will be treated like consent. (Smart, 1990, pp 10–14)

The inability to go beyond such binary meanings, concluding that the textual ambiguity of *Tess* presents us with a polarised scenario could, thus, be almost forgiven, for it is after all merely what happens in that other trial of fact, the court of law. Almost that is, until we recall the disinterested yet omniscient evidence of the narrator, an ideal third party witness available only in fiction. The voice clearly identifies the sexual encounter as an act of 'appropriation' and 'ruthlessness', concepts incompatible with the presence of consent.

To summarise: Professor John Sutherland assembles a critique of *Tess of the d'Urbervilles* based upon the premise that early readings of the text understood Tess to be largely the mistress of her own downfall; that it is only in recent years that the notion of Tess as overwhelmed 'victim' has emerged – 'She who was seduced in 1892 is she who was raped in the permissive 1960s' (Sutherland, 1996, p 203).

Juxtaposition of the text of *Tess* with Sutherland's gloss on it reveals significantly contestable points, both as to the actual content of the text and Sutherland's rhetorical and deductive elaborations of it.

At the heart of the debate lie the meanings ascribed to the words 'rape' and 'seduction' by commentators; each word carries cultural assumptions relating to the status and agency of female sexuality. Historical investigation reveals a complex background to the juristic gloss placed upon these cultural assumptions – both 'rape' and 'seduction' have complex legal histories, most notably in relation to the identification of women as property and the subsumption of any effective investigation of consent.

The text of *Tess* also provokes consideration of a particular point of law – that of cases concerning possible rape initiated upon a sleeping victim. Again, historical caselaw raises some discomfiting material.

The skewed vision of *Tess*, as presented by Sutherland, holds broader implications. The legal history of rape and seduction demonstrate a cultural ambivalence towards female victims of sexual exploitation, an ambivalence exhibited by Sutherland himself, and still very much in evidence in modern day law. Sutherland's thesis – that the 'seduction' of the 1890s becomes 'rape' in the 'permissive' 1960s – reveals a strange cultural implosion. If the 1960s heralded a new era of sexual freedom and conscience, with rape openly acknowledged as an event involving sexual predation and lack of consent, this is surely a welcome event. Yet attaching the label 'permissive' suggests regret, even hostility, that with this age of alleged sexual freedom comes an *unwanted* licence in the empowerment of victims, an *unfair* portrayal of men as exploitative. The battle continues, not least in court.

The serious question posed by *Tess* remains unanswered because sexual equality in the forest, in the courtroom and in the text exists largely in the ideal rather than the real. The serious question raised by Sutherland's treatment of the text, and of the evidence, is how far masculine readings, in the name of plausible textual scholarship or plausible justice in the courtroom, continue to dominate and shape feminine experience.

Selected Bibliography

Akdeniz, Y, 'The regulation of pornography and child pornography on the internet' (1997) 1(2) *The Journal of Information, Law and Technology*

Akdeniz, Y, Walker, C and Wall, D, *The Internet, Law and Society*, 2000, London: Longman

Aldgate, A, 'I am a camera: film and theatre censorship in 1950s Britain' (1999) 8(3) *Contemporary European History* 425–38

Allison, A (ed), *The Norton Anthology*, 3rd edn, 1983, New York and London: WW Norton & Co

Ashworth, A, *Principles of Criminal Law*, 2nd edn, 1995, Oxford: Clarendon

Atwood, M, *The Handmaid's Tale*, 1987, London: Virago

Baker, J, *An Introduction to English Legal History*, 2nd edn, 1979, London: Butterworths

Baker, J and Milsom, SFC, *Sources of English Legal History*, 1986, London: Butterworths

Ballard, JG, *Crash*, 1995, London: Vintage

Barker, M, Arthurs, J and Harindranath, R, *The Crash Controversy: Censorship Campaigns and Film Reception*, 2001, London: Wallflower Press

Barley, N, *Dancing on the Grave*, 1995, London: Abacus

Bavelas, J and Coates, L, 'Is it sex or assault? Erotic versus violent language in sexual assault trial judgments' (2001) 10(1) *Journal of Social Distress and the Homeless* 29–40

Chadwick, E, 'It's war, Jim, but not as we know it: a "reality check" for international laws of war?' (2003) 39 *Crime, Law and Social Change* 233–62

Clarke, S, *Social Theory, Psychoanalysis and Racism*, 2003, Basingstoke: Palgrave Macmillan

Cooper, D, *Existentialism*, 1990, Oxford: Blackwell

Cornish, W, *Law and Society in England 1750–1950*, 1989, London: Sweet & Maxwell

Dalton, C, 'Deconstructing contract doctrine' (1985) 94 *Yale Law Journal* 997–1114

Davis, Jr, W, 'The rape of Tess: Hardy, English law and the case of sexual assault' (1997) 52(2) *Nineteenth Century Literature* 221–31

Day, G, *Making Sense of Wales*, 2002, Cardiff: University of Wales Press

Dean, J, 'Zizek on law' (2004) 15 *Law and Critique* 1–24

Douzinas, C, Warrington, R and McVeigh, S, *Postmodern Jurisprudence*, 1991, London: Routledge

Dworkin, R, *Life's Dominion*, 1995, London: HarperCollins

Eagleton, T, *Literary Theory*, 1988, Oxford: Blackwell

Eagleton, T (ed), *Raymond Williams: Critical Perspectives*, 1989, Cambridge: Polity

Evans, C, *My People*, 1987, Harris, J (ed), Bridgend: Seren

Evans, I (ed), *Brewer's Dictionary of Phrase and Fable*, 1981, London: Cassell

Fish, S, *Doing What Comes Naturally*, 1989, Oxford: Clarendon

Gillon, R, *Philosophical Medical Ethics*, 1994, Chichester: John Wiley

Glannon, W, (1999) 'Responsibility and control: Fischer's and Ravizza's theory of moral responsibility' 18 *Law and Philosophy* 187–213

Good, B, *Medicine, Rationality and Experience: An Anthropological Perspective*, 1994, Cambridge: CUP

Goodrich, P, *Oedipus Lex*, 1995, Berkeley and Los Angeles: California UP

Hall, JC, *Sources of Family Law*, 1966, Cambridge: CUP

Hardy, T, *Jude the Obscure*, 1985a (first published 1896), London: Penguin

Hardy, T, *Tess of the d'Urbervilles*, 1985b (first published 1891), London: Penguin

Harris, E, 'Did the Athenians regard seduction as a worse crime than rape?' (1990) 40 *Classical Quarterly* 370–77

Hastings, J (ed), *The Dictionary of the Bible*, 1921, Edinburgh: T & T Clark

Hawkins, D, *Hardy at Home*, 1989, London: Barrie & Jenkins

Heaney, S, *The Government of the Tongue*, 1989, London: Faber & Faber

Helmholz, R, *Marriage Litigation in Mediaeval England*, 1974, Cambridge: CUP

Hess, H, 'Like Zealots and Romans: terrorism and empire in the 21st century' 39 *Crime, Law and Social Change* 339–57

Holohan, S and Featherstone, M, 'Multiculturalism, institutional law, and imaginary justice' (2003) 14 *Law and Critique* 1–27

Hom, RM, '*State v Moorman*: can sex with a sleeping woman constitute forcible rape?' (1987) 65 *North Carolina Law Review* 1246–66

Hunt, L, 'On improving people by political means', in La Follette, H (ed), *Ethics in Practice*, 2002, Oxford: Blackwell

Hutcheon, L, *A Poetics of Postmodernism*, 1988, New York and London: Routledge

Kennedy, H, *Eve Was Framed*, 1993, London: Vintage

Keown, J, 'No right to assisted suicide' (2002) 63(1) *Cambridge Law Journal* 8–10

Kiernan, K, 'The rise of cohabitation and childbearing outside marriage in Western Europe' (2001) 15 *International Journal of Law, Policy and the Family* 1–21

Kingdom, E, 'Cohabitation contracts and the democratization of personal relations' (2000) 8 *Feminist Legal Studies* 5–27

Larcombe, W, 'The "ideal" victim v successful rape complainants: not what you might expect' (2002) 10 *Feminist Legal Studies* 131–48

Larrabee, M, Weine, S and Woollcott, P, '"The wordless nothing": narratives of trauma and extremity' (2003) 26 *Human Studies* 353–82

Lees, S, *Carnal Knowledge, Rape on Trial*, 1996, London: Penguin

Lewis, J, 'Debates and issues regarding marriage and cohabitation in the British and American literature' (2001a) 15 *International Journal of Law, Policy and the Family* 159–84

Lewis, J, *Hollywood v Hard Core: How the Struggle over Censorship Saved the Modern Film Industry*, 2001b, New York: NYU UP

Maudsley, H, *The Physiology of Mind*, 1876, London: Macmillan

Metzl, J, 'Selling sanity through gender: the psychodynamics of psychotropic advertising' (2003) 24(1–2) *Journal of Medical Humanities* 79–103

Michelfelder, D, 'Our moral condition in cyberspace' (2000) 2 *Ethics and Information Technology* 147–52

Miller, J-A, *The Ethics of Psychoanalysis 1959–1960: The Seminar of Jacques Lacan*, Book VII, 1992, London: Routledge

Millgate, M, *Thomas Hardy: A Biography*, 1982, Oxford: OUP

Mills, C, '"Heart" attack: a critique of Jorge Garcia's volitional conception of racism' (2003) 7 *The Journal of Ethics* 29–62

Munro, C, 'Not the Last Picture Show' (2003) *Public Law* (Spring) 2–5

Murdoch, I, *The Sovereignty of Good*, 1970, London: Routledge & Kegan Paul

Murphy, W, The victim advocacy and research group' (2001) 11(1) *Journal of Social Distress and the Homeless* 123–38

Niebuhr, R, *The Nature and Destiny of Man*, 1943, London: Nisbet & Co

Oliphant, M (writing in 1855), cited in Allott, M (ed), *The Brontes: The Critical Heritage*, 1974, London: Routledge & Kegan Paul

Pateman, C, *The Sexual Contract*, 1988, London: Polity

Pedain, A, 'The human rights dimension of the Diane Pretty case' (2003) 62(1) *Cambridge Law Journal* 181–206

Porter, R, *A Social History of Madness*, 1987, London: Weidenfeld & Nicolson

Prins, A, 'What price the concept of psychopathic disorder?' (1995) 35(4) *Medicine, Science and Law* 307–15

Rayden on Divorce, 14th edn, 1983, London: Butterworths

Rooney, E, 'Tess and the subject of sexual violence', in Riquelme, JP (ed), *Tess of the d'Urbervilles: Case Studies in Contemporary Criticism*, 1998, Boston: Bedford

Rumney, P, 'Male rape in the courtroom: issues and concerns' [2001] *Criminal Law Review* (March) 205–13

Scruton, R, *Modern Philosophy*, 1994, London: Sinclair-Stevenson

Scull, A, *Museums of Madness*, 1979, London: Penguin

Showalter, E, *The Female Malady*, 1987, London: Virago

Silberfeld, M and Checkland, D, 'Faulty judgment, expert opinion and decision-making capacity' (1999) 20 *Theoretical Medicine and Bioethics* 377–93

Simmonds, N, 'Judgment and mercy' (1993) 13 *Oxford Journal of Legal Studies* 52

Simmonds, N, 'Protestant jurisprudence and modern doctrinal scholarship' (2001) 2 *Cambridge Law Journal* 271

Smart, C, 'Law's truth/women's experience', in Graycar, R (ed), *Dissenting Opinions: Feminist Explorations in Law and Society*, 1990, Sydney: Allen & Unwin

Smith, D, 'Relating to Wales', in Eagleton, T (ed), *Raymond Williams: Critical Perspectives*, 1989, Cambridge: Polity

Smith, R, *Trial by Medicine*, 1981, Edinburgh: Edinburgh UP

Stone, L, *Road to Divorce*, 1990, Oxford: OUP

Sutherland, J, 'Is Alec a rapist?', in *Is Heathcliff a Murderer: Puzzles in 19th Century Fiction*, 1996, Oxford: OUP

Thiroux, J, *Ethics, Theory and Practice*, 2nd edn, 1980, London: Collier-Macmillan

Thomas, RS, *Collected Poems 1945–1990*, 1993, London: Phoenix Giants

Tribe, D, *Questions of Censorship*, 1974, New York: St Martin's Press

Wakelin, A and Long, KM, 'Effects of victim gender and sexuality on attributions of blame to rape victims' (2003) 49(9–10) *Sex Roles* 477–87

Walker, D (ed), *The Oxford Companion to Law*, 1980, Oxford: Clarendon

Ward, I, 'Casting down imaginations: politics and poetry in the English republic' (2000) 21(3) *Journal of Legal History* 101–14

Weddle, D, '"Straw Dogs": they want to see brains flying out?' (1995) 5(2) *Sight and Sound* 20–25

Widdowson, P, *Hardy in History: A Study in Literary Sociology*, 1989, London: Routledge

Williams, B, 'Shame and autonomy', in *Shame and Necessity*, 1994, California: California UP

Williams, LR, 'Women can only misbehave' (1995) 5(2) *Sight and Sound* 26

Williams, M, '*Tess of the d'Urbervilles* and the law of provocation', in Freeman, M and Lewis, A (eds), *Law and Literature, Current Legal Issues*, Vol 2, 1999, Oxford: OUP

Williams, M, *Empty Justice: One Hundred Years of Law, Literature and Philosophy*, 2002, London: Cavendish Publishing

Williams, R, *The English Novel: From Dickens to Lawrence*, 1987, London: Hogarth Press

Witte, J, *Law and Protestantism*, 2002, Cambridge: CUP